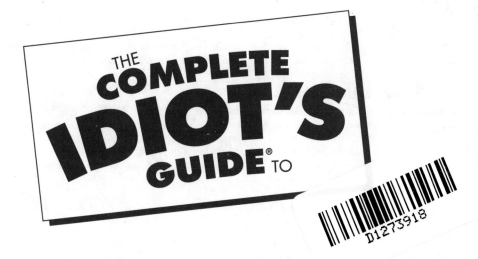

THE
COMPLETE IDIOT'S GUIDE® TO

Tax Breaks and Deductions

by Lita Epstein

ALPHA

A Pearson Education Company

In memory of my father, whose love of accounting helped me to learn about and appreciate the complexities of the tax code. He was always looking to uncover some new tax break.

Copyright © 2003 by Lita Epstein

THE COMPLETE IDIOT'S GUIDE TO and Design are registered trademarks of Pearson Education, Inc.

International Standard Book Number: 0-02-864439-5
Library of Congress Catalog Card Number: Available upon request.

04   03   02   8   7   6   5   4   3   2   1

Interpretation of the printing code: The rightmost number of the first series of numbers is the year of the book's printing; the rightmost number of the second series of numbers is the number of the book's printing. For example, a printing code of 02-1 shows that the first printing occurred in 2002.

Printed in the United States of America

For marketing and publicity, please call: 317-581-3722

The publisher offers discounts on this book when ordered in quantity for bulk purchases and special sales.

For sales within the United States, please contact: Corporate and Government Sales, 1-800-382-3419 or corpsales@pearsontechgroup.com.

Outside the United States, please contact: International Sales, 317-581-3793 or international@pearsontechgroup.com.

Publisher: *Marie Butler-Knight*
Product Manager: *Phil Kitchel*
Managing Editor: *Jennifer Chisholm*
Acquisitions Editor: *Gary Goldstein*
Development Editor: *Jennifer Moore*
Production Editor: *Billy Fields*
Copy Editor: *Krista Hansing*
Illustrator: *Chris Eliopoulos*
Cover/Book Designer: *Trina Wurst*
Indexer: *Tonya Heard*
Layout/Proofreading: *Angela Calvert, Mary Hunt*

Contents at a Glance

Contents

Foreword

Tax laws come and go. Congress fiddles with the tax code on a regular basis with any number of goals in mind: fiscal policy, social policy, international policy, and occasionally even based on the current economics of the country.

As a result, we have managed to create a labyrinth of tax legislation in the United States. There are very, very few professionals who understand even three fourths of content of the current tax laws.

It's no wonder that the average person frequently gives up on understanding their taxes. They turn over the preparation of their taxes to professionals and have little more involvement than providing their W-2s and a few related documents and waiting to sign their completed return.

What's wrong with that? Lot's. There are literally thousands of opportunities within the tax code for the average person to use to their advantage. Being unaware is the most common reason for not taking advantage of these opportunities.

What the average taxpayer needs is a guide to using the tax code strategically. Something that answers the questions: "What deductions are available to me?" "How can I reduce my tax burden?" and "Is there a more tax efficient way to achieve my goals?"

Drawing upon her numerous years of financial and retirement planning experience, Lita Epstein has created that guide. This book does not cover every aspect of the tax code specifically, but rather it helps the average taxpayer to learn how to ask the right questions, look in the right places, and begin to think strategically about their taxes.

You'll find the most commonly overlooked deductions and exemptions covered in-depth within the first few chapters.

The remainder of the book looks at strategic ways of handling life's taxing situations: paying for college education, planning for retirement, handling a divorce, and running a small business.

As a recognized expert in financial planning for women, Lita does a particularly good job of covering the tax consequences of divorce. If you've recently divorced, this book is worth its weight in gold for these chapters alone.

All in all, as a professional tax preparer, I wish more of my clients had read a book like this. A better informed client is easier to work with and allows me to fully advise the client for more strategic uses of tax planning.

Reading this book may not necessarily make you want to tackle your taxes on your own, though you'll certainly be better equipped if you do, but it will certainly help you be a more informed and better off taxpayer.

Shellie L. Moore, CPA

Introduction

As early television and radio celebrity Arthur Godfrey said, "I'm proud to be paying taxes to the United States. The only thing is—I could be just as proud for half the money." Godfrey's quote conveys the mixed feelings that most Americans have about taxes. On one hand, it's considered a patriotic duty for citizens to pay their taxes to keep our great country running smoothly. However, it's considered as much of a patriotic duty—if not more!—to take advantage of as many tax breaks, deductions, and credits as legally possible.

Although it's a fascinating topic, I won't be getting into the political discussion of whether taxes are a necessary evil or an evil that needs to be stopped. I'll let you fight that one out with your friends and neighbors. Instead, I've written this book from the perspective that the tax code exists and that we're not going to change it in time to file our next return. In other words, I'm trying to make the best of the current situation. You can use lots of sections in the tax code to reduce your tax bill while helping to do the things you want to do for yourself, your family, and your business. I'll be concentrating on these tax breaks and deductions, and how you can take the greatest advantage of them to minimize your tax bill.

Ready for a Trip?

Don't let taxes trip you up financially—instead take a journey with me through the world of taxes to find out how to take advantage of the numerous credits, deductions, and other breaks the IRS offers.

I've organized the book into seven parts:

Part 1, "Exploring Tax Basics," reviews the kinds of records you need to collect, what forms you should use, and how to claim exemptions and standard deductions. We'll also talk about the Alternative Minimum Tax.

Part 2, "Touring the World of Itemization," focuses on expenses you can deduct if you itemize taxes on Schedule A. These include medical expenses, taxes, interest, charitable donations, casualty and theft losses, employee expenses, job hunting expenses, professional fees, and fees for saving and investing.

Part 3, "Roaming for Credits," moves through the world of direct tax write-offs called credits. There are tax credits for children, elderly folks, and disabled folks, as well as electric cars, adoption, and other special-needs situations.

Part 4, "Wondering About Education," helps you sort out the various tax-advantaged ways you can save for your children's education, as well as further education for yourself. Then we'll move on to the tax credits and deductions that can ease the burden of education expenses.

Part 5, "Traveling to Retirement," reviews ways you can save for retirement, tax deferred or completely tax-free. We'll also look at the tax impacts of withdrawing your savings when you get to retirement.

Part 6, "Tripping Through Splitsville," talks about the complications in the tax code that can make your decision to split even more difficult to handle financially. We'll talk about ways to minimize the tax bite, and we'll discuss how alimony and child support impact your tax bill.

Part 7, "Taking a Business Trip," covers the tax benefits of using your home and car for business. This part also explores how to write off costs of buying equipment, insurance, and other business expenses. Finally, we'll take a quick look at tax-advantaged ways for small business owners to save for retirement.

Extras

Along the way, you'll find some road signs to help you navigate the world of taxes:

Taxing Terms

What do you get when you mix legalese with financial jargon and IRS idioms? A lot of taxing terms, which I'll define for you here!

IRS Idioms

Everyone from Abe Lincoln to Mark Twain to Charles Schwab has had something to say about taxes. Hopefully you won't find these quotes too *taxing* to read!

Audit Alarms

As many people who've been audited have discovered, you can take tax savings a tad too far. In these boxes, you'll find out what you can do to reduce your chance of being audited and which tax-saving tricks you must use with caution.

Tax Tips

Take advantage of the tax code with these helpful hints.

Revenue Ramblings

These aren't required reading, but you'll be a savvy taxpayer if you take the time to look them over.

Acknowledgments

Writing about taxes—with the many quirks in the tax code and the endless variables that can complicate even the simplest tax form—can be difficult. I've had lots of help with this book and want to take the time to thank all the key people. Thanks to Gary Goldstein, who guided this book through the approval process and helped make it a reality; Jennifer Moore, whose excellent editing helped to make things clearer; Krista Hansing, whose copyediting smoothed the rough spots; and Billy Fields, who coordinated the production.

Special Thanks to the Technical Reviewer

The Complete Idiot's Guide to Tax Breaks and Deductions was reviewed by an expert who double-checked the accuracy of what you'll learn here, to help us ensure that this book gives you everything you need to know about reducing your tax bill. Special thanks are extended to Shellie L. Moore, CPA, who did a wonderful job of helping me accurately explain this complicated world of taxes.

Trademarks

All terms mentioned in this book that are known to be or are suspected of being trademarks or service marks have been appropriately capitalized. Alpha Books and Pearson Education, Inc., cannot attest to the accuracy of this information. Use of a term in this book should not be regarded as affecting the validity of any trademark or service mark.

Part 1

Exploring Tax Basics

Our first stop on our tour of the wonderful (ha!) world of tax breaks and deductions is a quick review of tax basics. You probably know most of the information in this part of the book, but you may have forgotten some of it or never completely understood how it worked.

We'll be discussing record keeping, forms, tax brackets, exemptions, and standard deductions. We'll also spend a bit of time on that ticking time bomb—the Alternative Minimum Tax. Watch out! You could be its next victim.

Chapter 1

Getting Ready for Tax Season

In This Chapter

- ◆ Simplifying the paper chase
- ◆ Picking a tax form that works for you
- ◆ Knowing your brackets
- ◆ Beginning your tax journey

Unless you're among the few people who diligently file everything in exactly the right place as soon as it arrives, update your personal finance software with every check you write (being sure to add the proper codes to how the money was spent), and carefully categorize your receipts, tax time is probably, well, taxing! More than likely, you have to search all your drawers, the glove compartment of your car, and possibly even under some furniture to find the records you need at tax time. Now you know why it's called spring cleaning!

No matter how complicated or simple your finances are, you can save yourself a lot of grief—and maybe even a lot of money—at tax time if you spend some time organizing your records before you make the first mark on your tax form. It makes sense, then, that this first chapter will focus on gathering the forms and paperwork you'll need if you want to save the most you can on your taxes. Once we've covered that important territory, we'll look at the different tax forms you can use. Finally, we'll review tax brackets and find out where you fit.

Scouring Your Records

Pulling together your records can be a tedious and frustrating task, but the better you do it, the easier your taxes will be. Oh, and don't think that you can avoid organizing your records if you decide to have someone else prepare your taxes for you—they'll probably hand you a booklet telling you what paperwork they need from you.

Tax Tips

I'm not going to explain all the forms you'll collect in this chapter. That would take a book in itself. We'll be working together, learning about their use as we discuss the related issues throughout the book. For right now, just collect the forms.

Whether you are planning to go it alone or to seek help, this is one of those jobs you just can't pass off to someone else. Sorry!

I've included some charts and tips to help you organize your forms so that you end up with a well-organized pile of stuff to complete your tax forms. Luckily you need to do this only once a year. You may even want to promise yourself that you'll be better next week and keep your filing up-to-date. Don't we all wish?

First, you'll need that most basic of taxpayer information: your Social Security number. If you're married, you'll need your spouse's number as well.

Children

If you have children, you'll need more than just their Social Security numbers. You'll need the following information:

- Name
- Social Security number
- Birth date
- Child-care costs
- Educational costs
- Earned income

Make sure you have some paperwork to back up all your numbers. For example, pull together your canceled checks or invoices for any child-care costs. You'll also need your provider's name, address, and tax ID number or Social Security number. If you pay tuition, find those tuition bills and canceled checks. If you adopted a child during the year, you'll need to collect your receipts or canceled checks for legal fees, transportation, and other costs associated with the adoption.

Things can be more complicated if you're divorced. We'll take a closer look at issues involving divorce and what you can deduct in Part 6.

> **Revenue Ramblings**
>
> If you're not sure whether something is deductible, save the receipt and/or canceled check for it. It's better to have too much information than not enough!

Other Dependents

If you're helping your parents or other dependents, pull together the following information:

- Name/relationship
- Social Security number
- Months in your home
- Dependent's income
- Your support

You'll need to prove that you are providing more than 50 percent of his or her support to claim the relative as a dependent. If the relative you are supporting is not living with you, you'll need his or her address.

Income Information

Gathering your income information will probably be fairly simple. Most of the information arrives in your mailbox when you're already thinking about having to fill out your tax forms. As you receive year-end statements from your employers, financial institutions, and others from whom you earned income, collect them in a file. Some of the things you can expect to get in January and February include these:

- W-2 forms from your and your spouse's employers
- Form 1099-MISC for any work as an independent contractor or for miscellaneous income

> **Revenue Ramblings**
>
> By law, most year-end income statements are due by January 31 of the following tax year.

- Interest income—Form 1099-INT

- Dividend income—Form 1099-DIV

- Sale of investments—Form 1099-B (If you've sold investment assets, you will need information about how much it cost you to buy these investments.)

- State and local tax refunds—Form 1099-G

- Unemployment income—Form 1099-G

- Medical savings accounts—Form 1099-MSA

- Retirement income—Form 1099-R

- Social Security income—SSA-1099

- Scholarship records

- Gambling or lottery winnings—Form W2-G (If you've won big, be sure to collect proof of how much you spent to win that money.)

- Partnership investments—Schedule K-1 (Form 1065)

- S-Corporation Investments—Schedule K-1 (Form 1120-S)

- Broker's (or other financial institution) year-end statements

You'll also need to find any employee stock option or stock purchase plan information. This is critical only in the tax year that you exercised your option or sold your shares, but make sure that you keep good records about these employee benefits.

You'll need to collect some additional information in special circumstances. For example, if you are divorced and collecting alimony, you'll need bank statements or deposit records. If you're paying alimony, collect that information, too.

Audit Alarm!

CAUTION

If you've pulled money out of a retirement plan or deposited money into a plan, be sure to put your Form 5498 or 1099R from your financial institution in the stack. Taxes and penalties may have been taken out already, but you still must report it or you could end up with an audit.

If you've sold your residence, keep your sales information handy—but you probably won't owe taxes on it as long as you have lived there at least two years and the gain is less than $500,000 if you're filing a joint return with a spouse, or $250,000 if you're single. If you think your gain could exceed these limits, you should collect all records of major improvements you made to the property, as well as costs of selling the property. You'll also need information about costs when you purchased the property.

If you run a business, you'll need to find a lot more information, depending on the type of business you run. Life is a lot easier if you keep your business records in a standard accounting record format. You'll need invoices and billing information, bank statements, canceled checks for expenses, payroll records (if you pay anyone, including your children), records of major purchases for the business, inventory records, and vehicle records of mileage and expenses.

If you run your business from home, you'll need to calculate the percentage of the home you use for business purposes. Also, collect any information about your home expenses that are for utilities and other things used personally and by your business, such as phones, electricity, major repairs, and computer hook-ups. You may even be able to write off some of your homeowner's insurance premium.

If you have rental property, you'll need to either keep the profit and loss statements from your property manager handy, or begin collecting the information to put together your own version of a profit and loss statement. The records you'll need include canceled checks for paying expenses, records of rental income earned, mortgage interest paid on the property, property tax payments, and any other expenses related to the rental property.

Only you know how you earned income. If I've missed anything that helped you bring money into the house, collect those records, too.

Income Adjustments

Not all of your income will be taxable, but you'll need records to prove that fact. Contributions into retirement accounts are one of the largest *income adjustments* for many taxpayers. Be sure you gather your year-end statements for your retirement accounts. If you've made contributions into a medical savings account, you'll need information about that account and any of your canceled checks that show how the money was disbursed.

Some expenses can be used as adjustments as well. Save your Form 1098-E if you paid student loan interest. If you moved for the purposes of a job, be sure you have proof of all your costs related to that move.

Taxing Terms

Income Adjustments are items you can deduct from your income on the front of IRS form 1040 to calculate your Adjusted Gross Income. These include IRA deductions, student loan interest, medical savings accounts, moving expenses, one-half of the self-employment tax, retirement plan contributions, alimony, and savings penalties.

If you're self-employed, you could have adjustments for self-employed health insurance and pension plans. You also get to take an adjustment for half of your self-employed taxes paid to Social Security and Medicare. Be sure you keep records of those payments. You'll need them for adjustments and to prove that you actually paid those taxes.

Itemized Deductions

Taxpayers can choose to use the standard deduction allowed by the IRS or can itemize deductions based on their actual expenses. We'll be reviewing rules for the standard deduction in Chapter 3 and for itemized deductions in Part 2.

People typically itemize deductions if the total of their qualifying deductions exceeds the standard deduction allowed by the IRS. We'll talk more about that decision in Chapter 3. You won't know whether itemizing or taking a standard deduction is the way to go until you compare the two, so it's a good idea to collect the following information:

- **Medical and dental expenses.** You'll need all your medical bills or canceled checks, private health insurance premiums (only if paid for after taxes were taken out of your paycheck), Medicare premium payments (if you collect Social Security, you'll find the premium information on Form SSA-1099), and mileage records for all medical appointments. Medical expenses are discussed in detail in Chapter 4.

- **Taxes.** Be sure to have last year's state income tax return (if you owed money when you filed instead of getting a refund), proof of state and local taxes paid (you can find this information on your W-2s), canceled checks for estimated taxes paid, Form 1098 (which should be sent by mortgage companies and which lists interest expenses and real estate taxes), and tax bills on your real estate holdings. Taxes are discussed in detail in Chapter 5.

- **Interest.** As mentioned, you'll need Form 1098 from your mortgage company (if you threw that out by mistake, you probably can find the information on your January mortgage statement, or contact your mortgage company for another copy), mortgage loan closing statement if you bought a home or refinanced a loan during the year, and any investment interest paid (which you can find on your broker's statements). Interest is discussed in detail in Chapter 5.

- **Charitable donations.** Collect all your charity bills, receipts, and canceled checks; keep records of mileage you incur for charitable purposes; get receipts from charitable agencies to which you donated property (be sure they include the estimated value of property given—get expensive property appraised before you give the donation, and keep a copy of that appraisal for tax time); and collect year-end paychecks (if you have charitable donations taken out of your check). Charitable donations are discussed in detail in Chapter 6.

- **Casualty and theft losses.** Make a list of property damaged or stolen, find receipts or canceled checks that show how much you paid for that property (if you still have them), and find your insurance policy and any reports showing reimbursement you received. If you needed to get an appraisal to collect on your loss, find your bill or canceled check used to pay the bill; appraisal costs are deductible, too. Losses are discussed in detail in Chapter 7.

- **Job expenses.** If all your work expenses are 100 percent reimbursed by your employer, there is no need to collect these records for tax time. However, if you spend money related to your job that isn't reimbursed, here are the records you should collect: job travel information (invoices, receipts or ticket stubs for transportation, car mileage records, hotel bills, restaurant bills, and parking fee receipts), union dues, gifts to clients (be sure you have receipts that show date, cost, and description), invoices or receipts for supplies, proof of purchase for property that you use in your work, bills for purchasing or cleaning required uniforms or special work clothes, receipts or invoices for seminar fees, and proof of purchase for professional publications or books. You are also entitled to write off job search expenses, such as long-distance phone costs, resumé costs (including printing and mailing, as well as resumé services), transportation costs (which can include car mileage or other transportation fees), employment agency fees, and career counseling costs. If you take courses that are job-related, but for which your company doesn't reimburse you, you can deduct those costs as well. You'll need receipts, bills, or canceled checks for tuition, fees, and books; transportation receipts; and travel receipts if you had to take the course away from home. See Chapter 8 for more on job-related expenses.

CAUTION   **Audit Alarm!** _____

Today most companies deduct your medical insurance premiums from your paycheck before calculating taxes. Be sure you know whether your medical insurance was paid before or after the tax calculation—it should be indicated on your pay stub or W-2. You certainly don't want to miss the deduction if you are entitled to it, but if you haven't paid taxes on the premium and then you write off the payment as a deduction, you could end up being audited.

- **Other deductions.** Collect invoices or canceled checks for tax return preparation fees or tax software and book purchases, bank statements or invoices that show your safe deposit rental fees, IRA custodial fees if paid outside your IRA account, and costs for investment or other personal financial advice. See Chapter 8 for a list of other qualifying deductions.

Tax Payments

If you make quarterly estimated tax payments, be sure you keep your canceled checks or other records of those payments. If you applied a tax overpayment from the previous tax year toward the current, be sure you have records of that overpayment. If you filed for an extension on taxes and paid estimated taxes, don't forget to include those additional payments made with the extension.

Okay, that should do it. If I've missed something that you think might be deductible, certainly include that in the pile as well. I know it's a horrible job to pull all this together, but once it's done, the worst is over. Now you've got all the information you need in one place to complete your taxes. If you haven't already done so, group the papers in piles based on the type of tax information they are. For example, develop piles of medical receipts, taxes paid, investment information, interest paid, and so on. The more organized you are, the easier the rest of this task will be.

Choosing Your Forms

Now it's time to make your first big decision: the main tax form you'll use. Although the IRS publishes hundreds of worksheets, schedules, and miscellaneous forms, all filers must select from among three standard forms, which all additional forms must accompany:

- Form 1040EZ
- Form 1040A
- Form 1040

Form 1040EZ

Get it? "EZ" stands for easy. Sometimes the IRS actually *does* try to make things easy for us. Form 1040EZ is the simplest form, only one double-sided page, but you can't use it if you plan to claim any income adjustments, such as deductions for an IRA or student loan interest. Also, you can't itemize deductions. You must have less than $50,000 in taxable income. Your income must be from wages, salaries, tips, unemployment compensation, taxable scholarships and grants, qualified state tuition program earnings, or interest earnings of less than $400. If you are over the age of 65 or are blind and want to claim additional standard deductions (see Chapter 3), you can't use this simple form.

Form 1040A

If you're not planning to itemize, you may want to consider using Form 1040A. You can adjust your income on this form to show deductions for IRA contributions or student loan interest. You taxable income, however, can't exceed $50,000. In addition to the income types allowed in the Form 1040EZ, you can use this form if your income is derived from retirement sources, including pension and annuity payments, Social Security or railroad benefits, and IRA disbursements. You can also claim a number of credits, including the Child and Dependent Care Credit, Credit for the Elderly or the Disabled, Child Tax Credit), the Hope Credit and Lifetime Learning Credit (education credits), the Earned Income Credit, the Adoption Credit, and Rate Reduction Credit. We'll explore the credit types in Part 3.

> **Audit Alarm!**
> You may not be able to use Form 1040A if you received a sizeable capital gain distribution. If you're not sure that you qualify, check with a tax advisor.

Form 1040

If you don't qualify for one of the simpler forms, you're stuck with the 1040. Most people who want to take deductions use this form. The 1040 allows you to take the greatest advantage of the tax breaks and deductions that are discussed in this book. The 1040A is actually one page back-to-back, but you might need to attach lots of schedules and forms based on how many credits you can take, what types of investments you have, and whether you have a business. The number of schedules, credit forms, and worksheets that you'll need to attach depends on your individual tax situation.

Calculating Your Bracket

Tax brackets determine how much tax you have to pay based on your income. There are six tax brackets: 10 percent, 15 percent, 27 percent, 30 percent, 35 percent, and 38.6 percent. The tax bracket you are in represents how much tax you will pay on only a portion of your income. In other words, just because you are in, say, the 27 percent tax bracket doesn't mean that you are paying 27 percent in taxes on all of your

Taxing Terms

A progressive tax system requires wealthier citizens to pay higher taxes than those who are less well off.

earnings. Instead, you are paying 27 percent on the income range that falls in the 27 percent tax bracket. This is called a *progressive tax system.*

Everyone has some portion of income taxed at the lowest bracket of 10 percent. Here's the breakdown of the brackets for 2002 rates for a married couple filing jointly:

Earnings from $0 to $12,000 are taxed 10 percent.

Earnings from $12,001 through $46,700 are taxed 15 percent.

Earnings from $46,701 through $112,850 are taxed 27 percent.

Earnings from $112,851 through $171,950 are taxed 30 percent.

Earnings from $171,951 through $307,050 are taxed 35 percent.

Earnings above $307,051 are taxed 38.6 percent.

For a family with a taxable income of $60,000 after all adjustments and deductions, taxes are calculated as follows:

Income	Taxes
Up to $12,000 at 10%	$1,200
Between $12,001 and $46,700 at 15%	$5,205
Between $46,701 and $60,000 at 27%	$3,591
Total taxes	$9,996

Revenue Ramblings

You've probably heard politicians and others argue for instituting a flat tax rate of, say, 10 or 15 percent. These plans are developed without any tax breaks or deductions allowed. Let's go back to that $60,000 taxable earning level and add back what would be average deductions for earners at that level. Let's just guess that itemized deductions totaled $20,000. Let's assume that it's a family of four with four exemptions of $3,000 each, or $12,000. Also, we'll assume that adjustments for retirement contributions totaled $4,000. Total income without these adjustments was $96,000.

This family earning $96,000 would pay $9,600 in taxes, saving $396 if a flat tax rate of 10 percent was instituted. However, the family would end up paying $4,404 (total tax $14,400) more if a 15 percent flat tax rate were enacted. Be sure you understand the impacts on your personal taxes before supporting tax-simplification plans.

This family actually pays $9,996 in taxes, or 16.66 percent of its taxable income, even though its income falls in the 27 percent tax bracket. Only the income earned over $46,700 and below $112,851 will be taxed at the 27 percent tax rate.

Different tax rate tables are used depending on your filing status. The preceding table is for married people filing joint returns. There are also charts for single folks, married folks filing separately, and *heads of households* or surviving spouses.

Taxing Terms

A **head of household** is someone who isn't married but who has a dependent child or parent. To qualify, you must have paid more than half the cost of keeping up the home, as well as half the costs of the dependent person or persons.

People who are single (other than surviving spouses and heads of household) use the following brackets:

Earnings from $0 to $6,000 are taxed 10 percent.

Earnings from $6,001 through $27,950 are taxed 15 percent.

Earnings from $27,951 through $67,700 are taxed 27 percent.

Earnings from $67,701 through $141,250 are taxed 30 percent.

Earnings from $141,251 through $307,050 are taxed 35 percent.

Earnings above $307,051 are taxed 38.6 percent.

People who are married but decide to file separately use these brackets:

Earnings from $0 to $6,000 are taxed 10 percent.

Earnings from $6,001 through $23,350 are taxed 15 percent.

Earnings from $23,351 through $56,425 are taxed 27 percent.

Earnings from $56,426 through $85,975 are taxed 30 percent.

Earnings from $85,976 through $153,525 are taxed 35 percent.

Earnings above $153,526 are taxed 38.6 percent.

A person who is the head of a household but unmarried uses the following brackets:

Earnings from $0 to $10,000 are taxed 10 percent.

Earnings from $10,001 through $37,450 are taxed 15 percent.

Earnings from $37,451 through $96,700 are taxed 27 percent.

Earnings from $96,701 through $156,000 are taxed 30 percent.

Earnings from $156,001 through $307,050 are taxed 35 percent.

Earnings above $307,051 are taxed 38.6 percent.

Tax rates will be changing two more times because of the 2001 tax law, unless Congress decides to delay the changes. In 2004, the rates will drop 1 percent for the four highest tax brackets (27, 30, 35, and 38.6 percent). The 10 percent and 15 percent brackets won't change, but the higher brackets will be 26 percent rather than 27, 29 percent rather than 30, 34 percent rather than 35, and 37.6 percent rather than 38.6. There will be another 1 percent decrease for these same brackets in 2006, which is the final change planned at this time.

In 2008, there will be a change in the 10 percent bracket. Earnings up to $7,000 for single folks and $14,000 for married couples will be subject to the 10 percent tax rate. This is up from the current maximum of $6,000 for singles and $12,000 for married couples. The $10,000 earnings limit for the head of a household will remain the same.

The 2001 law was a massive revision of the tax code that will take effect in various stages over a 10-year period. Some deductions disappear partway during the time period, while others don't appear until five years down the road. We'll be pointing out the changes as we take our journey together.

Starting the Trip

Now that you know what financial information you need to gather, what basic tax forms you'll need, and what tax bracket you're likely to fall in, you're ready to start figuring out how to pay as little as legally possible.

The Least You Need to Know

- ◆ Collecting the information you need at tax time may be an arduous task, but it's the only way you'll be able to take advantage of tax breaks and deductions.

- ◆ To take advantage of most tax breaks and deductions, you'll need to file your taxes on Form 1040, not the simpler 1040EZ or 1040A forms.

- ◆ Rates for tax brackets are not necessarily the tax percentage you'll actually pay.

- ◆ Tax rates for the four highest income brackets are scheduled to decrease over the next several years.

Chapter 2

Exempting Options

In This Chapter

- ◆ Taking your claims
- ◆ Defining dependents
- ◆ Taking qualifying tests
- ◆ Running into the income limit

You may feel like you're back in first grade when you fill out the first page of the basic 1040 tax form, having to check boxes and add up ones, twos, and possibly even some fives and sixes. It may seem like kid's stuff, but each of those little numbers represents what the IRS calls an exemption, and they can add up to a lot of tax savings for you. We'll take a look at the kinds of exemptions you can take, what type of tests you need to pass to claim them, and what the limits to using them are.

Claiming You and Your Family

You and your spouse can each claim a personal exemption, and for each dependent you can claim a dependent exemption. In 2002, each exemption allows you to subtract $3,000 from your adjusted gross income (AGI), meaning that you won't have to pay taxes on that chunk of money. (The exemptions are in addition to your standard or itemized deductions, which are explained in the next chapter.) Each year the amount of the exemption is adjusted by the government based on an inflation index. The 2001 exemption was $2,900; be sure to check the number each time you fill out your 1040.

Taxing Terms

Personal exemption is the amount you can subtract from your adjusted gross income before calculating your taxes due for yourself and your spouse. This is in addition to your standard or itemized deductions.

Dependent exemption is the amount you can subtract annually from your adjusted gross income before calculating your taxes due for anyone that qualifies as your dependent. Your spouse is never considered your dependent.

Adjusted gross income (AGI) is the calculation of your income after adjustments for things such as retirement contributions, but before standard or itemized deductions and personal exemptions are made. This is the number at the bottom of the first page of IRS Form 1040.

The IRS tracks who claims whom as a dependent very closely using the Social Security numbers you must give for each person you claim as a dependent. This can get particularly tricky for students who are working but receive more than 50 percent of their support from their parents. In such situations, the parents can take a dependent exemption for the student, and the student—even though he or she must report earnings—cannot take a personal exemption.

Things can get murky when trying to figure who gets to claim whom after a death, divorce, or separation. If a spouse files separately, he or she can claim his or her spouse, provided that the spouse has no gross income and isn't someone else's dependent. If you become divorced or separated and there is a final divorce decree or separation agreement in place before the end of the tax year, you cannot take an exemption for your ex-spouse, even if you paid 100 percent of the former spouse's support. If a spouse dies, as long as you don't remarry during that year, you can claim your deceased spouse as a dependent.

Audit Alarm!

If you have any doubt about who is claiming whom as a dependent, be sure to sort it out before filing. The IRS can match dependents using the Social Security numbers you must provide.

Another area that can be confusing is how to handle the exemption if a dependent dies during the year.

A child who is born alive and dies shortly afterward can be claimed as a dependent, but a stillborn doesn't qualify. To claim a child who died shortly after birth, you must have proof, such as a birth certificate, that the child was alive at birth. Other dependents who die during the year—whether a child, a parent, or another relative—can be claimed as a dependent in the year they die, provided that they meet the other dependent tests we will discuss soon.

Be forewarned: Whether or not you can use these exemptions depends on your income and on the tax year. The phaseout of personal exemptions is one of those moving targets that changed several times during the life span of the 2001 tax law.

Passing the Tests

Dependents must past five so-called tests for you to claim them:

- Member of Household or Relationship Test
- Citizen or Residence Test
- Joint Return Test
- Gross Income Test
- Support Test

An individual must pass all five of these tests to qualify as a dependent. Failing even one of them disqualifies someone as a dependent. Let's start with the easier tests and work our way to the most difficult one.

Member of Household or Relationship Test

As long as the person is related to you, he or she may not need to live at your house to be considered a member of your household. Someone who isn't related to you may possibly pass the test, provided that he or she lives with you in your principal place of residence. You can't include housekeepers, maids, or servants as household members for exemption purposes if they work for you.

Members of household are allowed temporary absences and still qualify for the exemption. These temporary absences can be for special circumstances, such as illness, education, business, vacation, or military service. If someone goes to a nursing home for an indefinite period to receive medical care, he or she fits in this temporary absence category.

A relative who doesn't live with you could qualify as a member of your household if he or she is your ...

 ◆ Child, stepchild, grandchild, great-grandchild, or legally adopted child.

 ◆ Brother, sister, half brother, half sister, stepbrother, or stepsister.

 ◆ Parent, grandparent, or other direct ancestor, but not a foster parent.

 ◆ Brother or sister of your father or mother.

 ◆ Son or daughter of your brother or sister.

 ◆ In-law, including father, mother, son, daughter, brother, or sister.

Death or divorce doesn't end these relationships for tax purposes once they have been established by marriage.

Tax Tips

Member of household status can be a murky area when it comes to foster children and children you plan to adopt. Although you can claim a child whom you plan to adopt as a dependent even before the adoption is final, you can't claim a foster child unless that child lived with you for the entire year. As long as a child was placed with you for legal adoption by an authorized placement agency, this child can be claimed as a dependent even if he or she was in your household for less than a year.

Revenue Ramblings

If you help a foreign student, even if that student lives with you for a full year, he or she will fail the Citizen Resident Test and you won't be able to claim him or her. You may be able to use at least some of your expenses as a charitable contribution, though. We'll talk more about that in Chapter 6.

Citizen Resident Test

To claim a person as a member of your household, that person must be a U.S. citizen or a resident of Canada or Mexico for at least some part of the tax year. You can't claim someone who lives in Puerto Rico unless he or she is also a U.S. citizen. Odd, isn't it?

If your child was born abroad, he or she is a U.S. citizen, provided that you are a U.S. citizen and lived in the United States for at least 10 years before the child's birth. At least 5 of those 10 years must have been before the age of 14. Even if the child lives with a parent who is a nonresident alien in another country, the

U.S. citizen can claim the child as a dependent. If you legally adopt a child who isn't a U.S. citizen or resident, that child also may be able to pass the citizen test for tax purposes.

Joint Return Test

You can lose the right to claim someone who lives with you as a dependent if that person files a joint return with someone else. An example of this is if your child comes home to live with you while his or her spouse is on an overseas assignment. If the couple files a joint return, you cannot claim your child, even if he or she lived with you for a year.

The exception to this rule is if your child and his or her spouse would have a tax liability if they separately filed returns. As long as each had less than $3,925 in wages or other income (the standard deduction for married filing separately), together they would not have a tax liability. In this case, the couple wouldn't be required to file a return, although they might want to do so to get back money taken out for taxes from their wages. You can claim exemptions for both your child and your child's spouse if they pass the other dependency tests.

Gross Income Test

In most cases, you can't claim anyone who had *gross income* of more than $3,000 in 2002 (or the amount of the dependent deduction in future years). The only exception to this is for a child under the age of 19 or a full-time student until the age of 24.

If your dependent is disabled and attending a workshop at which he or she earns income, the income may not be included in the Gross Income Test. The key to getting this exemption from gross income is that the dependent must be permanently and totally disabled, and the primary reason for attending the workshop must be medical care. The income involved must come from activities at the workshop that are related to this medical care. These types of workshops must be operated in the United States or U.S. possessions and must provide special instruction to ease the disability of the individual.

Taxing Terms

Gross income can include any money, property, or services that are not exempt from tax. Rental receipts, gross business income, gross partnership income, unemployment claims, and some scholarship and fellowship grants count as gross income. Scholarships or grants that are only for tuition, fees, supplies, books, and equipment for specific courses are not considered gross income.

Support Test

The final test you must pass is to prove that you provide more than half a person's total support. However, as with all tax laws, there are special exceptions. Even if you are not providing more than 50 percent of a child's support, you may still be able to claim the child if no one person provides more than 50 percent of his or her support.

Divorced or separated parents also have different rules for passing the support test. We'll look at those rules more closely in Part 6.

Tax Tips

Even if you provide support for less than half the year, you may be able to claim a person as a dependent. The Support Test is based on the dollar amount spent, not the number of months the person has lived with you.

Just because a person gets funds, you may not necessarily need to include those funds when you figure the percentage of support received from you. Let's say that your mother gets money from Social Security and investment income, but she doesn't use it all for support (such as rent and food). You don't need to include the income not used by your mother for support when trying to figure out if she passes the dependent test.

If you pay your child wages or your child earns wages outside the home and then uses the money earned for support, you cannot include that money when calculating your support contribution.

Here are the key things to consider in the support calculations for each person you support:

◆ Lodging (Either rent paid or fair rental value—this is where you offset mortgage payments if you own a home. You must use a rental figure that is the reasonable market value you would charge if you rented to a stranger.)

◆ Food

◆ Utilities

◆ Repairs

◆ Clothing

◆ Education

◆ Medical or dental expenses

◆ Travel or entertainment expenses

◆ Charitable contributions for your dependent

◆ Payments for the care of a child or elderly parent

You may have other things to include, but be sure you can prove them as support costs.

When you've gathered all the numbers, calculate both the total amount of money needed to support the person and how much of that money you contributed. Then divide the amount you contributed by the amount of total support, as in the following calculation:

$$\frac{\text{Amount of Support Paid}}{\text{Total Support Needed}} = \text{Percentage of Support You Pay}$$

Let's work through an example for this test. We'll assume that your mother is living with you. Her total retirement income is $500 a month, or $6,000 per year. She contributes approximately $400 per month, or $4,800, toward her support needs. You pay approximately $800 per month (or $9,600) toward her support, whether it's toward the fair market value of the room you provide or the payment of food, medical bills, or other qualifying support payments. Total support for your mother in this example is $14,400, of which you pay 67 percent.

You figure your support percentage by:

$$\frac{\text{Amount of Support Paid: \$9,600}}{\text{Total Support Needed: \$14,400}} = 67\%$$

In this example, your mother qualifies as a dependent, provided that she meets the requirements of the other four dependency tests. If both of your parents are living with you, you must calculate their percentage of support separately.

Things can get complicated if more than one child is helping to support elderly parents. Sometimes no one is providing 50 percent of support. The children sharing in support costs must decide who gets to claim the parent as a dependent. The person who plans to claim the exemption must ask all others providing support to sign a Multiple Support Document, which the IRS provides as Form 2120, and then must file those documents with his or her tax forms.

Tax Tips

How do you decide which sibling should get the deduction for an elderly dependent parent if no one is providing 50 percent of support? Usually it makes the most sense to give it to the child who stands to benefit the greatest from the deduction because he or she is in the highest tax bracket.

Support for parents can be difficult to sort out, but it's usually easier than figuring support for children after a divorce or separation, which can often turn into a war between battling ex-spouses. We'll put off this discussion until Part 6, when we sort out all the tax issues in Splitsville.

Facing the Limits

Unfortunately, you can earn too much to be able to take advantage of the personal exemptions, whether for yourself, your spouse, or your dependents. If you are married filing separately, phaseout begins once you earn over $103,000. Single filers begin to lose the exemption write off once they earn more than $137,300. Head of household exemptions begin to phase out with earnings over $171,650, and married folks filing jointly begin to lose their exemptions with earnings over $206,000. Once you reach the income limit level, your personal exemptions begin to phase out gradually until you reach the level at which you lose them completely. The dollar amount of your exemptions is reduced by 2 percent for each $2,500 (or part of $2,500) once your income exceeds the adjusted gross income (AGI) limit for your filing status. If you are married filed separately, the 2 percent reduction is based on each $1,250 or part of $1,250. Eventually, if your income is high enough, the exemptions are wiped out completely.

The following table shows the personal exemption levels based on your status:

Phaseout of Personal Exemptions in 2002 Tax Year

Filing Status	Phaseout Begins	Phaseout Completed
Joint return	$206,000	$328,500
Head of household	$171,650	$294,150
Single	$137,300	$259,800
Married filing separately	$103,000	$164,250

The personal exemptions limit is one of those rules that hits married couples much harder than single folks. Two single people can earn a total of $274,600 before beginning to lose their personal exemptions, while a married couple's personal exemptions begin to phase out at $206,000. A married person filing separately is also hit much harder than a single person. For that person, the personal exemption begins to phase out at $103,000, or half the amount for a person filing jointly.

Let's take a closer look at how the phaseout provision works. Like almost everything related to taxes, the IRS provides you with a worksheet that you can use to figure out how the phaseout rules may impact your exemption amount.

Deductions for Exemptions Worksheet

1. The IRS asks you to compare your AGI to the phaseout limits based on your filing status. For example, a married couple with an AGI of less than $200,000 would not need to go any further, while a married couple earning $206,001 would need to complete the worksheet.

2. Multiply $3,000 by the total number of exemptions.   _____

3. Enter your AGI.   _____

4. Enter the amount at which the phaseout begins.   _____

5. Subtract line 4 from line 3.   _____

6. Divide line 5 by $2,500 ($1,250, if married filing jointly.) Always round up to the next highest whole number. For example, even a .001 would have to be increased to 1.   _____

7. Multiply line 6 by 2 percent.   _____

8. Multiply line 2 by line 7.   _____

9. Subtract line 8 from line 2.
   (This is the amount of your reduced exemptions.)   _____

This isn't as confusing as it looks, I promise! Let's practice filling out the worksheet for a family of four. We'll assume that the AGI for the couple filing a joint return is $300,000. The couple has two children. Their total for personal exemptions is 4.

Here's how the calculation would work for them.

1. Phaseout begins at $206,000 for married couples filing jointly, so they do need to complete the worksheet.

2. Multiply $3,000 × 4 exemptions. $12,000

3. Enter the AGI. $300,000

4. Enter the phaseout starting number. $206,000

5. Subtract line 4 from line 3. $94,000

6. Divide line 5 by $2,500. (The answer is 37.6, rounded to 38.)   38

7. Multiply line 6 by 2 percent.   .76

8. Multiply line 2 by line 7. $9,120

9. Subtract line 8 from line 2. $2,980

As you can see in this example, the couple will lose 76 percent of their exemptions, for a total of $9,120. Remember, this doesn't mean that they will pay $9,120 more in taxes, but only that they won't be able to subtract that amount from their AGI before calculating their taxes.

The good news for high earners is that, thanks to the tax law passed in 2001, this phaseout rule is going to gradually disappear. The phaseout is reduced by one third in tax years 2006 and 2007. There will be a further reduction of one third in tax years beginning in 2008 and 2009. There will be no phaseout in tax year 2010, but who knows what Congress will do with this provision by that time?

Now that we've got the exemptions out of the way, let's take a look at deductions.

The Least You Need to Know

◆ You can claim personal exemptions worth $3,000 each for yourself, your spouse, and your children or other dependents.

◆ To claim someone as a dependent, he or she must pass five tests.

◆ You can earn too much and lose your personal exemptions.

Standardizing Your Deductions

In This Chapter

- ◆ Figuring your standards
- ◆ Adding on extras
- ◆ Getting less than standard
- ◆ Losing it all
- ◆ A ticking time bomb

Although almost everybody hates to even think about taxes, almost everyone loves to talk about the deductions they took to avoid paying as much tax as legally possible (and maybe some breaks that aren't legal!). Finding tax deductions is a national pastime, and some people are better at playing the game than others.

As noted in Chapter 2, you can take deductions in one of two ways—by using standard tables based on your filing status or by itemizing deductions. We'll be concentrating on standard deductions in this chapter and we'll move to the world of itemization in the next part. We're also going to take a quick look at the ticking time bomb that, if it explodes, could eat up a lot of your deductions—the Alternative Minimum Tax.

Deciding on Deductions

Let's begin by defining the differences between standard and itemized deductions. The standard deduction is automatic. You don't need to figure anything out. Just write down the amount allowed based on your filing status. We'll look at the standard deduction tables later.

Itemization is a lot more work. You need to find receipts for all the things you spent money on that are tax deductible and add them up. Remember all that paperwork you collected in the first chapter? It will come in very handy when you start working on itemizing deductions.

A lot of people aren't sure when they should take the standard deduction and when they should itemize. Basically, you should itemize any time the amount of money you spent on eligible deductions is more than the standard deduction you're allowed. Now comes the hard part: What are eligible deductions? We'll be spending a good part of the rest of this book exploring exactly that topic. Before we get into the nitty gritty of deductions, I'll review the basics of when you'll likely have enough to make itemizing your deductions worth the effort in any one year:

IRS Idioms

The avoidance of taxes is the only intellectual pursuit that carries any reward.

—John Maynard Keynes

- ◆ You had large uninsured medical or dental bills.

- ◆ You paid interest and taxes on the home you own.

- ◆ You had large employee expenses that were not reimbursed.

- ◆ You suffered a significant loss from casualty or theft.

- ◆ You made sizeable charitable contributions.

All this will add up to the fact that your itemized deductions will be greater than the standard deduction you are allowed. You don't have to itemize every year. You need to do so only in the years that you will end up with a lower tax bill because your itemized deductions are high. If you are married filing separately, you must either both use the standard deduction or both calculate itemized deductions.

Standard Deductions

Let's review what the standard deductions are so you know whether it's even worth going through all the trouble of itemizing your deductions. The standard deduction is based on your filing status. Here are the standard deductions for the 2002 tax year:

Standard Deductions

Filing Status	Tax Year 2002
Married filing jointly	$7,850
Single	$4,700
Head of household	$6,900
Married filing separate returns	$3,925

You'll see that the marriage penalty shows up here as well. The combined standard deduction for two unmarried single people is $9,400, while a married couple filing jointly gets to take only $7,850. No wonder more people are living together without getting married!

Congress has finally decided to amend the tax laws to avoid the marriage penalty. The change is a gradual one, though, and doesn't start until 2005, with complete elimination by 2009. Here's how the marriage penalty related to standard deductions will be eliminated.

Tax Tips

There really isn't any part of the tax code that is called a marriage penalty. This political football actually stems from numerous inconsistencies of the tax code that result in many two-earner couples paying more tax than they would if they were filing as two single individuals.

Calendar Year	Standard Deduction for Joint Returns as a Percentage of Standard Deduction for Single Returns
2005	174%
2006	184%
2007	187%
2008	190%
2009 and beyond	200%

If you plan to take the standard deduction, all you need to do is put the amount for your filing status on the right line and subtract it from your income. Now that's easy. But we are talking about the federal government, so you know there will be exceptions to what appears to be a simple rule.

Can You Get Extras?

Your standard deduction is increased in two situations: If you're 65 or older, or if you are partially or totally blind.

You get to claim the extra deduction for the entire year, even if you turn 65 on January 1 of the following tax year. For example, if your sixty-fifth birthday is January 1, 2003, you qualify for the extra deduction in 2002.

You can qualify for the blind deduction if you are partially or totally blind. If you are partially blind, you will need a statement from a doctor certifying one of the following:

♦ Your vision is no better than 20/200 in your good eye with glasses or contact lenses.

♦ Your field of vision is not more than 20°.

The statement must also include the fact that your condition will never improve beyond these limits.

Additions to the standard deduction are allowed for yourself and your spouse, but for no one else on your return. You can claim your spouse on a joint return or on a return that you file separately if your spouse has no gross income and no one else claims an exemption for your spouse.

The additional standard deduction in 2002 is $900 for married filers and $1,150 for unmarried filers. If you are blind and over 65, you can claim two additional deductions. A couple who are both over age 65 and blind can claim as many as four additions at $900 each. Here's a table that shows the standard deduction with the additions allowed for age of over 65 and blindness:

Standard Deduction with Additions for over Age 65 and/or Blindness

Filing Status	Number of Additional Deductions	Total 2002 Standard Deduction
Married filing jointly or qualified widow(er)	1	$8,750

Filing Status	Number of Additional Deductions	Total 2002 Standard Deduction
($900 per addition)	2	$9,650
	3	$10,550
	4	$11,450
Single	1	$5,850
($1,150 per addition)	2	$7,000
Head of household	1	$8,050
($1,150 per addition)	2	$9,200
Married filing	1	$4,825
separate returns	2	$5,725
($900 per addition)	3	$6,625
	4	$7,525

When You Get Less

Not everyone gets to take the full standard deduction. If someone else gets to claim you as an exemption (for example, you are still a dependent of your parents), you may not be entitled to take a full standard deduction. The total deduction allowed is $750 or the dependent's *earned income* from a job plus $250. The highest this calculation can be is the standard deduction for a person based on his or her filing status, such as $4,700 for a single person in 2002.

Let's look at how this works. Say that a student earns $5,000 for part-time work while going through college. He also gets $300 in interest income, but this isn't included as earned income. The student is still being claimed on his parents' return as a dependent. To calculate the amount of his standard deduction, add his earned income of $5,000 plus $250, which totals $5,250. As a single person, his standard deduction would be $4,700. In this case, the student would qualify for the full standard deduction.

In another situation, a student who is still being claimed on his parents' return earns $1,000 in part-time work during the school year. To

Taxing Terms

For IRS purposes, **earned income** includes salaries, wages, tips, professional fees, and other amounts you were paid for work you actually performed.

calculate this student's standard deduction, you would add $250, for a total of $1,250. The total standard deduction allowed for this student would be $1,250.

If earnings plus the $250 are less than $750, the dependent can claim a $750 standard deduction on his or her form.

While no taxes may be owed by dependents earning less than the standard deduction, many will file tax returns anyway to get a refund of the taxes taken out of their paychecks.

When You Get None

If you meet any of the following criteria, you aren't allowed to claim any standard deduction:

♦ You are married filing a separate return, and your spouse plans to itemize deductions.

♦ You are filing a tax return in a short tax year because you are changing your annual accounting period.

Taxing Terms

A **nonresident alien** is an individual who is not a citizen or permanent resident of the United States. A **resident alien** is someone who is a permanent resident of the United States but not a citizen. A **dual-status alien** is an individual who was both a nonresident alien and a resident alien in the same year.

♦ You are a *nonresident alien* or a *dual-status alien*. Of course, no surprise, there is an exception to this last rule. If you are a nonresident alien who is married to a U.S. citizen or resident at the end of the year, you can elect to be treated as a U.S. resident. By making this choice, you do get to take a standard deduction as long as your spouse isn't itemizing his or her deductions.

If you find yourself in one of these situations, you can't take a standard deduction, but you may still itemize deductions.

Limitations on Itemized Deductions

Before we move on to exploring itemized deductions, let's look at two limitations that can decrease their value: the reduction of itemized deductions if you earn too much and the ticking time bomb, the Alternative Minimum Tax (AMT).

Reducing Itemized Deductions

We talked about the phaseout for exemptions after a certain earning limit in Chapter 2. Well, a similar thing can happen if you itemize deductions. Most of your itemized deductions will be reduced by 3 percent of the amount of your adjusted gross income (AGI) if your income exceeds a certain threshold. In 2002, these thresholds are $137,300 for people whose filing status is single, joint, or head of household. The threshold for married filing separately in 2002 is $68,650.

This limitation on itemized deductions is in addition to specific limitations placed on some of the itemized deductions, such as the reduction of 7.5 percent of your AGI for medical deductions. We'll look at how the specific reductions work as we explore each type of itemized deduction individually.

Deductions that might be limited under this overall rule include taxes, most types of interest expense, charitable gifts, job expenses, and most miscellaneous deductions.

Not all itemized deductions fall victim to this limitation. The deductions that are not reduced as part of this overall itemized deductions limitation include these:

Audit Alarm!

If you're subject to the overall limitation on itemized deductions, you should certainly compare the standard deduction to your reduced itemized deductions to be sure it's still worth itemizing. You may find that you will pay fewer taxes using the standard deduction.

- ◆ Medical expenses

- ◆ Investment interest expense

- ◆ Nonbusiness casualty and theft losses

- ◆ Gambling losses

To figure your reduction, you total all your itemized deductions subject to the limitation and then subtract 3 percent of your AGI. Whatever remains is your allowable itemized deduction amount. At least the limitation has a limit: The most you can lose is 80 percent of your itemized deductions.

Just as with the phaseout of exemptions, the rule limiting itemized deductions is set for extinction. Beginning in 2006 and 2007, the reduction will be cut by one third. In 2008 and 2009, the reduction will be cut by two thirds. The overall limitation will be eliminated beginning in the tax year 2010, unless Congress changes the rules again before then.

AMT: A Ticking Time Bomb

You may never have heard of the Alternative Minimum Tax (AMT)—and even if you know about it, you probably were never subject to it. In 2001, 1.4 million taxpayers were impacted by the AMT. The Congressional Joint Committee on Taxation projects that this number will jump to 35.5 million in 2010 without some fix by Congress before then.

The potential problem posted by the AMT time bomb is twofold. The first is that the AMT is not adjusted for inflation. The other is that the reductions to tax rates in the 2001 tax bill could throw about 18 million taxpayers under the AMT, which will reduce or completely eliminate the benefit of those new lower rates.

Revenue Ramblings

The idea of a minimum tax is not a new one. Congress first added the concept to the tax code in 1969. The purpose was to reinflate the tax bills of wealthy individuals who took advantage of tax credits, deductions, and other tax breaks to lower their tax liability to little or nothing. In order words, taxpayers who get a bit too aggressive taking advantage of special tax breaks have to test their tax liability under the AMT after they fill out their conventional tax forms. The taxpayer will pay the higher tax bill—whether it's the number from the conventional tax return or the AMT amount.

AMT tax rates are 26 and 28 percent, which are lower than the regular tax rates, but many of the deductions and credits can't be applied to a taxpayer's earned income to reduce the taxable income. Most miscellaneous deductions as well as personal exemptions are not allowed under the AMT, which is what will throw many middle-class families into the AMT pool. For example, interest on home equity loans is deductible on a conventional return up to $100,000, but if a taxpayer must use the AMT formula, interest paid on home equity loans used for purposes other than home improvement will not be allowed. As we tour the world of itemization in the next part, I'll point out the AMT losers.

Today most taxpayers are protected from the AMT because of its exemption mechanism. Couples filing jointly can exempt $45,000 from the AMT calculation, and singles or head of household filers can exempt $33,750. The new tax law did add a small, temporary increase of $4,000 for joint returns and $2,000 for unmarried individuals, but this lasts until only 2004. The new law also protects some personal tax credits, including the Child Tax Credit, Child and Dependent Care Credit, and Hope Credit and Lifetime Learning Credit (college tuition credits) from AMT reduction, at least through 2003.

Why didn't Congress fix the problem? The answer is plain and simple: It costs too much. The cost of the 2001 tax bill was projected over 10 years to be more than $200 billion. If Congress had fixed the AMT problem, it would not have been able to add some of its other favorite tax breaks and stay within the tax cut targets.

 IRS Idioms

"Every member of this Congress knows that we ought to do more about the alternative minimum tax than we do in this bill .... It is a major problem that needs to be addressed."

—Senator Charles Grassley (R-Iowa), then-chairman of the Senate Finance Committee in 2001

"We obviously have to address that situation, and we will in the future."

—Senator Max Baucus (D-Montana), the new chairman of the Senate Finance Committee in 2001

So who needs to calculate the Alternative Minimum Tax—IRS Form 6251? The IRS provides a worksheet to help you figure that out, but there are some tax breaks for which the IRS automatically requires you to calculate AMT (primarily tax breaks of the rich):

- Accelerated depreciation

- Exercising an incentive stock option and holding on to the stock

- Tax-exempt interest from private activity bonds

- Intangible drilling, circulation, research, experimental, or mining costs

- Amortization of pollution-control facilities or depletion

- Income or (loss) from tax-shelter farm activities or passive activities

- Percentage-of-completion income from long-term contracts

- Interest paid on a home mortgage not used to buy, build, or substantially improve your home

- Investment interest expense reported on Form 4952

- Net operating loss deduction

- Alternative minimum tax adjustments from an estate, trust, electing large partnership, or cooperative

If you don't understand what these tax breaks are, you probably aren't eligible for them. I won't go into detailed explanation here, but I will be covering many of them in Part 7, when I discuss small business tax breaks and deductions.

An AMT Form 6251 also must be filed for a child who is under the age of 14 with adjusted gross income over $5,350.

Even if your AGI is below the thresholds of $49,000 for filers who are married filing jointly, $35,750 for single or head of household filers, or $24,500 for married couples who are filing separately, you may need to fill out the form. The steps in the worksheet add back in an adjustment for medical expenses (even if you used the standard deduction), taxes paid, and miscellaneous deductions. If adding any of these numbers back in throws you over the threshold, you'll need to fill out the worksheet.

Tax Tips

If you use tax-preparation software, the AMT test is probably done for you automatically. If you don't use any of the tax breaks discussed already, you can complete the AMT worksheet in the 1040 package before going on to the complicated AMT Form 6251.

You probably didn't expect to spend so much time learning about the standard deduction. Unfortunately, no aspect of the tax code is simple. In the next chapter, we'll move on to everyone's favorite spot for tax deductions—the world of itemization.

The Least You Need to Know

- ◆ Your standard deduction is based on a set amount depending on your filing status, whether single, married filing jointly, married filing separately, or head of household.

- ◆ If you are over the age of 65 or are blind, you may be able to add to the amount of your standard deduction without having to itemize.

- ◆ If you make too much money, the limitation on itemized deductions may make it better for you to use the standard deduction.

- ◆ You may soon be affected by the Alternative Minimum Tax if Congress doesn't fix the problem.

Part 2

Touring the World of Itemization

Individual taxpayers can be their most creative when visiting this world, but you've got to be careful: It's also the area that the tax man monitors closely.

We'll review how deductions work for medical expenses, taxes and interest, charitable deductions, casualties or losses, and other miscellaneous expenses, which include job hunting, professional fees, and unreimbursed employee expenses.

THESE ARE OUR CHILDREN, OR AS WE LIKE TO CALL THEM--"OUR PRECIOUS LITTLE TAX DEDUCTIONS!"

Chapter 4

Your Medical Money Matters

In This Chapter

- ◆ Learning the limits
- ◆ What is allowed
- ◆ What is not allowed
- ◆ Giving some back

Most taxpayers find that pulling together all their medical bills and trying to get a tax deduction is an exercise in futility. The limit put on these deductions nearly erases any chance of deducting medical expenses unless you or a family member had a major—hence, expensive—illness during the tax year.

We'll take a look at what makes it so hard to claim medical deductions, what medical deductions are allowed, and what medical procedures are not deductible. We'll also review strategies for cutting your tax bill by using medical insurance and other strategies to reduce your taxable income.

Defining the Limits

Medical care is broadly defined in the tax code. It includes "diagnosis, cure, mitigation, treatment, or prevention of disease, and for treatments affecting any part or function of the body." Deductible items include your medical insurance premiums, the expenses of medical care, and the amounts you pay for transportation to get that medical care. Portions of qualified long-term care insurance contracts are also deductible.

With so many allowable deductions, you're probably wondering why so few people are able to take advantage of the tax break. It's because of the limit: You must subtract 7.5 percent of your adjusted gross income from your total medical deductions. For example, if your AGI is $50,000, your out-of-pocket medical expenses must exceed $3,750 (7.5 percent of $50,000) to begin claiming a deduction. Furthermore, the medical care must have been paid for during the tax year, *no matter when you received the services.* You can't deduct medical expenses that were paid by an insurance company or other source, whether paid to you, the patient, or the medical provider.

Audit Alarm!

Although we all enjoy collecting more than we spend, if you're reimbursed for more than your actual medical expenses, you may have to include the reimbursement as excess income.

Medical insurance premiums for most taxpayers are no longer included in their medical care deduction calculations because these premiums either are paid by their employer or are taken out of their paychecks before taxes are calculated. Anything paid with pre-tax dollars cannot then be deducted.

If your insurance premiums are deductible, the amount that can be deducted will be included in box 1 of your W-2.

Tax Tips

Many companies allow you to pay for medical expenses that will not be reimbursed by an insurance company or other source using a pre-tax medical expenses reimbursement account. These include co-payments and deductibles for medical care or other costs not covered. If you participate in the program, you can designate a monthly amount to be taken from your check before taxes are calculated. This lowers the amount of taxes taken out of your check. You then pay medical bills out of this account managed by your employer. Be careful, though: If the money goes unused, you don't get it back; it's forfeited to your employer.

Special Breaks for the Self-Employed

If you're self-employed and had a net profit for the year, you may be able to deduct up to 70 percent of the amount paid for health insurance for yourself, your spouse, and dependents. This 70 percent deduction can be taken on Form 1040 without being subject to the 7.5 percent limit. You can add the remaining 30 percent to your other medical expenses on *Schedule A*, but it will be subject to the limit. You cannot take the deduction for any month you were eligible to participate in any subsidized health plan offered by your employer or your spouse's employer. Beginning in 2003 you will be able to deduct 100 percent of your health insurance if you are self-employed.

Folks who are self-employed also have access to another tax-saving strategy, called the Medical Savings Account. This can also be used by small businesses with 50 or fewer employees. Participants combine a high-deductible health insurance plan with personal savings accounts using pre-tax dollars to pay for medical expenses that are not reimbursed. We'll take a closer look at this in Chapter 25.

Taxing Terms

Schedule A is the form that is used to calculate your itemized deductions. There are sections for medical and dental expenses, taxes, interest, gifts to charity, casualty and theft losses, job expenses, and miscellaneous deductions.

What You Can Deduct

Let's take a look at what medical expenses are deductible. Most of the deductions are in alphabetical order, but I have included special sections on long-term care, capital expenses, travel or transportation, and care for dependents with special needs. The rules for these deductions are much more complex.

Abortion (as long as it is legal).

Acupuncture.

Alcoholism. Expenses for inpatient's treatment at a therapeutic center for alcohol addiction are deductible, including meals and lodging provided by the center during treatment. You can also include in medical expenses transportation costs that you pay to attend meetings of an Alcoholics Anonymous Club in your community, if your attendance is pursuant to medical advice stating that membership is necessary for the treatment of a disease involving the excessive use of alcoholic liquors.

Ambulance.

Artificial limb.

Artificial teeth.

Birth control pills that were prescribed by a doctor.

Braille books and magazines for a visually impaired person when the cost is more than the cost of regular printed editions.

Car. You can include out-of-pocket expenses for your car, such as gas and oil, when you use your car for medical reasons. You cannot include depreciation, insurance, general repair, or maintenance expenses. If you don't want to use actual expenses, the standard mileage rate allowed for out-of-pocket expenses for your car when you use your car for medical reasons is 12 cents a mile. You can deduct the cost of special hand controls and other special equipment installed in a car for the use of a person with a disability. You also can deduct the difference in the cost of a car specially designed to hold a wheelchair and the cost of a regular car. You cannot deduct the cost of operating a specially equipped car, except as discussed under "Transportation," later.

Chiropractor, provided that the services are for medical care.

Christian science practitioner, provided that the services are for medical care.

Contact lenses, if needed for medical reasons. You can also include the cost of equipment and materials required for using contact lenses, such as saline solution and enzyme cleaner.

Crutches, whether you buy or rent them.

Dental treatment, including fees paid to dentists for x-rays, fillings, braces, extractions, dentures, and other medically necessary dental care.

Drug addiction, covering medical expenses for an inpatient's treatment at a therapeutic center for drug addiction. This includes meals and lodging at the center during treatment.

Eyeglasses and eye examinations needed for medical reasons.

Fertility treatments, to overcome your inability to have children. This includes *in vitro* fertilization and temporary storage of eggs or sperm. You can also deduct an operation to reverse a previous surgery that prevents you from having children.

Guide dog or other animal that will be used by a visually impaired or hearing-impaired person. You can also include the cost of a dog or other animal trained to assist persons with other physical disabilities. Amounts that you pay for the care of the specially trained animals are also medical expenses.

Health institute fees can be deducted only if the treatment is prescribed by a physician and the physician issues a statement that the treatment is necessary to alleviate a physical or mental defect or illness.

Hospital services.

Laboratory fees.

Laser eye surgery to improve vision, if it is done primarily to promote the correct function of the eye.

Lead-based paint removal from the surfaces of your home, to prevent a child who has or has had lead poisoning from eating the paint. These surfaces must be in poor repair (peeling or cracking) or within the child's reach. The cost of repainting the scraped area is not a medical expense.

Legal fees paid to authorize treatment for mental illness. However, you cannot include in medical expenses fees for the management of a guardianship estate, fees for conducting the affairs of the person being treated, or other fees that are not necessary for medical care.

Lifetime care, or "founder's fee," paid either monthly or as a lump sum under an agreement with a retirement home. The agreement must require that you pay a specific fee as a condition for the home's promise to provide lifetime care and must specify the amount for medical care.

Medical information plan expenses. These can be deducted for a plan that will keep your medical information in a computer data bank for later retrieval as needed for your medical care.

Medical services provided by physicians, surgeons, specialists, or other medical practitioners.

Medicines that are prescribed by a doctor. Insulin is included.

Mentally retarded care. If you pay for a special home to care for a mentally retarded dependent based on the recommendation of a psychiatrist to help the person adjust to life in a mental hospital to community living, the expenses are deductible. This does not include the home of a relative.

Nursing services, including giving medication or changing dressings, as well as bathing and grooming the patient, provided in your home or at another care facility. If the person providing the service also performs household and personal services, the time spent on nursing care must be broken out. Sometimes maintenance or personal care services can be included in medical expenses as part of a long-term care agreement. We'll cover long-term care issues in a special section later in this chapter. Some of these services may also qualify for the Child and Dependent Care Credit, which is covered in Chapter 9. If a live-in attendant was needed, some of the extra costs to house and feed the attendant may be deductible. This can include extra rent or utilities that you pay because you moved to a larger apartment to provide space for the attendant. Employment taxes you pay for a nurse, attendant, or other person who provides medical care can be included as a medical expense.

Operations, as long as they are medically necessary and not for unnecessary cosmetic surgery.

Oxygen and oxygen equipment to relieve breathing problems caused by a medical condition.

Prosthesis or artificial limb.

Psychiatric care, including the costs of supporting a mentally ill dependent at a specially equipped medical center where the dependent receives medical care.

Psychoanalysis for medical treatment, but not as part of your training to be a psychoanalyst.

Psychologist.

Sterilization, provided that it is a legally performed operation to make a person unable to have children.

Stop-smoking programs. However, you cannot include the cost of drugs that don't require a prescription, such as nicotine gum or patches, that are designed to help stop smoking.

Telephone equipment costs and repairs for special equipment that lets a hearing-impaired person communicate over a regular telephone.

Therapy received as a medical treatment.

Transplant medical expense payments that you make for surgical, hospital, laboratory, and transportation expenses for a donor or a possible donor of a kidney or other organ.

Vasectomy.

Weight-loss program expenses, provided that the program was started because of a physician's direction to treat an existing disease (such as heart disease). But you cannot include the cost of a weight-loss program if it is to maintain your general good health.

IRS Idioms

What is the difference between a taxidermist and a tax collector? The taxidermist takes only your skin.

—Mark Twain

Tax Tips

If you are disabled and have expenses that are necessary in order for you to be able to work, you should take them as a job-related business deduction rather than a medical deduction. The limits are much less in that category. We'll be covering this in greater detail in Chapter 8.

Wheelchair, when it is used mainly for the relief of sickness or disability and not just to provide transportation to and from work. The cost of operating and keeping up the wheelchair is also a medical expense.

X-ray fees.

Long-Term Care

As the U.S. population ages, more people will likely need long-term care services. These include necessary diagnostic, preventative, therapeutic, curative, treating, mitigating, rehabilitative services, and maintenance and personal care services for a chronically ill person based on a plan prescribed by a licensed health-care practitioner.

A chronic illness that requires thousands of dollars a year to pay for needed care can wipe out most family savings. Many folks are choosing to purchase long-term care insurance to protect against a devastating long-term illness. You can deduct qualified long-term care premiums, but there are deduction limits per person based on age:

- Age 40 or under: $230
- Age 41 to 50: $430
- Age 51 to 60: $860
- Age 61 to 70: $2,290
- Age 71 or over: $2,860

A qualified long-term care insurance contract is an insurance contract that meets the following standards set by the IRS:

- Is guaranteed renewable
- Does not provide for a cash surrender value or other money that can be paid, assigned, pledged, or borrowed
- Specifies that refunds (other than refunds upon the death of the insured or complete surrender or cancellation of the contract) and dividends under the contract must be used only to reduce future premiums or increase future benefits
- Generally does not pay or reimburse expenses incurred for services or items that would be reimbursed under Medicare, except where *Medicare* is a secondary payer or the contract makes per diem or other periodic payments without regard to expenses

You can also deduct expenses for qualified long-term care services that are not reimbursed. You can include in medical expenses the cost of medical care in a nursing home or home for the elderly for yourself, your spouse, or your dependents. This includes the cost of meals and lodging in the home if the main reason for being there is to get medical care.

Taxing Terms

Medicare is the health insurance provided to individuals when they reach the age of 65. Most have paid into the system all their life as a deduction from their paychecks. The government does allow people who have not paid into the system or who haven't paid enough to purchase this insurance.

Capital Expenses

If you need to install special equipment in your home or pay for other improvements to provide medical care for you, your spouse, or a dependent, these costs are deductible as a medical expense. The cost of permanent improvements that increase the value of the property may be partly included as a medical expense. If the value of the property is not increased by the improvement, the entire cost is included as a medical expense. These improvements can include the following:

- Constructing entrance or exit ramps for your home

- Widening doorways at entrances or exits to your home

- Widening or otherwise modifying hallways and interior doorways

- Installing railings, support bars, or other modifications to bathrooms

- Lowering or modifying kitchen cabinets and equipment

- Installing porch lifts and other forms of lifts, but generally not elevators

- Modifying fire alarms, smoke detectors, and other warning systems

- Modifying stairways

- Adding handrails or grab bars anywhere (whether or not in bathrooms)

- Modifying hardware on doors

- Modifying areas in front of entrance and exit doorways

- Grading the ground to provide access to the residence

Don't make the mistake of thinking that you can use this as an excuse to redesign your home for aesthetic reasons. Only reasonable costs to accommodate a home for a disabled person are considered medical care. Additional costs for personal pleasures are not medical expenses. For example, pools rarely qualify as a medical deduction.

Travel or Transportation

We already discussed the deductibility of costs for operating a car, but a lot more transportation-related costs can qualify for medical expenses. Any travel that is required to receive medical care is deductible, but you can't include a significant amount of personal pleasure, recreation, or vacation as part of the plans. What a shame!

Costs for lodging and meals can be included if you meet all these IRS requirements:

◆ The lodging is primarily for and essential to medical care.

◆ The medical care is provided by a doctor in a licensed hospital or in a medical care facility related to, or the equivalent of, a licensed hospital.

◆ The lodging is not lavish or extravagant under the circumstances.

◆ The amount you include in medical expenses for lodging cannot be more than $50 for each night for each person. For example, if a parent is traveling with a sick child, up to $100 per night can be included as a medical expense for lodging. Meals are not included in this limit. Meals that are not part of the inpatient care cannot be included as a medical deduction.

> **CAUTION**
>
> **Audit Alarm!**
>
> You can't spend much time on fun, though, if you need to take a trip for medical reasons or to attend a medical conference. At a conference, you must spend the majority of your time at the conference attending sessions on medical information to qualify for the deduction. Meals cannot be deducted.

◆ If you attend a medical conference that concerns the chronic illness of you, your spouse, or your dependent, you can deduct the amounts paid for admission and transportation to a medical conference.

Many types of transportation to get medical care can be deducted, including these:

◆ Bus, taxi, train, or plane fares or ambulance service

◆ Transportation expenses of a parent who must go with a child who needs medical care

◆ Transportation expenses of a nurse or other person who can give injections, medications, or other treatment required by a patient who is traveling to get medical care and is unable to travel alone

♦ Transportation expenses for regular visits to see a mentally ill dependent, if these visits are recommended as a part of treatment

Dependents with Disabilities

You can deduct payments to a special school for mentally impaired or physically disabled dependents, as long as the main reason for using the school is the resources available for relieving the disability. Examples of this include these:

♦ Teaching Braille to a visually impaired child

♦ Teaching lip reading to a hearing-impaired child

♦ Giving remedial language training to correct a condition caused by a birth defect

You can also deduct the cost of meals, lodging, and ordinary education supplied by a special school if the main reason for being there is the resources that the school has to offer. You cannot include in medical expenses the cost of sending a problem child to a special school for benefits that the child may get from the course of study and the disciplinary methods.

Tuition fees for a special school for a dependent with severe learning disabilities caused by mental or physical impairments, including nervous system disorders, can be deducted as medical expenses, provided that the school is recommended by a doctor. This can also include tutoring fees for a teacher who is specially trained and qualified to work with children who have severe learning disabilities, provided that the tutoring is recommended by a doctor.

You also can deduct advance payments to a private institution for lifetime care, treatment, and training of your physically or mentally impaired child upon your death or when you become unable to provide care. The payments must be a condition for the institution's future acceptance of your child and must not be refundable.

Things You Can't Deduct

Although you can deduct a lot of things, some medical expenses don't qualify for a deduction. Here are the no-nos, in alphabetical order:

Baby-sitting, child care, and nursing services for a normal, healthy baby.

Controlled substances.

Cosmetic surgery that is primarily for improving the patient's appearance and that does not meaningfully promote the proper function of the body or prevent or treat illness or disease. Procedures such as face-lifts, hair transplants, hair removal (electrolysis), and liposuction generally are not deductible. If the surgery is necessary to improve a deformity arising from a congenital abnormality, a personal injury resulting from an accident or trauma, or a disfiguring disease, you may be able to deduct the costs.

Dancing lessons.

Diaper service.

Electrolysis or hair removal.

Hair transplant.

Health club dues.

> **Tax Tips**
>
> You might be able to cover the costs of some of these items with the Child and Dependent Care Credit (see Chapter 9).

Household help, unless part of a qualified long-term care plan as mentioned previously.

Illegal operations and treatments.

Maternity clothes.

Nonprescription drugs and medicines.

Nutritional supplements.

Personal use items.

Swimming lessons.

Weight-loss program, unless for treatment of a particular disease.

Unexpected Income from Medical Expenses

Sometimes you get money back in a later year that you already deducted as a medical expense. You might need to pay taxes on this money. I'll review a few of the scenarios; however, the adjustments can be complicated. If you find yourself in any of these situations, you may want to seek the advice of a tax advisor.

Reimbursements After Deduction

Sometimes you receive a reimbursement for a medical expense you deducted in a previous year. You will generally need to report this already deducted expense as income in the year you receive it. If you didn't deduct a medical expense in the year you paid it, either because your medical expenses were not more than 7.5 percent of your adjusted gross income or because you didn't itemize deductions, you don't need to report it as income the year you receive it.

Sale of Medical Property

You may have a taxable gain if you sell medical equipment or property that you previously deducted as a medical expense. The taxable gain is the amount of the selling price that is more than the equipment's adjusted basis. The adjusted basis is the portion of the equipment's cost that was not deductible because of the 7.5 percent limit used to compute the medical deduction.

Settlement of a Damage Suit

If you receive money as part of a settlement of a personal injury suit, the portion that covers previous years' medical expenses must be reported as income if you used the medical expense to reduce your taxes. If any part of the medical reimbursement is for future medical expenses from the personal injury, you must reduce your future medical expenses by the amount received until it is completely used. In other words, future medical bills will not be deductible until the settlement funds for medical expenses are exhausted.

It's never fun to discuss medical problems, and when you combine them with tax issues, it can be a particularly unpleasant combination. But if you ever find yourself in a situation in which you, your spouse, or a dependent needs serious medical care, it's important to know that there are ways you can ease the financial burden.

The Least You Need to Know

- ◆ Few people get to deduct their medical expenses because they must exceed the tax code limitation. You must have expenses that total more than 7.5 percent of your adjusted gross income.

- ◆ Many people pay their medical insurance premiums and even some medical bills using pre-tax income, which reduces the amount of money taken out of their paychecks.

- ◆ You can deduct only medical expenses that are not reimbursed by an insurance company or other source.

- ◆ You may qualify for medical expense deductions for long-term care expenses, improvements to your home for medical reasons, and transportation to a medical conference.

Outlays for Taxes and Interest

In This Chapter

- ◆ Deducting taxes
- ◆ Taking advantage of mortgage interest
- ◆ Reducing investment costs
- ◆ Other personal breaks

Taxes and interest payments on loans are a big part of everyone's financial liabilities. Unfortunately, the IRS doesn't let us deduct many of those costs from our annual tax bill.

Federal taxes, for example, are not deductible. And although interest expenses generated on credit card balances used to be deductible, they aren't anymore.

The IRS does make some exceptions to its ban on deducting personal interest and taxes, including some biggies, like some taxes and home mortgage interest. In this chapter, we'll take a look at what taxes and interest are deductible on good old Schedule A. We'll also briefly review taxes and interest related to your trade or business, but we'll leave most of that discussion for Part 7.

Recovering Taxes on Income

The federal government is nice enough to let us deduct all state and local income taxes that we've paid. The first place to find information on how much you've paid in state and local taxes is your W-2, which will list any money that your employer deducted from your salary to pay state and local income tax. But the fun doesn't stop here. You can find other deductible state, local, and foreign taxes that you've paid on some of those forms you collected in Chapter 1. Still got that stack? Pull it out and look for any of the following:

♦ If you got lucky and won money gambling, you'll get a W-2G, which may show local or state taxes that you paid.

♦ People who work as independent contractors or who receive other miscellaneous income may have state and local taxes that were taken out from their payment and that show up on Form 1099-MISC. Folks receiving retirement income shouldn't forget to check the Form 1099-R for state or local taxes that may have been deducted.

CAUTION

Audit Alarm!

Remember, any taxes and interest deductions that you take may be limited if your adjusted gross income in 2002 exceeds $137,300 ($68,650 for a couple who is married filing separately), as we discussed in Chapter 3. If your income exceeds this limit, you will have to reduce your itemized deductions by 3 percent of your adjusted gross income. Investment interest expense is not subject to this limitation.

♦ If you're self-employed, don't forget to deduct those estimated tax payments you made for state or local taxes during the year. Also, if you underpaid your state or local taxes from the year before, you had to pay them in the current tax year when you filed your state or local tax forms. Be sure to find that proof of payment so you can deduct them this year.

Generally, all state and local taxes are deductible in the year you actually pay them. You can take advantage of this fact and increase your deductions in a tax year by paying your fourth-quarter estimated state and local taxes, usually due in January, by December. For example, if you want to have more write-offs for 2002, you should pay your fourth quarter estimated state and local taxes by December 2002. If you wait until January 2003, you'll have to deduct them on your 2003 tax return.

If you are a married couple that has decided to file federal taxes separately, you can deduct only the amount of your own individual state and local income tax allocated based on your personal gross earnings. The only exception to this is if you are jointly and individually liable for the full amount of the state and local income taxes. If that is the case, you and your spouse can deduct the amount each actually paid on separate federal returns.

If you pay foreign income taxes, you can take them as a deduction or a credit. Most folks in this category have investments overseas from which foreign income taxes are deducted. Others work overseas. You cannot take the deduction or credit if the foreign income taxes were paid on income that is exempt from U.S. tax. In most cases, you are better off taking a credit, which directly reduces your tax bill dollar for dollar, rather than a deduction, which only reduces the amount you use to calculate your tax bill on taxable income. We'll be taking a closer look at tax credits in Part 3. If you invest overseas, any foreign taxes paid will show on your year-end statement from your broker.

> **Tax Tips**
>
> Don't forget to include as tax deductions any estimated payments for the previous year's taxes made in January of the current tax year. People have a tendency to forget those estimated taxes when they are calculating their local and state tax deductions because they paid them so long ago.

Breaks for Home Ownership

Interest and taxes that you incur at the time you purchase your home or that you incur to pay off your mortgage or to pay property taxes to state and local governments are probably among your highest deductions on your Schedule A. Let's take a look at what you can and cannot deduct for your personal residence.

Real Estate Taxes

First, let's review real estate taxes. You can deduct any state, local, or foreign taxes on real property, provided that the taxes are based on the assessed value of the property and that all property taxes under the jurisdiction of the taxing authority is charged uniformly. This legalese is intended to prevent people from setting up a local "tax" for themselves and their friends and then writing that money off.

You also must have an ownership interest in the property. For example, if you pay taxes for a relative who owns the property, you won't be able to deduct those taxes. There's no limit to the number of properties for which you can deduct taxes, but you must not rent out the property for more than 14 days to deduct the taxes on Schedule A. If you rent the property for more than 14 days, you'll need to deduct those taxes on Schedule E, "Supplemental Income and Loss."

Audit Alarm!

You usually can't deduct taxes charged for local benefits and improvement that increase the property value. Examples of this type of tax include assessments for streets, sidewalks, water mains, and sewer lines. Services such as trash collection or water that are billed separately usually are not deductible, either.

Tax Tips

Ministers and military personnel qualify for special benefits. Even though ministers and members of the armed services don't have to pay federal taxes on housing allowances, they can deduct the real estate taxes they pay on their homes.

When you get your copy of the tax bill from your taxing authority, be sure to put it with your other paperwork that you'll need at tax time. You'll find all the details you need about your tax payments and how they were allocated on this bill. If taxes for property improvements or local services are individually itemized, you probably won't be able to deduct them. If you can't find your tax bill and your taxes are paid out of the escrow payments from your mortgage account, you can use your year-end statement from your finance company to find out how much you paid in property taxes.

Property taxes are divided between buyer and seller in the year a home changes ownership. The split is based on the number of days each actually owned the property. You can find out how much you paid on the closing statement. (That statement will also come in handy when you start figuring out your deductible interest, which is discussed later in this chapter.) If you're divorced or separated and have an agreement in place stating that you must pay the real estate taxes for a home owned by you and your spouse, you may be able to deduct part of the payments as real estate taxes and part as alimony. We'll look at this tricky issue more closely in Chapter 18.

Interest Deductions

For many people, the interest they pay on their mortgage is the largest single chunk of cash they can deduct on Schedule A. You can deduct interest from your principal residence and a second home, such as a vacation condominium. Gee, another good reason to buy that place at the beach!

You must be the one legally liable for the mortgage. You can't deduct interest on mortgage payments you make for someone else. The debt on your home must also be secured, which means that you must have put up your home as collateral to get the loan.

Taxing Terms

A **secured loan** is one in which the loan assets are backed by property that belongs to the borrower, which decreases the risk for the lender. The assets may be forfeited to the lender if you cannot afford to make the payments. This is why you should always be cautious when you take out additional loans against your home, such as a second mortgage or an equity line of credit. You could lose the property if you can't make the payments.

You probably will be able to deduct all of your home mortgage interest, but some high earners may lose a portion of the tax deductibility of their home mortgage interest. There are three categories of mortgage debt:

- **Mortgages taken out before October 13, 1987.** Interest on this debt, also known as grandfathered debt, is fully deductible.

- **Mortgages taken out after October 13, 1987.** Interest on this debt, also known as home acquisition debt, which you used to buy, build, or improve your home, can be deducted only if your total mortgage debt, including grandfathered debt, is $1 million or less ($500,000 or less if you're married and filing separately) during the tax year. Interest paid above that loan amount is not deductible.

- **Home equity debt.** This is mortgage debt that you took out after October 13, 1987, for use toward items that were not for the purchase of your home or to build or improve the home you own. Total interest on home equity debt is deductible only if total home equity loans are $100,000 or less and all your mortgage loans totaled no more than the fair market value of your home. If your total debt exceeds $1 million ($500,000 if you're married and filing separately) the amount allowed for home equity debt is limited by that calculation as well. You also can lose the interest deduction completely if you fall under the Alternative Minimum Tax (see Chapter 3).

If your mortgage payment is late you may be able to deduct at least part of your late fees. The official IRS position is that you can deduct as home mortgage interest a late payment charge if it was not for a specific service performed in connection with your mortgage loan. You may need to check with your mortgage company to find out how much of the late fee is interest and how much is related to services because of the late payment.

You can't deduct interest on more than two homes. You may even be able to deduct the interest on a second home that you rent out part of the year. The second home can be one that you don't occupy, one that you occupy only part of the year, or one that you rent out. You must use the property yourself more than 14 days or 10 percent of the number of days that it was rented or held out for resale during the year for which you want to deduct mortgage interest. For example, if you rented the home for 180 days, you would need to use that home yourself for at least 18 days to deduct the interest on Schedule A. If you don't meet that criteria, the interest can still be used as an expense against your income when calculating your net rental income. If you don't rent the second home during the year, you can deduct the mortgage interest even if you didn't use the home.

If you own more than two homes, you must choose which two you want to use for mortgage interest deductions. You don't have to choose the same two each year, but your principal residence must be one of the two. You also must use the same second home for the entire year. For example, you can't use the mortgage interest of one home for six months and then pick a different second home for the remaining six months.

For rental property that doesn't qualify within these home mortgage limitations, you'll need to use a Schedule E and write off the mortgage interest as an expense on that form.

In the year that you buy and sell property, there are special interest considerations:

Mortgage prepayment penalty   If you must pay a penalty for paying off your mortgage early, you can deduct the penalty as home mortgage interest, as long as that penalty was not charged for a specific service performed or cost incurred in connection to your mortgage loan.

Points   When you close a mortgage loan, you frequently must pay points. These can be called loan origination fees, maximum loan charges, loan discount, or discount points. Even if the seller pays these points for you, you can deduct them as an interest expense. If the mortgage is for the initial purchase of your primary residence, you can deduct them entirely in the first year. Points for a mortgage on a second home or a refinance must be deducted over the term of the mortgage. For example, if the term is 30 years, you can deduct $1/30$ of the points each year.

If you paid points on a mortgage for your primary residence or to improve your primary residence, you'll still have to pass the following tests to deduct the points fully in the year you paid them:

- Points must be a standard business practice in the area you took the loan.

- The amount you were charged for points must not be more than is generally charged in the area.

- Points were not charged in lieu of other settlement costs, such as appraisal fees, title fees, attorneys fees, inspection fees, and property taxes.

- You did not borrow the funds used to pay the points from either the lender or the mortgage broker.

- You must take the mortgage to buy or build your primary residence.

- The points must be calculated as a percentage of your mortgage's principal amount.

- The points are shown on the settlement statement.

CAUTION

Audit Alarm!

Sellers cannot deduct points paid for the borrower as an interest expense, but you may be able to use them as a selling expense to reduce any profit on the sale of home. This doesn't help many people selling their primary residences: Profits on the sale of your primary residence are exempt from capital gain, provided that they are below $500,000 for a couple filing jointly and $250,000 for all other taxpayers provided the home was your personal residence two of the last five years.

Even if you don't meet all these criteria, you can deduct the points over the life of the loan. You always have the option to deduct the points over the life of the loan, but it usually makes more sense taxwise to deduct them fully in the year that you close the loan if the points qualify for this deduction. If you pay your loan off early and haven't yet deducted all the points paid, you can write off the amount of points not yet deducted in the year you pay your loan off.

Any refund you receive on interest payments must be used to reduce the interest deduction if received in the same year. Otherwise, an interest refund is considered taxable income.

Folks who receive government assistance have special considerations when determining whether they can deduct their interest expense. If you receive mortgage assistance payments under section 235 of the National Housing Act and part or all of your interest on your mortgage is paid for you, you cannot deduct

Tax Tips

As with tax payments, ministers and military personnel who get a housing allowance that is not taxable as income can still deduct their home mortgage interest.

the interest that you did not pay yourself. (You can still deduct any real estate taxes you paid.) The good news is that these mortgage assistance payments do not need to be reported as income.

Another government program that reduces your interest deduction is the Mortgage Interest Credit. In this case, you must reduce your interest deduction by the amount of the credit. We'll talk about the credit in greater detail in Chapter 11.

Deducting Investment Interest

Interest you pay when you borrow money to make an investment is deductible, but it's limited to your net investment income. This income can include interest income, dividend income, annuity income, royalties not received in your business, and any other investment income passed through to you from a corporation or trust. Your investment income can include the part of your child's interest and dividends that you chose to report on your tax return.

If you have investment income, you'll be able to deduct investment interest expenses you incurred to …

- Buy stocks or bonds.

- Lend money to someone else.

- Buy land for investment purposes.

- Buy stock in your employer's company.

- Take a margin loan on stock you own through your broker.

Your broker will report most of your investment interest. Another possible place you may find investment interest is on a Schedule K-1 that you received from a limited partnership you use for investment purposes.

Taxing Terms

Capital gain is any profit you make from the sale or exchange of your home or other investments.

Capital gain can be included as part of your net investment income, but it usually doesn't make sense to handle capital gain this way. If you include capital gain as part of your net investment income calculation, you must then include the gain as part of your ordinary income, and it will be taxed at your regular tax rate. Most people are better off using the lower capital gain rate (20 percent for most taxpayers, and 10 percent for taxpayers in the 15 percent tax bracket).

Personal Deductions

Remember that personal interest is *not* deductible. This means that you can't deduct interest on car loans (unless you use the car for business); interest on federal, state, or local income tax (when you owe back taxes); finance charges for credit cards, installment contracts, or revolving charges for personal expenses; or late payments to a utility. Loan fees, credit investigation fees, service charges, and annual credit card fees are not deductible, either.

That doesn't leave many personal expenses to deduct. However, if you live in a state that has a *personal property tax*, you can deduct that tax. To qualify for a deduction, the state or local tax must be charged on personal property, based on the value of the personal property, and charged on a yearly basis even if collected more or less than once a year. If the personal property tax on your car is partially based on weight and partially based on value, only the portion based on value is deductible.

Most car license fees are not deductible, but they have been allowed for at least part of the fee in Arizona, California, Colorado, Connecticut, Georgia, Indiana, Iowa, Maine, Massachusetts, Minnesota, Mississippi, Montana, Nebraska, Nevada, New Hampshire, Oklahoma, Washington, and Wyoming. (Part of the fees in these states is based on the value of the vehicle. The portion based on value is deductible.)

Personal taxes and fees that aren't deductible include estate, inheritance, legacy, or succession taxes; fines; gift taxes; and license fees, such as ones you pay for marriage, your driver's license, or your pet. If you are including income as a beneficiary of an estate, you can deduct estate tax as a miscellaneous deduction. We'll talk more about miscellaneous deductions in Chapter 8.

> **Taxing Terms**
>
> **Personal property taxes** vary state-by-state. Many states tax personal property such as cars, trucks, motorcycles, trailers, buses, mobile homes, motor homes, boats, boat motors and aircraft. States seem to be getting more aggressive about this tax now that state budgets are so tight.

Student Loan Interest

The U.S. government wants its population to be well educated, so it makes all kinds of tax allowances for expenses related to getting an education. For example, you can write off up to $2,500 of interest paid on a loan used to pay your college expenses, your spouse's expenses, or the expenses of one of your dependents. You can even claim this deduction if you don't itemize your taxes. Before January 1, 2002, this deduction was allowed on only the first 60 months of interest, but the 2001 tax law erased that limitation and now interest is deductible for the life of the loan.

The deduction is phased out for joint filers beginning with adjusted gross incomes above $100,000, and it isn't available at all for couples once their joint income is above $130,000. For single taxpayers, the phaseout range begins at $50,000, and the deduction is lost fully once earnings exceed $65,000.

Parents can deduct education loan interest as long as the loan is used solely to pay college expenses. Mixed-use loans are not deductible. If the student loan was taken out by the child, parents can't deduct the interest even if they are the ones paying off the loan. As with other loan payments, only the person legally liable for the loan payments can claim the deduction.

This can create a situation in which no one can deduct the interest. A child who took out the student loan won't be eligible to deduct the interest, either, if he or she is still claimed as a dependent on the parent's return. Children will be able to claim the interest payments as deductions when they are no longer claimed as dependents.

If you take out a home equity loan to finance a college education, you can deduct the interest, but only as a mortgage expense on Schedule A.

We'll cover other tax breaks for education expenses in Chapter 13.

Writing Off Business Taxes and Interest

Although you can deduct business taxes and interest on Schedule A, you may find it more advantageous to write off those expenses as part of your small business. If you write them off as business expenses, it will reduce the amount you have to pay in self-employment taxes for Social Security and Medicare payments *in addition* to reducing your federal income taxes. We'll talk about business tax breaks in Part 7.

This brings up an important point: When you can take deductions or credits in different ways, you should calculate where you get your greatest tax reduction advantage and go that way. The tax game is one in which you want to stay within the law but use any advantage available to reduce your tax bill as much as legally possible. Is all this talk about saving money making you feel generous? I hope so, because in the next chapter we're going to take a look at how giving your money to charity can help reduce your tax bill.

IRS Idioms

The income tax has made more liars of more Americans than golf.

—Will Rogers

The Least You Need to Know

♦ You can deduct most of the state and local income taxes you pay. You may even be able to deduct foreign taxes that you pay, as long as the income wasn't exempt from U.S. federal taxes.

♦ Most personal interest is no longer deductible; the big exceptions are interest paid on your first and second homes and on your investments.

♦ Limitations govern the amount of home mortgage interest you can deduct once your mortgage tops $1 million if you are married filing jointly, or $500,000 for all other taxpayers. Deductions for interest on home equity lines are limited to the first $100,000 borrowed.

Chapter 6

Giving Your Share

In This Chapter

- ◆ Tax-deductible donations
- ◆ Deduction limits
- ◆ Aiding foreigners
- ◆ Helping yourself

Itemizing your charitable deductions lets you do something that feels good and gives you a tax cut, to boot. You get to pick whom you want to give your money to (within some limits). You can even write off some expenses or give away something that you just don't need anymore and take advantage of a deduction at the same time.

If you're one of the lucky few with a major increase in the value of an asset, you may even be able to avoid capital gain taxes, have a donation to write off, and live on the money for a while.

No matter what kind of donation you want to deduct, the IRS stipulates that you must have given the charitable gift voluntarily without expecting anything of equal value in return.

You'll probably find at least one charitable deduction that is just right for you.

Who Can Receive

First, let's look at who you can give your money to so that it qualifies as a charitable organization in the eyes of the IRS. The most common eligible groups that receive donations are community chests, corporations, trusts, funds, or foundations that were established and are operating for religious, charitable, educational, scientific, or literary purposes. Groups that work to prevent cruelty to children or animals are also eligible.

War veterans' organizations, such as posts, auxiliaries, trusts, or foundations organized in the United States or its possessions are eligible for your deductible donations. You also can deduct gifts to U.S. fraternal societies, orders, and associations, provided that the money will be used solely for one of the approved purposes just mentioned. If you give a gift to a nonprofit cemetery corporation, that, too, can be deducted, as long as it is not used for a specific cemetery plot or crypt.

Tax Tips

You can find out whether a charity to which you are thinking of giving a contribution qualifies in the eyes of the IRS at the GuideStar website (www.guidestar.com/index.jsp), which lists more than 850,000 charities recognized by the IRS as non-profit organizations. If you're wondering whether your community foundation is an acceptable recipient for your funds, you can check it out at the Community Foundation Locator (www.cflocate.com/search/index.cfm). You can also check with the IRS at the Tax Exempt/Government Entities Customer Service line: 1-877-829-5500.

Federal, state, or local governmental organizations also qualify as recipients of tax-deductible contributions. Governmental organizations of a U.S. possession or in Puerto Rico are eligible as well. Indian tribal government groups also pass the eligibility test. You can even give to foreign charitable organizations and deduct the money, as long as the organizations are located in Canada, Mexico, or Israel. These foreign organizations must meet all the standards discussed for U.S. organizations to qualify for a tax deduction.

Who Can't Receive

Now that you know who can receive your deductible contributions, let's review the organizations that don't qualify:

State bar associations that are not a political subdivision of the state and that have private as well as public purposes, and to which your contribution is unrestricted.

Chambers of commerce.

Civic leagues and associations.

Communist organizations.

Country clubs and other social clubs.

Foreign organizations, except those already mentioned.

Homeowners' associations.

Labor unions. (Dues may be deductible as a miscellaneous itemized deduction. We'll cover that in Chapter 8.)

Political organizations and candidates.

Revenue Ramblings

Contributions and donations to organizations with 501(c)3 designations are tax deductible to the donor for federal and, generally, state income tax purposes. The term "501(c)3" is part of the United States Federal Internal Revenue Code that exempts organizations from federal income tax if they are organized and operate exclusively for religious, charitable, scientific, testing for public safety, literary, or educational purposes; to foster national or international amateur sports competition; or for the prevention of cruelty to children or animals. Groups that claim 501(c)3 and that accept donations must be very careful that their activities are not seen as lobbying for a cause. Most organizations that want to keep their charitable status are careful to educate the public but not to lobby politicians. Sometimes this can be a very fine line.

Contributions to individuals aren't deductible, either. Even if you give a donation to a qualified organization and specify that it should be used for a certain needy individual, the contribution isn't eligible as a deduction. This includes paying someone's hospital bill, even if the hospital meets all the other giving criteria. So be sure that you don't specify an individual when you write out that check if you want to be able to deduct it!

Another deductible no-no is writing a check to your clergyman or religious leader if he or she can use the money for anything desired, such as for personal needs.

Donation Types

You don't have to give cash or a check to take a deduction. You can also donate clothing, property, and other types of assets. Some of the expenses you incur may be deductible as well, but you can't deduct anything for the value of your time or services. Let's take a look at the rules of the different types of donations that the IRS allows.

Cash

A cash contribution can be given using cash, a check, a credit card, or a payroll deduction. The IRS has two levels of proof, depending on the size of the contribution. Your receipts will suffice if the donation was less than $250, but you'll need written proof, in the form of a letter, from the organization that received the donation if you donate $250 or more at one time.

If you make regular donations of less than $250, they each count separately. For example, if you send $50 a month to a charity for a total of $600 in a year, your receipts will be sufficient. The more stringent rules apply only to single donations of $250 or more.

For contributions less than $250, you should keep copies of any canceled check or letter acknowledging your gift. If you don't have a canceled check, you should keep a record of the check number, the amount, the date posted, and the name of the recipient. For donations made by electronic transfer or credit card, you should keep a log of the amount, the date posted, and the receiving organization. Small cash donations should be kept in a log with the date of the contribution and the recipient. If you get a button or other trinket for your donation, hold on to it so you have proof of a cash donation.

For contributions of $250 or more, you must receive a written acknowledgement of each contribution from the charitable organization that received the donation. If you've made more than one donation in a year, the organization can give you a statement at the end of the year that shows your total contributions. The acknowledgement letter must …

- Show the contribution amount.
- Indicate whether goods or services were given as a result of your contribution. Token items or membership do not need to be listed.
- Describe the goods or services received and state their value. If the only benefit is an intangible religious benefit that is not sold as a commercial transaction, value does not need to be estimated, but the benefit should be described.

You should get a copy of this letter by the time you file your taxes.

If you elect to make payroll deductions for charity, you should keep a copy of your pay stubs, W-2, or other document furnished by your employer as proof of the donation. For a donation of $250 or more taken from any one paycheck, you'll need a pledge card or other document from the charitable organization stating that no goods or services were provided for the donation.

As you've probably figured out by now, if you're a pack rat, it helps at tax time—as long as you can find everything!

Expenses

Although you can't deduct the value of your time or services, you can deduct expenses that you incur while providing those services. These expenses can include the costs of operating your vehicle and costs for meals while you perform the services.

To claim your car expenses, you'll need to keep records of the organization you serviced, the date you used your car for charitable purposes, and your mileage. You can write off 14 cents per mile. You have the option of deducting actual expenses rather than mileage, but to do this you must show that the cost of operating the car was directly related to the charitable service.

You also can write off out-of-pocket expenses, as long as you have written acknowledgment from the charitable organization that you incurred these expenses and that they were not reimbursed. The organization would need to give you a letter stating ...

- A description of the services performed.

- A statement regarding whether you were reimbursed for any part of these expenses.

- A description with a good-faith estimate of the value of any goods or services you provided.

- A statement of any intangible religious benefits you may have received.

If you pay expenses for your child so that he or she can do volunteer work, you can't deduct any of those expenses.

Tax Tips

You've probably noticed the per mile reimbursement for charitable purposes is higher than the 12 cents per mile for medical purposes. When you get around to using you car for business purposes it's even higher: 36.5 cents per mile. Be sure you carefully track the mileage and its purpose when you use your car for different purposes on the same trip.

> ### Revenue Ramblings
>
> Fortunately, you probably won't have to go chasing the written documentation needed for the IRS. Most charitable organizations are familiar with what you need and send it to you without asking. The IRS will even penalize a charitable organization that doesn't give you the proof you need. There is a penalty of $10 per contribution and can be as high $5,000 per fund-raising event or mailing. The charity can avoid the penalty if it can show that the failure was due to a reasonable cause.

Noncash

If you give contributions of property rather than cash, there are four sets of rules based on different levels of giving:

- Less than $250

- $250 but not more than $500

- More than $500, but not more than $5,000

- More than $5,000

For noncash contributions less than $250, you'll need to keep records of the charitable organization that received the donation, the date and location you made the donation, and a description of the property donated. If you can get a written acknowledgment of the donation with this information, it's even better. You don't need this receipt, however, especially if the donation was left at an unattended drop site.

You'll also need to note the fair market value of the property donated and the cost or basis of the property if you must reduce the property by its appreciation (which we'll cover later in this chapter). You'll need to keep records of the amount of the reduction and how you figured it. When your gift exceeds $250 in value but is worth less than $500, the only additional piece of information you'll need is a written acknowledgment from the organization before you file your taxes that states ...

- A description of the property you donated. A value is not required.

- An indication of whether you received any goods or services because of your contribution. This does not include member benefits or a token gift.

- A description of the value of the goods or services you received. If the only value you received was an intangible religious benefit, the acknowledgment must state that.

When your noncash gift exceeds $500, requirements get stiffer. For contributions that exceed $500 but are less than $5,000, you'll need written acknowledge from the charitable organization that states ...

♦ A description of the donated property.

♦ The date of the contribution.

♦ The date that the contribution was acquired by the donor.

♦ A description of how the donor acquired the property.

♦ The donor's cost or adjusted basis. The only exception to this is for publicly traded securities or property that was held for longer than 12 months.

♦ The fair market value of the contribution.

♦ The method for determining the fair market value, whether it was by appraisal, thrift shop value, catalog, market quote, or comparable sales.

You'll also need to file Form 8283, "Noncash Charitable Contributions," along with your Schedule A.

If the contribution exceeds $5,000, you'll need all the information just listed, *plus* you must have the property appraised instead of using one of the other methods mentioned to determine property value. You will not need an appraisal for publicly traded stock, however. If you are donating *securities* that are not publicly traded, you won't need the appraisal unless the contribution is above $10,000.

If you donate two or more items of property whose total more than $5,000 in value, you'll need to get an appraisal for these items as well. You can't get this appraisal from the organization receiving the gift, from the organization from which you bought the item, from the taxpayer, or from someone who is related to any of these entities. In other words, if you want to be sure the IRS will accept the appraisal, you'd better get it from a third party who has no interest in the transaction. So don't rely on Uncle Jim or Cousin Betty to tell you what the property is worth!

Taxing Terms

Securities include any investment instrument that is issued by a corporation, government, or other organization. The only exceptions to this are insurance policies or a fixed annuity. Publicly traded securities are available on the open market. Privately traded securities are not available for general sale to the public.

Reporting Benefits

Sometimes you give money to an eligible organization and get some of it back in goods or services. If you donate to public radio or public television, you might receive a magazine subscription or tickets to a show as a thank-you gift, for example. When that happens, you must subtract the value of the benefit from your contribution.

Other items that you must subtract the value of include raffle tickets, bingo games, and lottery tickets. The costs of buying tickets or playing bingo (or any game of chance) are not deductible. (Shucks. I bet you were deducting those raffle tickets! Don't you wish you didn't know?)

Audit Alarm!

If you buy something at a charity auction, you must reduce the market value of the item you purchased and deduct only the amount you spent above that market value. That's also true if you got a meal as part of a ticket that you bought to attend a function run by a charitable organization. You must subtract the value of the meal from your deductible contribution. Many organizations will include the value of the meal on your ticket or other documentation.

Some folks make a contribution to a qualified retirement home in which they or a family member will live. As long as the retirement home qualifies as a charitable organization, you can deduct your contribution. However, you can't deduct any contribution that is for room, board, maintenance, or admittance. If the contribution helps you get a larger unit, it's not deductible, either.

If you send your child to a private or parochial school, or send a relative to a nonprofit day-care center, you can't deduct the tuition or fees. Furthermore, you can't deduct a fixed amount that is required by the institution, even if it is called a "donation." Remember, donations must be voluntary.

Student Aid

If you host a foreign student in your home, you may be able to deduct a portion of your expenses each month. You must have a written agreement with a qualified charitable organization that runs a program to provide educational opportunities for students. American students also qualify as long the other criteria are met.

The student cannot be a dependent or relative and must be a full-time student in the twelfth grade or a lower grade at a U.S. school. You can deduct up to $50 of expenses for each full month the child lives with you. As long as the child spends 15 days with you, a full month can be counted in your calculations. You can get more details about this deduction in IRS Publication 526, "Expenses Paid for Student Living with You."

Finding the Limits

Unfortunately, in the eyes of the IRS, you can be too generous. The IRS imposes three limits on charitable donations, depending on the kind of charity.

You can deduct donations that exceed 50 percent of your adjusted gross income (AGI), provided that the donations are to the following kinds of organizations:

♦ Churches and their associations or conventions

♦ Educational organizations

♦ Hospitals and some of their associated medical research organizations

♦ Publicly supported charities

♦ Private operating foundations

♦ Private nonoperating foundations—if they distribute all their contributions to charities within 2½ months of the foundation's year end

♦ Some private foundations that pool their contributions in a common fund and donate to public charities

Taxing Terms

A **private foundation** is a foundation operated by a company or family that doesn't get money from the general public. A foundation that engages in charitable activities is called an **operating foundation. Nonoperating foundations** give money but don't run their own charitable activities.

If you want to donate more than 50 percent of your AGI and you aren't sure whether a organizations fits within these limits, make sure you ask before you give. You can call the IRS at 1-877-829-5500.

Stricter limits are placed on your donations if they involve capital gain or are given to certain organizations. You can give only 30 percent of your AGI if ...

♦ The gift is property with a capital gain that is given to an organization that qualified under the 50 percent rule, mentioned previously. You can skirt this rule if you decide to deduct the fair market value of the gift by the amount that would have been long-term capital gain if you had sold the property.

♦ The cash or property gift does not include capital gain but is given to an organization that's not on the 50 percent list, such as a veteran's organization, fraternal society, nonprofit cemetery, or private nonoperating foundation.

The greatest restriction is placed on property gifts that have a capital gain and are given to organizations that don't qualify under the 50 percent rule. You are limited to a deduction of only 20 percent of your AGI in any one year.

You can carry over donations that exceed the limits for as many as five years after you make the donation until the donation is completely used. If you haven't used up the donation in five years, you've then lost it as a deduction.

Tax Tips

If you hold property with a large capital gain, it might make sense to donate the property instead of making a cash contribution, as long as the contribution fits within the limits. For example, let's say you bought stock more than a year ago for $1,000 that is now worth $10,000. You plan to make a $10,000 donation to your favorite charity that qualifies under the rules we've just discussed. Instead of making the donation by cash, give the charity your stock. This way you not only get a charitable deduction, but you also avoid having to pay the capital gain tax. If it's stock that you still want to own, you can give away the stock and buy new shares at current market value. You avoid the capital gain tax and still own the stock.

Living on Donations

Now that you know the limits, I'll tell you about a loophole in the law for folks who have a large capital gain. By structuring things properly, you could end up living on the money made from the sale of the property, avoid paying capital gain tax, and still getting a charitable donation. This is a very complex transaction, so don't try this without the help of a financial advisor.

Let's say that you bought a home 30 years ago for $80,000. Today that home is worth $1 million. Don't laugh—the way real estate values have jumped in many areas of the country, a lot of people are finding that their homes have skyrocketed in value. If you don't have anyone to whom you want to leave this property and are planning to move out of the home to something smaller, you can use what's called *a charitable remainder annuity trust* to get a stream of income for as long as you and your spouse are living (or for however long you specify) and give the remainder of the trust to your favorite charity after you die. You can even avoid all capital gain on the property if the donation is structured correctly.

To set up a charitable remainder annuity trust, you would first need to work with an attorney to transfer your title to the property into the name of a charitable trust you establish. You can designate that this trust will pay you a certain percentage of interest income per year, and you can even elect to serve as trustee yourself. The trust then sells the property and avoids capital gain tax because it has a charitable purpose. You can then place the cash from the sale of your home into investments of your choice. You can get yearly income for the rest of your life and your spouse's life, as long as you designate both lives when you set up the initial trust.

In addition to getting the yearly income, you would get a charitable tax deduction in the year you established the trust. If it exceeds your allowable limits, as we discussed, you can carry over the deduction for up to five years.

If you have children to whom you want to give the property, you can use part of your tax savings to buy a life insurance policy naming your children as beneficiaries that will give them the value of the property in cash. Let the lawyers work all this out so it's done right, to ensure that it won't cost your children their inheritance or unnecessary taxes.

This is just one example of the way you can use charitable trusts. Wealthy folks have a myriad of options, including various kinds of trusts and private foundations to make charitable donations, protect the rights of their heirs to their property, and cut their taxes at the same time. If you are one of the lucky few in this situation, don't try to do it yourself. Seek advice from an attorney and an accountant who specialize in estate planning, to be sure you are selecting the best option given your set of circumstances.

Although most people don't give money to charity for the tax break, if you're already planning to give, make sure you know how to make the most of it come tax time.

> **Taxing Terms**
>
> A **charitable remainder annuity trust** usually is funded with a gift of cash, property, or marketable securities. The trust pays fixed income to one or more persons for life or for a selected term of up to 20 years. The annuity amount, which is set when the trust is established, does not change. The amount must be at least 5 percent of the initial trust value. After the income interest ends, the trust assets go to the qualified charitable institution to be used as directed in the trust document.

The Least You Need to Know

◆ Charities to which you make donations must be qualified under federal rules before you can deduct the donations on your tax return. Make sure you know whether your charity of choice is qualified.

◆ You can't deduct the value of your time or services, but you can deduct the expenses you incur when doing charitable activities.

◆ Limits govern the percentage of your adjusted gross income that you can deduct, depending on the type of contribution and the type of charitable organization.

◆ You may be able to avoid capital gain tax by contributing your property or securities rather than giving cash.

Chapter **7**

Recovering Some Losses

In This Chapter

- ◆ Losing your stuff
- ◆ Declaring thefts
- ◆ Proving loss
- ◆ Calculating value

Losses of cash or property are devastating. No one wants to have property stolen or damaged or destroyed, whether by accident or nature. If it happens, though, you can deduct any losses for which you didn't receive reimbursement.

The loss must exceed 10 percent of your adjusted gross income after you subtract $100 from the value of the loss. Business losses have different rules; we'll cover those in Chapter 25. If you run a business out of your home and have lost both business and personal assets, you can take a partial personal deduction and a partial business deduction.

Making the Most of Losses

Let's first take a look at the rules for casualty and theft losses that you can deduct on Schedule A, what you need to prove the loss, how you value losses, and how you claim them.

Losses from Casualties

Losses from casualties include the damage, destruction, or loss of property caused by an identifiable event that is sudden, unexpected, and unusual. To qualify as sudden, it must be an event that was swift and not something that happened gradually or progressively. For example, a building that finally falls because of normal exposure to wind and weather would not qualify because the loss was due to progressive deterioration. To qualify as unexpected, it must be an event that is ordinarily unanticipated and unintended. To qualify as unusual, it must be an event that doesn't happen every day and that isn't a part of your typical daily routine.

Although the following reads like a list of recent disaster movies, it's actually a list of the disasters that are acceptable to the IRS for claiming a loss due to casualty:

Earthquake

Fire

Flood

Hurricane

Landslide

Lightning

Mine cave-in

Shipwreck

Sonic boom

Storm

Tornado

Vandalism

Volcanic eruption

Losses from a car accident also may be deductible, provided that they were not caused by your willful negligence or the negligence of someone driving your car. Fires are not deductible if you set them or paid someone to set them for you. In other words, you can't burn down your old home and then claim the deduction. That method of renovation just won't cut it.

Articles, such as an expensive china set, that are broken under normal usage conditions, even if accidental, don't qualify as a casualty loss. However, if your finger gets slammed in a door and an expensive diamond ring is smashed, the loss may be deductible from the unexpected accident.

Damages in your home caused by a faulty appliance, such as a burst water heater, are deductible, but the cost of fixing of the water heater is not. The same is true if you are a victim of faulty construction. The damage to your personal property is deductible, but you can't deduct the cost of fixing the defect.

Losses incurred from termite or moth damage are not deductible because they are considered to be progressive deterioration. Most damage caused by drought is also considered to be progressive and thus doesn't qualify, but if the loss is related to your trade or business, you can deduct it as a business expense. In some court cases, the cracking of foundation walls caused by soil shrinkage during a drought were allowed as a deduction, so it's certainly worth checking out if you have a loss from drought conditions.

Tax Tips

If you're a victim of a presidentially declared disaster, the IRS may postpone your tax deadlines for 120 days. These include deadlines for filing income and employment tax returns, paying income and employment taxes, and making contributions to your IRAs, whether a Roth or a traditional IRA. You will also have the option to deduct the loss in the current tax year or in the year immediately preceding the year the casualty occurred. You get to decide which year will give you the better tax break.

Losses from Theft

Now that you know what qualifies as a casualty, let's take a closer look at theft rules. A theft is the act of taking or removing property with the intention of depriving the owner of its use. The theft must be illegal within the state where it occurred, and it must be done with criminal intent.

If you discover the theft in a different year than the one in which it happened, you deduct the theft in the tax year in which it was discovered. For example, if your house was burglarized during the last week of December 2002 while you were on vacation and you discover the theft in January 2003, you would write off the loss in 2003.

The following crimes qualify as theft for tax purposes:

Blackmail	Kidnapping for ransom
Burglary	Larceny
Embezzlement	Robbery
Extortion	Threats

If you happen to mislay or lose property, that doesn't qualify as a theft.

How to Prove Your Losses

To take a casualty deduction, you must prove that the loss actually happened and that the property is worth what you claim it is. The type of proof you need will depend on the loss.

For losses from casualty, you'll need the following:

- The type of casualty and when it occurred. If there were any media reports, such as newspaper coverage of the fire or other disaster, keep them to help prove the event in case of an audit. Police and insurance reports will help as well. Pictures can tell the story strongly. You don't need to submit the pictures or other kind of proof with your tax return, but hold on to them in case you are audited.

- Proof that the loss was a direct result of the casualty.

- Proof that you were the owner of the property or had the legal responsibility for the property because of a lease arrangement.

> **Revenue Ramblings**
>
> It's a good idea to take pictures of valuable items and put them in a safe place outside your home. Photos not only help if you need to report a loss for tax purposes, but they're also helpful for insurance purposes. Pictures taken after the casualty will help to establish the condition and value of the damaged property.

For losses from theft, you'll need this:

- The date and time you discovered the missing property.

- Proof that your property was stolen. A police report is critical for proving theft, so be sure you call as soon as possible after discovery. Insurance reports also help to build your proof of loss.

- Proof that you owned the property.

You will have the burden of proving the value of the property and the fact the casualty or theft happened. You can never have too much proof, but you can have too little.

Calculating Your Loss

Your next difficult task will be to place a value on the loss. You will need to work through the following steps:

1. Determine the adjusted basis of your property before the casualty or theft. The adjusted basis of an item is its original cost, increased by any improvements and decreased by any *depreciation* or tax credits.

2. Determine the decrease in fair market value (FMV) after the casualty or theft. Fair market value is the price for which you could sell your property to a willing buyer when neither of you is under any duress to buy or sell.

Taxing Terms

Depreciation is a deductible expense through which you write off a portion of the wear and tear on property over the life of the property. There are many different methods for depreciating property. We'll cover those in greater detail in Part 7.

3. Determine whether your adjusted basis or the decrease in value is less. You subtract your insurance reimbursement from the amount that is less. Whatever remains is the amount that you can deduct.

You'll need to calculate the individual value of each item that was lost. You may have already done some of these calculations with an insurance adjuster, in which case you can use those values.

Let's assume that your house was burglarized and that you lost a stereo, television, and personal computer (PC). The following table shows you how to calculate their value for tax purposes:

Calculating Fair Market Value for Tax Loss

	Stereo	Television	PC
Cost	$600	$500	$1,200
FMV before theft	$400	$300	$800
FMV after theft	$0	$0	$0

In this case, the fair market value before theft is less than the cost, so you would use the fair market value when calculating your loss. Add $400 for the stereo, $300 for the television, and $800 for the PC, to come up with the total loss of $1,500. Let's say that insurance paid $1,000; the remaining $500 can be used to calculate your tax loss.

Unfortunately, you won't be able to deduct the full amount. As mentioned previously, you will have to subtract $100 plus 10 percent of your AGI.

To calculate the tax loss based on IRS rules:

$500 - $100 = $400

You must then subtract 10 percent of your adjusted gross income. In this case, if your AGI exceeded $4,000 (10 percent of $4,000 = $400), you would not be able to deduct the loss at all. As you can see, you have to experience significant losses to deduct them from your taxes.

If your loss is the result of damage or vandalism and you are able to repair the property so that it is useable again, the costs of repairs can be included when calculating your tax loss, provided that you meet the following tests:

- ◆ The repairs were needed to restore your property to its condition before the casualty occurred.

- ◆ You are not claiming an expense that is excessive for the type of repair.

- ◆ The repairs did not increase the value of the property before the casualty; they just took care of fixing the damage.

- ◆ The repair restores the damaged property to its condition before the loss.

Tax Tips

If you've suffered a significant loss, the best way to prove the value of the property is to hire an appraiser. Be sure you pick someone who is familiar with your property before and after the casualty or theft and who is aware of the sales of comparable property in the area. For example, if your house was damaged in a storm, consider contacting the appraiser who prepared the appraisal for your mortgage company. He or she would be familiar with both the house before the loss and your current real estate market.

Any fee that you pay for the appraisal can't be written off as part of the loss, but you can include it in the miscellaneous itemized deduction section of your taxes (this is discussed in Chapter 8).

Mixing Business and Pleasure

If you lost property related to your trade or business, you should write it off as a business expense (we'll cover this in more detail in Chapter 25).

The advantage of writing it off as a business expense is that it reduces your AGI—you don't have to reduce the loss first by $100, then by 10 percent of your AGI, which is required for personal losses.

If the property is partially used for business and partially used for personal reasons, you can split the loss between business and pleasure. For example, if you use your computer 70 percent for business and 30 percent for personal reasons, you would split the loss on this computer based on these percentages. If you have depreciated the item as a business expense, you would need to consider that depreciation when calculating the item's adjusted basis at the time of the casualty or theft.

Losses at Your Bank

If your bank, credit union, or other financial institution becomes insolvent or files for bankruptcy, you might be able to claim a loss. Any money lost that is not covered by federal deposit insurance can be written off. You can chose one of three options for writing off the loss:

- As a casualty loss

- As an ordinary loss

- As a nonbusiness bad debt

You should choose the type of loss that will give you the greatest tax-reduction benefit.

You can deduct the loss the fastest as a casualty loss. When using this option, all you'll need to make a claim is a reasonable estimate of how much is lost. You don't need to wait until all matters are resolved to claim your loss. The disadvantage of this method is that you will have to reduce your loss by $100 plus 10 percent of your adjusted gross income.

Your next option is to report the loss as an ordinary loss. In this case, the loss would be reported with your miscellaneous itemized deductions and would be reduced by only 2 percent of your AGI. There are limits, though. You can deduct only $20,000 of the loss ($10,000 if married filing separately). You can't select this option if your account was federally insured. You must be able to reasonably estimate the amount of the loss before it can be claimed.

If you choose the third option, a nonbusiness bad debt, you must wait until all matters are settled and the actual loss, rather than just an estimate, is known. Once the numbers are known, the loss is written off as a short-term capital loss on Schedule D, "Capital Gains and Loss."

Getting Reimbursed

If your insurance company or other source reimburses you for your loss, you must subtract that reimbursement from the value of the property before writing off the loss. You'll need to estimate the reimbursement you expect for the loss, even if you didn't receive it by the end of the tax year in which you plan to report the loss. If your property is covered by insurance and you don't make a claim, you can't write off the portion of the loss that would have been reimbursed if you had filed the claim.

When you receive your reimbursement, if it is for more than the adjusted basis of your property, you have what is called a gain, and you may have to pay taxes on it. If you lose property that you held for more than 12 months, the gain is considered a capital gain. Property lost that was held for fewer than 12 months would be reported as an ordinary gain. Tax rates are lower for a capital gain—20 percent (10 percent if your current income tax rate is 15 percent or lower). An ordinary gain is reported as current income and taxed at your current income tax rate.

Sometimes you can delay reporting a gain in the tax year you receive it. For example, let's say that your rental house was totally destroyed and that you received cash from the insurance company. You can postpone reporting your gain for two years, to give you time to replace the property. As long as you reinvest the insurance proceeds in like property, you will not have to report the gain until the property is sold. If you have money left after you buy a new house, you may have to report the gain at that time. If your property was taken from you through condemnation, you have three years to replace the loss. If you lost your property during an act that was declared a disaster by the president, you have four years to find a replacement.

Revenue Ramblings

Sometimes you'll get reimbursement from an emergency disaster fund—whether set up by your employer, another private entity, or the government—or cash gifts from relatives or friends. As long as you use this money to repair or replace your losses, you don't have to report it as income, but it will reduce the amount you can deduct on your taxes for the loss.

Audit Alarm!

Disaster relief that you receive for food, medical supplies, or other forms of assistance does not have to be subtracted when you are calculating your casualty loss unless the funds were used to replace or repair your lost or destroyed property. Disaster unemployment assistance payments are treated as unemployment benefits and are taxable.

Completing the Forms

When you report a casualty or theft loss, you'll have to fill out a special form—Form 4684, "Casualties and Thefts"—and put the results of that form on your Schedule A. If you experienced more than one casualty or theft during a year, you'll need to fill out a separate form for each loss, add the final numbers, and report the loss on Schedule A. You will need to attach Form 4684 to your return when you file it with the IRS.

Now that you know how to handle any losses for theft or casualty, we'll consider the leftovers, or miscellaneous deductions. This is where you get to deduct anything not already mentioned that qualifies as an itemized deduction.

The Least You Need to Know

- ◆ Casualty losses are damage, destruction, or loss of property caused by an identifiable event that is sudden, unexpected, and unusual.

- ◆ Theft is the act of taking or removing property with the intention of depriving the owner of its use. The theft also must be illegal within the state where the theft occurred, and it must be done with criminal intent.

- ◆ Deductions for casualty or theft losses are limited. You can deduct only losses not reimbursed, and you must reduce your loss by $100 plus 10 percent of your adjusted gross income.

- ◆ You'll need proof of the loss and proof of the value of the property lost to claim the deduction.

Chapter 8

Miscellany:
The Itemizing Catchall

In This Chapter

◆ Miscellaneous types

◆ Limiting deductions

◆ Avoiding limits

◆ What you can't deduct

After itemizing your medical expenses, taxes and interest payments, charitable donations, and losses, you might still have a long list of things you'd like to deduct. Here's your last chance: If the IRS allows you to deduct it on Schedule A, you'll probably find it in this chapter; if not, you're most likely out of luck.

Although it might seem arduous to take the time to scan the deduction types and determine whether your expenses qualify, it's worth it. You may be surprised by what you find.

Two Percent Limit Deductions

Most miscellaneous deductions face the 2 percent limit, which means that the total amount you can deduct must exceed 2 percent of your adjusted gross income before you are able to deduct anything. (I'll point out the few that are not subject to this limitation as they come up.) In addition, if your 2002 income exceeds $137,300 ($68,650 for a couple who is married filing separately), you may have to reduce your miscellaneous itemized deductions by 3 percent of your adjusted gross income.

> **Revenue Ramblings**
>
> In addition to the 2 percent limit and the income limit, some deductions face other limits, such as 50 or 60 percent on business meals and entertainment not reimbursed by your employer. I'll do my best to try to navigate these very murky areas and clear them up for you.

Deductions that are subject to the 2 percent limit fall into three categories in the Miscellaneous section of Schedule A: unreimbursed employee expenses, tax preparation fees, and other expenses. To make things easier for you to find, I'll alphabetize the deduction items under each of these three groups.

Unreimbursed Employee Expenses

Your employee expenses must pass three tests to qualify as a tax break:

◆ Your expenses must be paid during the tax year.

◆ The expenses must have been used to carry on your trade or business of being an employee.

◆ The expenses must be ordinary and necessary. "Ordinary" means that it is a common and accepted expense in your type of trade or business. "Necessary" means that the expense is appropriate and helpful to your trade or business.

> **Tax Tips**
>
> If you can convince your employer to reimburse you for what would otherwise be unreimbursed business expenses instead of paying you that amount of your salary, you should take advantage of this option. Your employer will not have additional costs, but your taxable salary will be lower. Reimbursed employee expenses are not subject to the 2 percent limitation. For example, let's say that each year you spend $1,000 on unreimbursed costs for marketing materials. You convince your employer to reduce your salary by $1,000 instead of making you pay for those materials out of pocket. The employer then makes these materials a $1,000 reimbursed employee business expense. Your taxable salary is now $1,000 less, so you pay less taxes on that and the marketing materials are no longer subject to the 2 percent limitation rule.

If your expenses pass these three tests for your particular trade or business, you can deduct them—as long as they were not reimbursed by your employer. If you received a partial reimbursement, you'll need to subtract that from your calculations.

Remember, we're looking at only unreimbursed employee expenses. Business expenses for your own small business are covered in Part 7.

Now let's take a look at the 2 percent deduction types:

Business bad debt is a loan you make for business purposes that is not repaid. The main motive for incurring the debt must be related to your business or trade to qualify. If you are never repaid this money, but you had to make the loan to keep your job, you can write off the debt.

Business liability insurance premiums can be written off if you pay for protection against personal liability for wrongful acts on the job.

Damages for breach of employment contract are deductible expenses if you pay your former employer for damages attributable to the pay you received from your employer. This can happen when you don't perform the services for which you were contracted to perform or the services were not performed to the satisfaction of your employer.

Depreciation on computers or cellular telephones can be deducted if you buy these items for the convenience of your employer and they are required as a condition of your employment. For example, if you must use your computer or cell phone during your regular working hours to carry out business for your employer, it will usually pass the convenience test. To pass the required test, you must not be able to properly perform your duties without these tools. We'll talk about depreciation methods in Chapter 24.

Dues to chambers of commerce and professional societies can be deducted if the membership helps you to carry out the duties of your job. Qualifying organizations include bar associations, medical associations, boards of trade, business leagues, civic or public service organizations, real estate boards, and trade associations. You can't deduct the membership dues if the primary purpose of the organization is to conduct entertainment activities or provide entertainment facilities for members or their guests. Sorry, you can't deduct airline, hotel, or luncheon club dues. If part of your dues are for lobbying or political activities, you may not be able to deduct that part of your dues. We'll talk more about nondeductible expenses later in this chapter.

Education that is work related can be deducted even if you are not working toward a degree. The purpose of the education must be to maintain or improve skills required in your present work or required by your employer or the law to keep your salary, status, or job. If your education meets any of these tests, you can deduct expenses for tuition, books, supplies, laboratory fees and similar items, and certain transportation costs.

Tax Tips _____

You may be better off using one of the education tax credits to write off education expenses. We'll discuss those in Chapter 14. Even if your education doesn't qualify under the rules discussed in this chapter, you may still be able to use the education tax credit.

Taxing Terms _____

Principal place of business means that you use a part of your home regularly and exclusively for administrative or management activities of your trade or business, and that you have no other fixed location where you conduct substantial administrative or management activities of your trade or business.

Travel as education cannot be deducted if it constitutes a form of education. For example, a Spanish teacher who travels to Spain to maintain or improve his or her familiarity with the Spanish language and culture cannot deduct the cost of the trip as an educational expense.

Home office expenses can be at least partially deducted if you use a part of your home regularly and exclusively for business purposes. You may also be able to deduct the depreciation of your home. Your home office should be used ...

♦ As your *principal place of business* for any trade or business.

♦ As a place to meet or deal with your patients, clients, or customers in the normal course of your trade or business.

♦ In the case of a separate structure not attached to your home, in connection with your trade or business.

♦ For regular and exclusive business use that is for the convenience of your employer and not just appropriate and helpful in your job.

We'll cover the details of what is deductible for home office use in Chapter 22.

Job search expenses can be deducted if you are looking for a new job in your present occupation, even if you don't get a new job. You can't deduct these expenses if you are looking to change occupations, if you took a substantial break between jobs, or if you are looking for your first job. Employment and outplacement agency fees can be deducted if you pay these fees to find a new job in your present occupation. Resumé costs for typing, printing, and mailing copies of a resume to prospective employers are deductible if you are looking for a new job in your present occupation. Travel and transportation expenses incurred if you travel to an area to look for a new job in your present occupation may be deductible. You can deduct the travel expenses if the primary purpose of the trip is to look for a new job. If you mix business and pleasure, the amount of time you spend on personal activity must be compared to the amount of time you spend looking for work to determine the trip's deductibility. If most of your time is spent on personal entertainment activities, you can't deduct the travel expenses to and from the area, but you can deduct the expenses of looking for a new job in your present occupation while in the area.

Legal fees that are related to keeping or doing your job are deductible.

Licenses and regulatory fees paid to state or local governments for your trade, business, or profession are deductible.

Occupational taxes that you are charged at a flat rate by a locality for the privilege of working or conducting a business in that locality are deductible.

Research expenses if you are a college professor can be deducted, including travel expenses for teaching, lecturing, writing, or publishing on subjects that relate directly to your field of teaching. You cannot deduct the cost of travel that is purely for the purpose of furthering your education.

Tools used in your work can be deducted. If the tools wear out and are thrown away within one year of the date of purchase, you can deduct their cost all in one year. Otherwise, you can depreciate the cost of tools over their useful life.

Travel, transportation, meal, entertainment, and gift expenses also might be deductible for an employee who has ordinary and necessary business-related expenses for travel away from home, local transportation, entertainment, and gifts. To deduct these expenses, though, you will have to file an additional Form 2106 or a 2106 EZ. Travel expenses can include the costs of getting to and from the business destination, meals and lodging while away from home, taxi fares, baggage charges, and cleaning and laundry expenses. The amount you deduct for meals and entertainment is limited to only 50 percent of what you actually spend, including taxes and tips. Gift expenses are limited to $25 per recipient.

Transportation expenses locally can be deducted if they are costs incurred while traveling from one workplace to another when you are not traveling away from home. They include the cost of transportation by air, rail, bus, and taxi, and the cost of using your car. Car expenses can be charged at the standard business mileage rate of $36\frac{1}{2}$ cents per mile, or you can figure out your actual costs of operating the vehicle related to your business use. If you work at two places in a day, whether or not for the same employer, you can usually deduct the expenses of getting from one workplace to the other.

Tax Tips

Some types of employees get to deduct more of their meal and entertainment expenses. If you're an air transportation employee, interstate truck operator, interstate bus driver, railroad employee, or merchant marine, you may be eligible to deduct a greater share, thanks to the 2001 tax law. The percentage that qualifying employees can deduct gradually increases to 80 percent under the new law. The changes are as follows:

Beginning in Tax Year	Deductible Percentage
2002	65%
2004	70%
2006	75%
2008 and beyond	80%

Union dues and expenses for membership are deductible. You can also deduct assessments for benefit payments to unemployed union members, but you can't deduct the part of the assessments or contributions that provide funds for the payment of sick, accident, or death benefits. Also, you can't deduct as a miscellaneous expense contributions to a pension fund, even if the union requires you to make the contributions. (We'll talk more about retirement tax-reduction benefits in Part 5.) Amounts paid toward lobbying and political activities are generally not deductible.

Work clothes and uniforms can be deducted if you wear them as a condition of your employment and if the clothes aren't suitable for everyday wear. You can deduct their initial costs as well as the cost of their upkeep. Types of workers who generally are able to deduct the costs of their work clothes and uniforms include delivery workers, firefighters, health-care workers, law-enforcement officers, letter carriers, professional athletes, and transportation workers. Musicians and entertainers can deduct the cost of theatrical clothing and accessories that are not suitable for everyday wear. You also can deduct the cost of protective clothing required in your work, such as safety shoes or boots, safety glasses, hard hats, and work gloves. Military personnel on full-time active duty can't deduct the costs of their uniforms, but armed forces reservists who are restricted from wearing their uniforms except while on duty can deduct them. You can deduct the cost of your uniforms if you are a civilian faculty or staff member of a military school.

Tax Tips

You should deduct the expenses for preparing tax schedules related to profit or loss from business on Schedule C or C-EZ, rentals or royalties on Schedule E, or farm income and expenses on Schedule F. Deduct expenses of preparing the remainder of the return on Schedule A.

Tax-Preparation Fees

Fees to prepare your taxes are deductible in the year you pay them. These fees include the cost of tax-preparation software programs and tax publications. They also include any fee you paid for electronic filing of your return.

Other Expenses

You may be able to deduct other expenses not related to tax-preparation or unreimbursed business expenses. These expenses include money spent to …

◆ Produce or collect income that must be included in your gross income.

◆ Manage, conserve, or maintain property held for producing such income.

◆ Determine, contest, pay, or claim a refund of any tax.

The following types of expenses fit in the "other" category:

Appraisal fees paid to figure a casualty loss or the fair market value of donated property can be deducted.

Certain casualty and theft losses for damaged or stolen property used in performing a service as an employee are deductible. In these cases, the losses are subject to only a 2 percent limit rather than the higher limits we discussed in Chapter 7.

Clerical help and office rent expenses related to your investments or for collecting the taxable income on them are deductible.

Depreciation on a home computer, if you use it to produce income or manage investments, is deductible.

Excess deductions of an estate, if the estate's total deductions are higher than the gross income from the estate, can be deducted.

Fees to collect interest and dividends paid to a broker, bank, trustee, or similar agent to collect your taxable bond interest or dividends on shares of stock, are eligible for deduction. However, you cannot deduct a fee you pay to a broker to buy investment property, such as stocks or bonds. You must add the fee to the

Taxing Terms _____

An activity that you don't operate with a profit motive is a hobby and the income is considered by the IRS to be **hobby income,** not business income. The most important difference is that hobby losses are not deductible the way business losses are. There is an excellent article on this topic at taxes.about.com/library/weekly/aa061200a.htm.

cost of the property. Fees paid for the sale of securities should be used to figure gain or loss from the sale on Schedule D and cannot be deducted on Schedule A.

Hobby expenses can be deducted, but only up to the amount of *hobby income.*

Indirect deductions of pass-through entities are expenses passed through from entities such as partnerships, S corporations, and mutual funds that are not publicly offered. For example, if you're a member of an investment club that is formed solely for the purpose of investing in securities and the club is a partnership, you can deduct your share of the partnership's operating expenses as miscellaneous itemized deductions. If the investment club partnership has investments that also produce nontaxable income, you can't deduct your share of the partnership's expenses that produce the nontaxable income.

Investment fees and expenses paid to manage your investments that produce taxable income can be deducted. You can't deduct the fees if they are paid by the funds within your retirement plan, such as an IRA.

Legal expenses that you incur in attempting to produce or collect taxable income or a tax refund can be deducted. You can also deduct legal expenses related to doing or keeping your job, tax advice related to a divorce, or expenses to collect taxable alimony.

Loss on deposits can be deducted if you can reasonably estimate the amount of your loss on money deposited in a bankrupt or insolvent financial institution, provided that none of your deposit was federally insured. Generally, these losses can be deducted in the current year even though the exact amount has not been finally determined. When you make this choice, you cannot change it without IRS approval. If you are a 1 percent or more owner or officer of the financial institution involved, or if you are related to someone who is, you can't take this loss as a miscellaneous deduction.

Repayments of income also qualify as deductible. If you had to repay income reported in an earlier tax year, you may be able to deduct the amount you repaid. This is not a common occurrence, but let's say your employer made an error on your check and demands repayment after you've filed taxes based on income received. If the amount you had to repay was ordinary income of $3,000 or less, the deduction is subject to the 2 percent limit. If it was more than $3,000, see "Repayments Under Claim of Right," in the next section; you may be able to avoid the 2 percent limit.

Repayments of Social Security benefits are deductible as well. If the amount of income indicated in net benefits on your Form SSA-1099 ("Social Security Benefit Statement") and Form RRB-1099 ("Payments by the Railroad Retirement Board") totals a negative figure, you may be able to take a miscellaneous itemized deduction subject to the 2 percent limit. The amount that you can deduct is the part of the negative figure that represents an amount you included in gross income in an earlier year.

Safe deposit box rent can be deducted if you use the box to store taxable income-producing stocks, bonds, or investment-related documents.

Service charges on *dividend reinvestment plans* can be deducted if they were payments for holding the shares acquired through the plan, for collecting and reinvesting dividends, or for keeping individual records.

Trustee's administrative fees for IRAs are deductible if they are billed separately and paid by you in connection with your IRA.

Taxing Terms

Dividend reinvestment plans are plans that let you choose to use your dividends to buy additional stocks instead of getting the dividends in cash. They can be bought through a broker or directly from the company.

Deductions Not Subject to the 2 Percent Limit

Some deductions are not subject to the 2 percent limit. These are placed in a special section called "Other Miscellaneous Deductions" on Schedule A.

The following deductions get this special treatment:

Amortizable premium on taxable bonds. If the amount you pay for a bond is greater than its stated principal amount, the excess is a called bond premium. You can elect to *amortize* the premium on taxable bonds. The amortization of the premium is generally an offset to interest income on the bond rather than a separate deduction item. Whether this is a deductible expense, and whether it is subject to the 2 percent limit, depends on the year you acquired the bond. If you have a bond premium, you can get more details about how it should be reported in IRS Publication 550, "Investment Income and Expenses."

Certain casualty and theft losses can be deducted free of the 2 percent limit if the damaged or stolen property was income-producing property (property held for investment, such as stocks, notes, bonds, gold, silver, vacant lots, and works of art).

Taxing Terms

Amortization is the way you can recover an investment cost for an intangible asset. This is similar to depreciation for a tangible asset. An **intangible asset** is something for which you have rights of ownership, but it is not a material item.

Gambling losses, up to the amount of gambling winnings, can be deducted in this section. You cannot deduct gambling losses that are more than your winnings.

Impairment-related work expenses can be deducted if you have a physical or mental disability that limits your ability to be employed or that substantially limits one or more of your major life activities, such as performing manual tasks, walking, speaking, breathing, learning, and working. If you have such an impairment, you can deduct your impairment-related work expenses. Impairment-related work expenses are ordinary and necessary business expenses for attendant care services at your place of work, and other expenses in connection with your place of work that are necessary for you to be able to work. You'll need to complete Form 2106 or Form 2106-EZ if you are an employee.

Repayments under claim of right work this way: If you had to repay more than $3,000 that you included in your income in an earlier year because at the time you thought you had an unrestricted right to it, you may be able to deduct the amount you repaid or take a credit against your tax. See IRS Publication 525 on repayments for more information.

Nondeductible Expenses

People often think that they can deduct certain expenses, when in reality those expenses are not deductible. Here are some of the common items people deduct by mistake:

Adoption expenses are not a miscellaneous deduction, but they may be deductible as part of the Adoption Credit.

Campaign expenses are not deductible, even if you must pay fees for qualification or registration. Legal fees that are paid to defend charges that arise from participation in a political campaign also can't be deducted.

Check-writing fees on a personal account cannot be deducted, even if you earn interest on the account.

Club dues cannot be deducted if the membership is for a club that is organized for pleasure, recreation, or other social purpose. This includes business, social, athletic, luncheon, sporting, airline, and hotel clubs.

Commuting expenses between your home and your main or regular workplace are not deductible. If you haul tools, instruments, or other items in your car to and from work, you can deduct only the additional cost of hauling the items. For example, you can deduct the rent on a trailer to carry the items.

Fines or penalties paid because you violated a law are not deductible. These include parking tickets, tax penalties, and penalties deducted from teachers' paychecks after an illegal strike.

Health spa expenses are not deductible, even if you have a job that makes it a requirement to stay in excellent physical condition.

A **home security system** is not deductible for personal reasons, but if you got the security system because you want to protect business assets, you may be able to deduct part of its cost as an unreimbursed employee expense.

Homeowners' insurance premiums for fire, theft, and liability protection or for mortgage insurance are not deductible, but may be partially deductible if you have a home office as a business deduction. More about that in Chapter 22.

Investment-related seminars are not deductible for attending a convention, seminar, or similar meeting for investment purposes.

Life insurance premiums are not deductible unless they are premiums required as part of your divorce agreement for your former spouse. In this case, they may be deductible as alimony expenses.

Lobbying expenses are not deductible, even if they are incurred for research, preparation, planning, or coordination of lobbying efforts. This includes dues paid for lobbying expenses as part of your membership in a tax-exempt organization, unless these expenses are an ordinary and necessary expense of carrying out your trade or business.

Lost or mislaid cash or property cannot be deducted, unless if you can prove that the loss resulted from an identifiable event that was sudden, unexpected, or unusual. We discussed these types of events in greater detail in Chapter 7. An example of this type of loss is catching your hand in a car door that was accidentally slammed and breaking the setting on your diamond ring. If the diamond is never found, the loss of that diamond would qualify as a casualty.

Lunches with co-workers are not deductible, unless they are part of a trip away from home for business purposes.

Meals while working late are generally not deductible, unless they qualify as an entertainment expense or you are traveling away from home for business purposes.

Personal legal expenses are not deductible, even if the result of the legal proceeding could be the loss of income-producing property. These include expenses for legal fees related to child custody, personal injury, will preparation, property claims or settlement in divorce, and civil or criminal charges resulting from a personal relationship.

Political contributions to a political candidate, a campaign committee, or a newsletter fund are not deductible. Advertisements in convention bulletins and admissions to dinners or programs that benefit a political party or political candidate also don't qualify for a tax deduction.

Professional accreditation fees, including the fees for initial certification to practice accounting, bar exams and other expenses to secure admission to the bar, and medical and dental license fees for initial licensing, are not deductible.

Relief fund contributions made to a private plan that pays benefits to any covered employee who cannot work because of any injury or illness not related to the job do not qualify for a tax deduction.

Residential telephone service for the first line to your residence is not deductible, even if it is used for your trade or business. Only the long distance for specific business calls is deductible.

Stockholders' meeting expenses aren't deductible. You can't deduct your transportation and other expenses paid to attend stockholders' meetings for companies in which your only interest is that you own stock, even if you think that the information you will learn will be useful for making investment decisions.

Tax-exempt income expenses incurred to produce tax-exempt income are not deductible.

Travel expenses for another individual cannot be deducted for your spouse, a dependent, or another person who accompanies you on a business trip.

Voluntary unemployment benefit fund contributions made to a union or private fund are not deductible. You can deduct contributions as taxes if state law requires you to make them to a state unemployment fund that covers you for the loss of wages from unemployment caused by business conditions.

Wristwatches are not deductible, even if you must know the correct time to do your job.

That's it! If you didn't find a personal expense listed in this chapter or any other chapter in this part of the book, chances are good that it's not deductible as an expense on Schedule A. Don't give up hope yet, though—maybe your expense will qualify for a credit. These wonderful benefits are covered in the next part of the book.

The Least You Need to Know

- Most deductions that qualify as miscellaneous deductions are subject to the minimum reduction of 2 percent of your adjusted gross income. A few are not subject to this reduction.

- Only 50 percent of the cost of meals and entertainment is allowed.

- Some employees can deduct more than 50 percent of their meals and entertainment deductions if they fall within certain industry categories.

- You can't deduct most expenses that you incur when changing jobs for work in a new career field or for the costs of getting your first professional licenses or certifications as a miscellaneous expense.

Part 3

Roaming for Credits

When you roam this area of the tax code, you may find a lot of red tape and hoops you must jump through—but it's definitely worth the effort. Tax credits are better than deductions because they are subtracted directly from your tax bill. Deductions are subtracted from the income on which your tax is calculated.

Chapter 9

Crediting Your Children and Dependents

In This Chapter

- ◆ Credit options
- ◆ Limiting benefits
- ◆ Passing more tests
- ◆ Calculating credits

Kids aren't cheap! The IRS recognizes that raising children eats up a significant chunk of many families' resources, and good old Uncle Sam tries to ease that burden by giving parents a break at tax time. If you have children, two types of credits are available to help reduce the tax bite: the Child Tax Credit and the Child and Dependent Care Credit.

Each credit has different qualifying rules and income limitations. Lower-income folks may even be able to get a refund on part of their Social Security taxes if they qualify.

Child Tax Credit

We'll start with the Child Tax Credit, which is by far the easier of the credits to figure out and claim. If you qualify for it, you get a $600 credit for each qualifying child under the age of 17.

The new tax law passed in 2001 raised the credit from $500 to $600 beginning in 2001. The credit will increase to $700 in 2005, to $800 in 2009, and finally to $1,000 in 2010. Also, the new law exempted the Child Tax Credit from being reduced by the Alternative Minimum Tax, which we discussed in Chapter 3.

Who Qualifies

Now that you know how much you can save on your tax bill, let's look at the rules for qualification. Your child must …

- Be under the age of 17 by the end of the current tax year.

- Be a citizen or resident of the United States.

- Have been claimed as a dependent.

By the way, a child, for the purpose of the tax credit, can be …

- A son or daughter.

- A stepson or stepdaughter.

- An adopted child.

- A grandchild.

- An eligible foster child. To qualify as an eligible foster child, he or she must have been placed with you by an authorized placement agency. Children whom you cared for as your own and who are your brother, sister, stepbrother, stepsister, or descendent (such as a child of your brother, sister, stepbrother, or stepsister) also qualify.

Facing Limits

Unfortunately, you can earn too much to qualify for this tax break. If your adjusted gross income (AGI) is above $110,000 for married couples filing jointly, $75,000 for a single parent, or $55,000 for a married person filing separately, the allowable tax credit will be reduced. The tax credit is reduced by $50 for every $1,000 of AGI over the threshold amounts.

Let's work through an example together. A couple who is filing jointly has earnings that total $120,000 AGI, which is $10,000 above the allowable threshold of $110,000 for a married couple filing jointly. They first need to divide the amount that is above the allowable threshold (in this case, $10,000) by $1,000, which equals 10. They must then multiply 10 by $50 to figure out their tax credit reduction; this number is $500. The couple has two children and would qualify for a $1,200 credit if they didn't exceed the income limit. After subtracting their reduction amount of $500, their tax credit is $700, which is still a nice tax savings.

Taking Claim

You can claim the tax credit when you file using Form 1040 or Form 1040A. As you might expect, you'll find a Child Tax Credit worksheet in the 1040 instruction packet, to help you figure out whether you qualify for the tax credit and how much you should take.

The form is relatively simple and has only five steps. You use this worksheet to calculate the amount of the possible credit and adjust it by the amount of taxes paid, if less than the credit allowed. You can't write off more than your actual tax liability. If you find that you can't take the full credit, you'll need to complete Form 8812 to calculate whether you are entitled to any additional Child Tax Credit. You may be able to recover some of the lost credit by using the Additional Child Tax Credit form.

Child and Dependent Care Credit

The Child and Dependent Care Credit is higher than the Child Tax Credit, but it's based on your actual expenses for taking care of a child or qualified dependent rather than a fixed sum determined by the IRS. Also, you can use the credit only if you are working or looking for work and if you pay someone to take care of your child or dependent.

You can take up to a $720 credit if you have one qualifying dependent and up to a maximum of $1,440 if you have two or more qualifying dependents.

Taking the Tests

You must pass six tests to qualify for the credit. Tired of tests? Don't despair—the taxes savings are worth the effort.

Qualifying Person Test. Any dependents you are claiming must be under the age of 13 at the time the care was provided or must be physically or mentally unable to care for themselves. Your spouse can qualify if he or she is unable to care for himself or herself. Your qualifying dependent or spouse must be someone for whom you can claim an exemption. If you are divorced or separated, you can claim the exemption for a dependent child only if you are the *custodial parent* or if the custodial parent signed a Form 8832, "Release of Claim to Exemption for Child of Divorced or Separated Parents."

Tax Tips

You can claim the credit for a child in the year he or she turns 13. The credit is based on your child-care expenses, not on the number of months that you provide the care. So don't stop claiming your deduction prematurely!

Taxing Terms

The **custodial parent** is the person who has primary care, custody, and control of a minor child or children.

Keeping Up a Home Test. You qualify as a person keeping up a home if you paid more than 50 percent of the costs of keeping up that home. The home must be both your primary residence and the primary residence for the child or dependent you are claiming. The home can qualify as the dependent's primary residence even if he or she doesn't live there all year. Exceptions to the full-year rule include birth, death, or temporary absence because of sickness, school, business, vacation, military service, or custody agreement. When figuring the costs of keeping up a home, you should include rent, mortgage interest, property taxes, utility charges, home repairs, insurance on the home, and food costs. You can't include expenses for clothing, education, medical treatment, vacations, life insurance, transportation, or mortgage principal in the home cost calculations.

Earned Income Test. To claim the credit, you and your spouse, if filing jointly, must have earned income. Earned income includes wages, salaries, tips, other employee compensation, and net earnings from self-employment. If you have a net loss from self-employment, it reduces your earned income for this test. Strike benefits and disability pay also are considered earned income. For the purposes of this test, your spouse is considered as having earned income for any month that he or she is a student or is unable to care for himself or herself.

Work-Related Expense Test. The expenses that you use in figuring this tax credit must be expenses that allowed you to work or look for work. If you're married, generally you and your spouse must work or be looking for work unless you or your spouse is a full-time student or requires care by another person. If you looked for work but ended up with no earned income for the year, you don't qualify for this credit. Volunteer work, whether unpaid or nominally paid, doesn't count as work for this test. If you don't work for part of the month, even if this is because of illness, you must separate expenses for days worked and days not worked. Only the expenses on days worked can be included in the calculation for this tax credit.

Joint Return Test. In most cases, married couples must file a joint return to take the credit. If you're legally separated or are living apart from your spouse, you may be able to file a separate return and still take the credit. Legal separation must be based on a decree of divorce or separate maintenance agreement. If you're married and living apart, you'll need to prove that your home was the home of the qualifying dependent for more than half the year, that you paid more than half the costs of keeping up the home for the year, and that your spouse didn't live with you for the last six months of the year.

Provider Identification Test. You must identify all people or organizations that provide care for your child or dependent. This should include the name, address, and taxpayer identification number. If the person providing care is an individual, you can use his or her Social Security number. For an organization, you'll need the employer identification number. If the provider organization is tax exempt, such as a church or school, you won't need the number; instead, you can write "tax-exempt" on the tax form where the number would otherwise be noted. You can get the number from the provider's Social Security card or driver's license (if the state is using the Social Security number to issues licenses), the W-4 form if he or she is your employee, or a letter or invoice from the providing organization. If your employer is the provider, you'll need a statement from your employer that this is part of your employer's dependent-care plan.

Getting the Credit

Let's assume that you've passed all these tests. Now we'll look at how to figure the tax credit. You can include only the expenses for care that was provided in the year the care was received. For example, if you prepaid 2003 expenses at the end of 2002, you can't claim the 2003 expenses in 2002. You'll have to wait to claim those prepaid expenses on the 2003 return. Up to $2,400 of expenses is eligible for use in calculating the credit, if you have one qualifying dependent, and up to $4,800 is eligible if you have two or more dependents.

You may be able to claim 2001 expenses paid in 2002, but you will need to figure those expenses separately. There is a line on Form 2441 for claiming the previous year's expenses. If a state social services agency pays you a nontaxable amount to help you cover your dependent-care expenses, you cannot count the expenses that were reimbursed as work-related expenses.

Audit Alarm!

You may be able to use medical expenses paid to care for a qualifying dependent who requires outside care as work-related expenses and as deductible medical expenses on your itemized deductions. You can claim the medical expenses either way, but you can't claim the same expenses as both a work-related expense for the purposes of this credit and a medical deduction. You have to choose one. You should pick whichever will result in your greater tax savings.

Tax Tips

If you have the option to participate in an employer-sponsored plan, compare the employee dependent-care benefits with the possible loss of this tax credit, and decide which will result in the greatest tax reduction.

If your employer pays your dependent-care benefits, whether directly to the care provider or to you, you can't use this credit for expenses paid by the employer plan, even if the payments were made using money deducted from your salary. Some employers permit employees to deduct a portion of their salary before taxes are taken out to pay child and dependent-care expenses. This means that your salary is reduced not only for federal income tax purposes, but also for calculating Social Security and Medicare taxes and state and local taxes.

Facing the Limits

In addition to passing the tests, you're faced with three possible limits that could reduce or totally wipe out this tax credit for you.

Earned Income Limit. Your work-related expenses used to calculate the credit can't exceed either your earned income, if you are single at the end of the year, or the lower amount of your earned income or your spouse's earned income, if you are married at the end of the year. If your spouse died during the year and you're filing a joint return as the surviving spouse, you should consider only your income when figuring out this limit. If your spouse is a full-time student or someone who requires outside care, his or her earned income for the purposes of calculating this limit is $200 per month if you have one qualifying dependent, or $400 per month if you have two or more dependents. If your spouse works during any of the months in the year, you should use the actual earnings if they are higher.

Dollar Limit. As stated previously, there is a dollar limit on the amount of work-related expenses you can use to calculate the credit. If you have one qualifying dependent, the maximum amount you can use in figuring the credit is $2,400. If you have two or more dependents, the maximum is $4,800. This limit is based on expenses during the tax year. The number of months you paid these expenses is not relevant in calculating the dollar limit.

Reduced Dollar Limit. If you received dependent-care benefits from your employer, even if they were deducted from your own salary, the amount you can use in calculating the work-related expenses is reduced by your employee benefits. For example, if your employer pays $1,000 toward your work-related dependent-care expenses, then your allowable expenses are reduced dollar for dollar by that amount. We'll assume in this example that you have one child, which means that you can use up to $2,400 to calculate the credit. Since your employer paid $1,000, the amount you can use to calculate the credit is now only $1,400.

Credit Calculations

We're finally ready to look at how the credit is calculated. If you're still interested, it must mean that you passed the tests and know your limits.

First, let's look at what expenses can be included. You can include any expenses that are for the care of a qualifying dependent or spouse if the main purpose of the expense is for the person's well-being or protection. You don't need to look for the cheapest care option for the expenses to qualify. When calculating expenses, don't include costs for food, clothing, education, or entertainment.

CAUTION

Audit Alarm!

Education expenses so that your child can attend first grade or higher are not expenses that can be included when calculating this credit.

To determine how much your credit will be, multiply your work-related expenses (after you have applied the limits) by a percentage based on the following table:

If your adjusted gross income is …		
Over:	**But Not Over:**	**Your Percentage Is:**
$0	$10,000	30%
$10,000	$12,000	29%
$12,000	$14,000	28%
$14,000	$16,000	27%
$16,000	$18,000	26%
$18,000	$20,000	25%
$20,000	$22,000	24%
$22,000	$24,000	23%
$24,000	$26,000	22%
$26,000	$28,000	21%
$28,000	No limit	20%

Let's practice calculating the credit. We'll assume that a married couple filing jointly has an adjusted gross income of $100,000, with each earning equal amounts.

They have two children and spent $800 a month (total $9,600) on eligible work-related childcare expenses. They don't have employer benefits for child care. They meet the earned income limit, which means that they aren't subject to the reduced dollar limit and so can use $4,800 when calculating their credit. According to the table, their percentage is 20 percent (because their income is over $28,000). The couple would multiply $4,800 × 20 percent to get a credit of $960.

Beginning in 2003, the maximum percentage will increase to 35 percent, which will increase the maximum credit allowed for lower-income folks to $1,050 (now $720) for one dependent, and $2,100 (now $1,440) for two or more dependents. The amount of expenses that can be included in the calculations will increase as well in 2003. Eligible expenses will increase to $3,000 for one qualifying dependent or spouse, which is up from the current max of $2,400. If you have two or more qualifying dependents, the max increases to $6,000, which is up from the current max of $4,800.

Even though the couple in our example are not low-income earners, they will benefit from the change in the tax law because of the higher expenses allowed. Once the new law goes into effect in 2003, this couple would be able to take a credit of $1,200 ($6,000 × 20%), which is $240 higher than currently allowable.

The credits you receive for your kids probably won't even come close to covering the expense of raising a child, but it's a good start!

The Least You Need to Know

- You can take a Child Tax Credit for each of your eligible children of $600, provided that you don't exceed the income limitations. This credit is exempt from the Alternative Minimum Tax.

- You are entitled to the Child and Dependent Care Credit based on a percentage of your eligible care expenses.

- Both the Child Tax Credit and the Dependent and Child Care Credit were increased as part of the 2001 tax law.

Using Your Elderly and Disability Credits

In This Chapter

- ◆ Qualifying rules
- ◆ Earning caps
- ◆ Credit calculations
- ◆ Knowing your limits

Seniors or disabled folks who are getting little from Social Security, non-taxable pensions, or other income sources may qualify for up to $1,125 using the Credit for the Elderly or the Disabled. The income level caps are strict, so you really must be living at or below the poverty line to take advantage of this credit.

Folks who are permanently and totally disability and who have taxable income from a public or private employer also can qualify for this credit, provided that they don't exceed the income limits.

We'll review the rules and show you how to figure this credit.

Who Qualifies

Anyone who is 65 or older by the end of the tax year and who is a U.S. citizen or resident can qualify for this tax credit, as long as income remains below the strict limit set by law. Nonresident aliens don't qualify unless they're married to a U.S. citizen or resident at the end of the tax year.

People who are retired and *permanently and totally disabled* are also eligible for this credit. Anyone who has stopped working because of his or her disability is considered retired for the purpose of claiming this credit.

Tax Tips

If you're a nonresident alien and your spouse is a U.S. citizen or resident, you can file as a U.S. resident if you choose to. However, if you chose to file as a U.S. resident, all your worldwide income could be taxed. For more information about your filing choices as an alien, read IRS Publication 519, "U.S. Tax Guide for Aliens."

Taxing Terms

To be considered **permanently and totally disabled** according to the IRS, you must be unable to "engage in any substantial gainful activity because of your physical and mental condition." You'll also need to provide certification from a physician stating your condition and that it is either expected to last for 12 months or more or that the condition will result in your death.

Employment, in this context, is work you do for pay or profit. It doesn't include taking care of yourself or your home. Unpaid work on hobbies, individual therapy or training, clubs, social programs, and other activities are permitted, but by doing so you may prove that you are able to engage in substantial gainful activity and thus lose your disability status. It's one of those catch-22 situations. You'll get bored just sitting around, but if you do too much, you may prove that you are no longer disabled.

Income Limits

If you're 65 or older, you don't need to have taxable income to qualify. However, if you're trying to qualify for this credit based on disability, you must have taxable disability income. This income must come from your employer's accident, health, or pension plan, and it must be included in your income as wages (or payments instead of wages) for the time you are absent from work. For example, a lump-sum payment for accrued annual leave that you receive when you retire upon disability must be considered salary, not a disability payment. When you reach the mandatory retirement age at your former place of work, you're no longer considered disabled. You are now just considered retired by the IRS, and thus you will qualify for the credit even if you don't have taxable income.

The following table shows the income limits that you must not exceed to qualify for the credit.

Income Limits for the Elderly and Disability Credit

Filing Status	AGI Less Than or Equal To	Nontaxable Social Security or Other Nontaxable Pension, Less Than or Equal To
Single, head of household, qualifying widow(er) with dependent child	$17,500	$5,000
Married couple filing jointly—both qualify	$25,000	$7,500
Married couple filing jointly—only one qualifies	$20,000	$5,000
Married filing separately	$12,500	$3,750

If you're married filing separately, you can't live with your spouse at any time during the year to qualify for the credit. You must not exceed the income limit for AGI or the income limit for Social Security/nontaxable pensions to qualify for this credit.

Figuring Your Credit

It's time to crunch some numbers. You'll calculate your credit using Schedule R if you file using Form 1040, or Schedule 3 if you use Form 1040A. There is a four-step process:

1. Determine your initial amount, or nontaxable income limit.

2. Total any nontaxable Social Security and nontaxable pensions or disability benefits.

3. Determine your excess adjusted gross income.

4. Determine your credit.

Step 1: Initial Amount

The initial amount is the total income allowed for your nontaxable income, whether it's from Social Security, a nontaxable pension plan, or nontaxable disability income.

You can use the preceding table, "Income Limits for the Elderly and Disability Credit," to figure out your initial amount. For example, if you're a married couple filing jointly and only one of you is 65, the initial amount is $5,000.

Step 2: Nontaxable Benefits or Income

Now it's time to add up all your nontaxable benefits or income. Remember all those documents I wanted you to gather in Chapter 1? It's time to use them. On the SSA-1099 form, which is the form you get from Social Security reporting your payments for the tax year, you'll find your nontaxable retirement or disability benefits. You'll look for the amount of the disability income before any deductions to pay premiums on supplementary Medicare. Disabled folks need to use the compensation amount before any workman's compensation was deducted.

Retired railroad employees receive a different form: RRB-1099. For railroad retirees or disabled railroad workers, the nontaxable pension benefits are in Tier 1 on the form.

Veterans must include any pension, annuity, or disability payments, unless they are being made for personal injuries or sickness resulting from active service in the armed forces, the National Oceanic and Atmospheric Administration, or the Public Health Service.

Any other nontaxable pension, annuity, or disability payments that are excluded from federal taxes for any reason should be added in this step.

When you've added all nontaxable benefits or income you receive, you'll have your total nontaxable benefits, or income amount.

Step 3: Excess Adjusted Gross Income

Next, you need to calculate your excess adjusted gross income. To do this, subtract from your AGI the following amount based on your filing status:

◆ $7,500 if you are single, head of household, or a qualifying widow(er) with a child.

◆ $10,000 if you are married filing a joint return.

◆ $5,000 if you are married filing separately and you and your spouse did not live in the same household at any time during the year. If you did live together, you can't take this tax credit.

Then divide your result by 2.

Step 4: Determine Your Credit

Add the amounts you figured in steps 2 and 3, and subtract that total from the initial amount in step 1. Finally, multiply the answer by 15 percent (.15) to get your credit.

Walking Through an Example

Confused? Let's work through an example together. We'll assume you're single and have an adjusted gross income of $8,500, plus you receive $4,000 in Social Security benefits.

Step 1. Initial amount: $5,000

Step 2. Nontaxable pensions: $4,000 (This is your Social Security income of $4,000, which you found on your Form SSA-1099.)

Step 3. Excess AGI ($8,500 — $7,500 ÷ 2): $500 (AGI minus $7,500 for single people, divided by 2.)

Step 4. Credit: $75 ($5,000 [from Step 1] – 4,500 [$4,000 from Step 2 + $500 from Step 3] = 500 × .15)

As you can see from this example, you really can't have much income to qualify for this credit. This example used a total of $12,500, which is $1,040 per month, and that just barely qualified.

Credit Limits

The credit is limited by the amount you actually pay in taxes. If the credit due you is more than your actual taxes paid, the credit will be limited to the taxes paid. You can't get a refund based on this credit.

You also may face limits on the amount of the tax credit if you claim the Child and Dependent Care Credit. Claiming both credits can get very confusing. You must use your dependent care credit first and then your disability credit. The Credit Limit Worksheet in your 1040 or 1040A instructions will help you calculate the limits. The IRS will figure your credits for you as well, if you find this just too confusing. The IRS has local taxpayer assistance centers if you need help with filing.

IRS Idioms

If Einstein and the agents of the Internal Revenue Service cannot understand the Tax Code, then the ordinary taxpayers of the U.S. are entitled to a little help.

—Warren Magnuson, former U.S. Senator

The 2002 tax bill extended this credit until 2003 and also exempted it from the Alternative Minimum Tax. At least that ticking time bomb we mentioned in Chapter 3 won't affect this credit.

In the next chapter, we'll take a look at other credits available to you in special situations.

The Least You Need to Know

- ◆ You can get a tax credit if you are at least 65 and have limited income.
- ◆ If you are permanently and totally disabled with limited income, you can get a tax credit.
- ◆ You must consider both your taxable and nontaxable income when calculating the Credit for the Elderly or the Disabled.

Tax Credit Potpourri

In This Chapter

- ◆ Tax-reducing credits
- ◆ Getting taxes back
- ◆ Increasing your refund

Even if you don't have kids and are under age 65, you may qualify for tax credits. The IRS will give you credits if you adopt a child, buy an electric car, get mortgage assistance, or overpay taxes in certain circumstances. There are also education tax credits, but we'll be talking about tax breaks related to educating you and your family in Part 4. Business tax credits are discussed in Part 7.

Naming the Credits

Two types of credits exist: those that you can use to subtract from your tax bill and get it down to zero, and those that allow you to get a refund of certain taxes already paid.

Most of the tax credits let you write down your taxes to zero but won't allow a refund. However, you may be able to carry that credit forward or backward to other tax years and reduce your tax liability. Credits you can carry over include these:

- Adoption Credit
- Electric Vehicle Credit
- Foreign Tax Credit
- Minimum Tax Credit
- Mortgage Interest Credit

We'll review those first. Then we'll take a look at the credits that actually let you get back money based on the credit, even if it exceeds your tax liability. Any unused credit is refunded to you in the same tax year. These include …

- Credit for Excess Social Security Tax or Railroad Retirement Tax Withheld.
- Credit for Tax on Undistributed Capital Gain.
- Earned Income Credit.

Now that you know the names, let's see how they work and find out if you qualify.

Credits Without a Refund

We'll start with the nonrefundable credits. I've put them in alphabetical order so that it will be easier for you to find the ones that fit your situation.

Adoption Credit

The 2001 tax law doubled the Adoption Credit beginning in 2002, which makes this an even bigger boon for people who adopt a child with special needs. Not only did it double the actual credit maximum from $5,000 to $10,000, but it also doubled the amount of modified adjustable gross income allowed before the credit begins to phase out from $75,000 to $150,000. If your income exceeds $150,000, the tax credit will be reduced.

Most credits have different income rules for single and married folks, but this one allows the same credit no matter what your filing status is. If you adopt a special-needs child, beginning in 2003 you may be able to claim a $10,000 credit even if your actual expenses were lower. Clearly, the government is looking to increase the number of children adopted. Are you ready?

Other changes in the new tax law have made this tax credit even more valuable. It was permanently protected from that ticking time bomb (the Alternative Minimum Tax)—and if your employer provides adoption assistance, up to $10,000 of it is exempt, meaning that you won't have to report it as taxable income.

Let's take a look at how all this works. First things first—how does the government define an eligible child? The child must be under 18 or someone who physically or mentally relies on a caregiver, and must be classified by a state as a child with special needs. When determining special-needs qualification for purposes of this credit, the child must meet the following criteria:

◆ Must be a citizen or resident of the United States or a U.S. possession

◆ Cannot or should not be returned to his or her parents' home, and probably would not be adopted without adoption assistance provided to the adoptive parents

States consider a number of factors in determining a special-needs adoption, including ethnic background, age, minority or sibling group, and emotional handicap. A foreign child cannot be treated as a special-needs child when figuring the credit (the government doesn't want foreign adoptions considered special needs adoptions), but the adoption of a foreign child still qualifies for the adoption credit.

Audit Alarm!

If you attempt to adopt an eligible child who is a U.S. citizen or resident, but you were not successful, you can still use the credit to reduce your taxes for qualified adoption expenses. If the child is not a U.S. citizen or resident, this credit can be used only if the adoption is finalized.

Next, you need to figure out what expenses qualify for the credit and what expenses don't. Qualifying expenses include adoption fees, court costs, attorney fees, and traveling expenses, including meals and lodging costs associated with the legal adoption of a child.

Expenses that don't qualify include these:

◆ Costs that violate state or local law

◆ Surrogate parenting costs

◆ Adoption of your spouse's child

◆ Expenses paid using funds from federal, state, or local programs

◆ Expenses allowed as a credit or deduction under any other federal income tax rule

◆ Expenses paid by your employer or any other person or organization

You can claim this credit for each child you adopt, as long as each child meets all other qualifications for this credit. If you adopted a child in this tax year, use Form 8839, "Qualified Adoption Expenses," to figure out your credit. You can carry this credit forward into later tax years. Form 8839 provides lines for you to track your multiyear credit calculations.

Electric Vehicle Credit

Thinking about trying out that new electric car? If you do, you could end up with a tax credit as well. Hmmm ... tempted?

You can take a credit of up to $4,000 for each vehicle placed in service in any given tax year. The credit is equal to 10 percent of the vehicle's cost, but if you buy the vehicle for business purposes, you must reduce the cost of the vehicle by any *Section 179* deduction before figuring the credit. You can't take the credit if you will be using the car primarily outside the United States.

Because this is the IRS we're talking about, your electric car will have to meet certain rules to qualify. It must ...

 ♦ Have at least four wheels and be manufactured primarily for use on public streets, roads, and highways. Nope, that electric golf cart won't qualify.

 ♦ Be powered primarily by an electric motor that draws its power from rechargeable batteries, fuel cells, or other portable sources of electric current. You can't use this credit for hybrids such as the Honda Insight or Toyota Prius, which are powered by both gas and electric.

 ♦ Be originally used by you. In other words, used electric cars don't count.

 ♦ Be acquired for your own use, not for resale.

Taxing Terms

Section 179 is a tax rule that lets business folks deduct up to $24,000 for new property in the year this property was put into service rather than having to depreciate the property over a number of years. In 2003, the amount increases to $25,000. We'll be talking more about this rule in Chapter 24.

Nope, you can't start a business of buying these cars to get the credit and then sell them to your neighbors. Shucks!

Foreign Tax Credit

If you pay taxes to a foreign government or U.S. possession, you may be eligible to take the Foreign Tax Credit and reduce your U.S. tax bill. This credit is designed to prevent a double tax burden when both the U.S. government and a foreign country tax your foreign income. Generally, if the foreign tax rate is higher than the U.S. rate, you won't have to pay U.S. tax on the foreign income. If the foreign tax rate is lower than the U.S. rate, U.S. tax on the foreign income will be the difference between the rates. This tax credit can reduce U.S. taxes only on foreign source income. It can't be used to reduce U.S. taxes on U.S. income.

You can take a Foreign Tax Credit or deduct your qualified foreign taxes as itemized deductions, but as we've discussed, a credit is usually better because it reduces your tax bill dollar for dollar. You also may be able to carry over to the next tax year or carry back to a previous tax year any tax credit that is in excess of the amount allowable for the current tax year. U.S. citizens, resident aliens, and nonresident aliens who paid foreign income tax and who are subject to U.S. tax on foreign source income may be eligible to take this tax credit. For the tax to qualify for the credit, it must meet these four tests:

> **Tax Tips**
>
> If you have foreign income, things can get rather complicated. You can find more detailed information on the Foreign Tax Credit in IRS Publication 514, "Foreign Tax Credit for Individuals" (www.irs.gov/pub/irs-pdf/p514.pdf).

- ◆ The tax must be imposed on you.

- ◆ You must have paid or accrued the tax.

- ◆ The tax must be the legal and actual foreign tax liability.

- ◆ The tax must be an income tax (or a tax in lieu of an income tax).

You can't take the Foreign Tax Credit in the following situations:

- ◆ For taxes on excluded income. U.S. citizens working abroad can exclude up to $80,000 foreign earned income, as well as some income for excess housing costs. This excluded income cannot be included when figuring the Foreign Tax Credit. More information on this exclusion can be found in IRS Publication 54, "Tax Guide for U.S. Citizens and Resident Aliens Abroad" (www.irs.gov/pub/irs-pdf/p54.pdf).

- ◆ For taxes for which you can take only an itemized deduction. These taxes are either income taxes that you chose to take as an itemized deduction or foreign taxes paid that are not income taxes.

- ◆ For taxes on income related to foreign oil.

- ◆ For taxes on foreign mineral income.

- ◆ For taxes from international boycott operations.

◆ For taxes of U.S. persons controlling foreign corporations or partnerships.

◆ For taxes on income related to foreign oil and gas extraction.

If you work in a country that has been sanctioned by the United States, you can't take a Foreign Tax Credit for income taxes paid or accrued to those countries. Sanction countries include countries for which …

◆ The Secretary of State has designated the country as one that repeatedly provides support for acts of international terrorism.

◆ The United States has severed or does not conduct diplomatic relations with the country.

◆ The United States does not recognize the country's government, unless that government is eligible to purchase defense articles or services under the Arms Export Control Act.

Countries that fell into the sanctioned category in 2002 were Balkans, Burma, Cuba, Iran, Iraq, Liberia, Libya, North Korea, Sierra Leone, Sudan, and Yugoslavia. This list may grow as the war on terrorism heats up. You can find the current list online at www.treas.gov/offices/enforcement/ofac/sanctions/index.html.

Revenue Ramblings

Some foreign countries may require you to participate in or cooperate with an international boycott that the U.S. government opposes. If your foreign income tax was paid to one of these countries, you also won't be able to use the Foreign Tax Credit. Each calendar quarter, the U.S. Department of Treasury publishes a list of these countries. Just to give you an idea of the countries involved, one recent list included the countries Bahrain, Iraq, Kuwait, Lebanon, Libya, Oman, Qatar, Saudi Arabia, Syria, United Arab Emirates, and Republic of Yemen. You can get more information about the list by writing to:

Internal Revenue Service
International Section
P.O. Box 920
Bensalem, PA 19020-8518

There is a limit to how much your Foreign Tax Credit can be. To calculate your maximum tax credit, first divide your taxable income from sources outside the United States by your taxable income from all sources. Then multiply that result by your U.S. income tax liability to get your maximum tax credit. Here's the calculation:

$$\frac{\text{Taxable Income from sources outside the United States}}{\text{Taxable Income from all sources}} = \text{U.S. Income Tax} = \text{Maximum Credit}$$

You must do this calculation separately for income categories:

◆ Passive income.

◆ High withholding tax interest.

◆ Financial services income.

◆ Shipping income.

◆ Certain dividends from a domestic international sales corporation (DISC) or a former DISC.

◆ Certain distributions from a foreign sales corporation (FSC) or a former FSC.

◆ Any lump-sum distributions from employer benefit plans for which the special averaging treatment is used to determine your tax.

◆ Sanctioned income (also known as Section 901j income).

◆ Income re-sourced by treaty.

◆ General limitation income. This is all other income not included in the previous categories.

You can claim exemptions from the foreign tax limitation if your only foreign income for the tax year is passive income. Passive income includes dividends, interest, rents, royalties, annuities, and net gain from various investment transactions (for more details, see IRS Publication 514).

Passive income doesn't include export financing interest, high-taxed income, active business rents and royalties, gains or losses from the sale of inventory property, and any category specified previously as a separate income category.

If you're subject to the limits, you must figure your limits on a separate Form 1116 for each of the categories of income.

Tax Tips

Mutual funds with foreign investments may sometimes pass credits on foreign taxes to their stockholders. Check your mutual fund statements in the pile you collected in Chapter 1 to see if any mutual funds included a Foreign Tax Credit.

Minimum Tax Credit

We talked about the ticking time bomb called the Alternative Minimum Tax (AMT) in Chapter 3. If your deductions or credits were limited by the AMT during the previous tax year, you may be able to use the Minimum Tax Credit to reduce the current year's taxes. The amount of this credit cannot reduce your current year's tax below your current year's tentative alternative minimum tax.

You may be eligible for this credit if you …

◆ Paid Alternative Minimum Tax in the previous calendar year.

◆ Had an unused minimum tax credit that you are carrying forward from the previous tax year.

◆ Had unallowed qualified Electric Vehicle Credits in the previous tax year. In other words, you qualified for the credit in a previous tax year, but couldn't use it because you didn't have enough tax liability.

You can figure out whether you are entitled to use this tax credit by completing Form 8801, "Credit for Prior Year Minimum Tax."

Mortgage Interest Credit

The Mortgage Interest Credit helps lower-income individuals afford home ownership. If you qualify, you can claim the credit each year for part of the home mortgage interest you pay.

You may be entitled to take the Mortgage Interest Credit if you got a mortgage credit certificate (MCC) issued by a state or local government. The certificate must be used in connection with the purchase of a home, qualified rehabilitation of a home, or qualified home improvement.

Taxing Terms

Mortgage credit certificates are issued by state or local government entities and are usually related to a new mortgage for the purchase of your main home. Occasionally they include funds for qualified rehabilitation or home improvement. The MCC shows the certified credit rate you use to figure your credit. It also shows the amount of your debt (called the certified indebtedness amount, for some strange reason). Only the interest on that amount qualifies for the credit.

When calculating the credit, you can include only the debt incurred up to the level specified on the MCC. You multiply the rate specified on the certificate by the interest you paid on your mortgage for the year. If the mortgage amount is higher than the amount specified on the certificate, you must calculate the interest allocated to the certified level. To figure the allowable portion of the mortgage interest, use this calculation:

$$\frac{\text{Certified indebtedness amount on your MCC}}{\text{Original amount of mortgage}} = \text{Percentage of allowable mortgage interest}$$

Multiply this percentage by the amount of interest paid each year. This gives you the allowable amount of interest. Multiply that amount by the rate specified in the MCC. If the certificate credit rate is more than 20 percent, the credit cannot be more than $2,000.

I know this sounds confusing. Let's practice the calculation. We'll assume that a buyer purchased a home using a mortgage loan totaling $100,000. The certified indebtedness on the certificate was $80,000. Interest for the year totaled $8,000. The certificate rate is 15 percent. Here's how the Mortgage Interest Credit would be calculated in this example:

$$\frac{\$80,000}{\$100,000} = 80\% \text{ (Allowable percentage of interest)}$$

$$\$8,000 \times 80\% = \$6,400 \text{ (Interest allowable for MIC calculation)}$$

$$\$6,400 \times 15\% = \$960 \text{ (Mortgage Income Credit)}$$

Your credit is limited to the amount of your current year tax liability, but you can carry forward any unused portion of your credit over the next three tax years. You report the credit using Form 8396, "Mortgage Interest Credit."

If you claim this credit and itemize your deductions, you must reduce your home mortgage interest deduction by the amount of your current-year MIC.

If you refinance your original mortgage loan on which you had been given an MCC, you'll need to get a new MCC for the new loan before you can use this tax credit. The entity that issued your original MCC may reissue an MCC after

CAUTION

Audit Alarm!

If you take an MCC credit and sell your home during the first nine years of ownership, you'll have to repay a portion of the credit you took. Be sure you understand the tax implications before you decide to sell.

you refinance, but this must be done within one year of the date of refinancing. So, if you're using the credit and plan to refinance, check with your issuing authority to be sure that all the needed paperwork is in place and that you are entitled to a new MCC.

Credits That Allow a Tax Refund

All the credits we've discussed so far in this chapter are limited by the amount of your liability in the current tax year. Now we'll take a look at the ones that can result in a refund of more taxes than you actually paid in for the year.

Excess Social Security or Railroad Retirement Taxes

Social Security and Railroad Retirement taxes (RRTA) both have maximum wage caps. Any money earned above that cap should not be taxed for Social Security or Railroad Retirement.

The cap for Social Security is 6.2 percent of wages, up to $84,900 in 2002. This cap is adjusted each year. Railroad Retirement taxes are based on two tiers. The Tier 1 limit is the same as the Social Security limit. The Tier 2 cap is $63,000 in 2002. The formula for figuring Tier 2 tax is more complicated. For more information about this tax, visit the U.S. Railroad Retirement Board site (www.rrb.gov/field.html).

If your Social Security or Railroad Retirement taxes exceed the amount you should have paid, you can get the amount refunded using this tax credit. Most often this happens if you work for more than one employer and your total earnings were higher than the cap. For example, let's say that you worked for one employer and earned $70,000, and then you worked for a second employer and earned $30,000. Both employers would have taken out the 6.2 percent Social Security tax. Because total earnings were $100,000 in this example, excess Social Security taxes were taken out on the $15,100 of income above the $84,900 cap. You would be eligible for a refund of that excess tax.

Audit Alarm!

If you worked for only one employer, your employer must pay you back. You are not eligible for the tax credit. Also, if you file a joint return, you must calculate any excess taxes separately for you and your spouse.

Both Form 1040 and Form 1040A have lines designed for "Excess Social Security and RRTA tax withheld." Worksheets are included in the instructions to figure out the credit allowed.

Undistributed Capital Gain

If you're an investor in real estate investment trusts (REITs) or mutual funds, you may receive capital gain distributions even if you don't actually get cash. Instead, investors frequently reinvest their dividends and capital gain.

Taxing Terms

A **real estate investment trust** invests in real estate property and mortgages. The REIT pools the capital of many investors and purchases income property or mortgage loans. REITs are traded on major exchanges just like stocks. Their primary advantage is that they are much more liquid than investing in real estate property directly. You know that it can take a while to sell your home, but a REIT can be traded rather quickly on a major exchange.

If your mutual fund or REIT paid tax on any capital gain, you're allowed a credit on the tax because it's considered paid by you. Your REIT or mutual fund will send you Form 2439, "Notice to Shareholder of Undistributed Long-Term Capital Gains," if you're entitled to this credit. There's a line called "Other Payments" in the Form 1040 "Payments" section where you can claim this credit. You'll need to attach Form 2439 to your tax return; that's one of the forms you should find in your Chapter 1 pile if you're entitled to this credit.

Earned Income Credit

The Earned Income Credit (EIC) was created for low-income working individuals and families to offset the burden of Social Security taxes and provide a work incentive. The credit reduces the amount of federal tax owed and can result in a refund check.

Income and family size determine the amount of the credit. The following table shows the income eligibility limits based on 2002 adjusted gross income amounts.

	Two or More Children	One Child	No Children
Individual return	$33,178	$29,201	$11,060
Joint return	$34,178	$30,201	$12,060

If you fall below these income limits, the maximum credit amount allowed in 2002 is $4,140 if you have two or more children, $2,506 if you have one child, and $376 if you have no qualifying children. Qualifying children must be under the age of 19 (age 24 if a child is a full-time student) or must be permanently and totally disabled. There are no age limits for children permanently and totally disabled.

A qualifying child includes your son, daughter, adopted child, grandchild, stepchild, or foster child; the child also must have lived with you for more than half the year.

You figure the credit by using a special worksheet included as part of the EIC instructions in the 1040, 1040A, and 1040EZ tax packages. This tax credit isn't reduced by the AMT.

Tax Tips

You can find out more about the Earned Income Credit in IRS Publication 596, "Earned Income Credit." You can find it online at www.irs.gov/pub/irs-pdf/p596.pdf.

You may even be able to get advance payments on this credit during the tax year. You'll need to file Form W-5, "Earned Income Credit Advance Payment Certificate," with your employer. To qualify for this advance, you must have at least one qualified child living with you. After you've filed this form with your employer, your employer will pay part of the credit to you in advance throughout the year. Any portion not received in advance would then be claimed on your tax return.

We've finally reached the end of our trip through credits. There are still some that you'll be introduced to in Chapter 13 for educational purposes, and I'll be sure to mention any business credits in Part 7. Remember, tax credits are generally more beneficial than deductions because they reduce your tax bill dollar for dollar, while tax deductions reduce the taxable income that is used to figure your tax bill.

The Least You Need to Know

- Tax credits are available if you adopt a child, buy an electric car, or pay foreign taxes.

- Low-income earners have additional tax credits for mortgage interest and earned income.

- If you overpay your Social Security or Railroad Retirement taxes, you can get a refundable tax credit.

- You may be eligible for a refundable tax credit if you have undistributed capital gain.

Part 4

Wondering About Education

You can learn new things and take a tax deduction as well! We'll look at credits and deductions that the IRS makes available to ease your burden of education expenses. We'll also review some tax breaks that make it easier for you to save for your education or the education of your children.

12

Tapping Your IRAs

In This Chapter

◆ IRA flavors

◆ Covering your Coverdell

◆ Taking from tradition

◆ Buying bonds

You're probably aware of the tax advantages of saving for retirement using tax-free or tax-deferred Individual Retirement Accounts (IRAs), but you may not have considered the option for education savings. In fact, until 2002 the old Education IRA allowed you to deposit only $500 per child each year. Certainly, this wasn't enough to build a significant college savings.

Congress changed all that with the 2001 tax bill by increasing the annual savings level of Education IRAs, now known as Coverdell Education Savings Accounts (ESAs), to allow annual contributions of up to $2,000 per child beginning in 2002. These accounts are no longer limited to paying higher education expenses. You can use the money saved to pay for elementary and secondary school expenses as well.

Your contributions and any gains on those contributions can be withdrawn tax free, provided that you use the money for qualified education expenses.

You read it right: You never have to pay taxes on your investment gains as long as you use the money for education. Now that's a nice tax break!

Before this new law, parents used to tap their tax-advantaged retirement accounts to pay for education. Today there are numerous alternative tax-advantaged savings options, so you no longer have to drain your retirement funds to send your child to college.

In this chapter, we'll look at how Coverdell ESAs work, who can use them, and what impact these accounts may have on your child's chances of getting financial aid. We'll also take a brief look at the rules for using your other types of IRAs, if you choose that route. Finally, we'll consider the option of buying bonds to finance education.

IRAs Come in Many Flavors

You probably hear the term *IRA* tossed about a lot, but you may not realize that there are actually four types of IRAs available for retirement (plus, the Coverdell ESA used to be a type of IRA). All IRAs offer you the opportunity to save money without taxes on the gains until you take out the money. In fact, the Roth IRA allows you to save money totally tax-free. You don't even have to pay taxes on investment gains when you withdraw the money in retirement.

IRAs and Coverdell ESAs can be invested in stocks, bonds, mutual funds, or cash accounts through your bank, broker, credit union or mutual fund company. I'll briefly describe each of the IRAs here, but we'll talk about the retirement tax advantages and rules for each in greater depth in Part 5. The following is a list of the four retirement types:

- **Traditional tax-deductible IRA.** If your income is low enough, this IRA allows you to deduct your contributions from your income in the year you deposit the money, up to a set limit each year. Your money grows tax deferred until you take it out at retirement. You have to pay taxes on all the money withdrawn in retirement, and you may have to pay penalties if you withdraw the money before age 59$\frac{1}{2}$.

- **Traditional non–tax-deductible IRA.** You can deposit up to a set limit each year in this type of IRA. Your contributions are not tax deductible, but your money will grow tax-deferred until you start taking it out at retirement. In retirement you pay taxes only on the gains. You may have to pay penalties and taxes on any gains that you withdraw before you reach age 59$\frac{1}{2}$.

- **Roth IRA.** As long as you don't earn too much, you can deposit money in this type of IRA up to a set limit each year. Your contributions are not tax deductible, but your money grows tax-free and you *never* have to pay taxes on the gains—as long as you wait until you reach age 59¹/₂ to take out the money and the money has been in the IRA for at least five years.

- **Spousal IRA.** You can use any of the three types of IRAs mentioned to deposit funds in a Spousal IRA. You must have income that at least matches the amount you've deposited in the other IRAs, but your spouse doesn't have to earn his or her own income, as long as you file taxes jointly.

All of these IRAs allow you to withdraw funds without penalties to pay college education expenses. You'll have to pay taxes on all the money withdrawn from the traditional deductible IRAs, but you will have to pay taxes on only the gains withdrawn from a Roth IRA or non deductible traditional IRA. We'll take a closer look at these options later in this chapter, but first let's zoom in on the advantages and disadvantages of using the tax-advantaged savings plan developed for education—the Coverdell ESAs.

What Is a Coverdell ESA?

The law defines a Coverdell ESA as a "trust or custodial account created to pay the qualified education expenses of the designated beneficiary of the account." Yikes, what a mouthful of legal jargon. Let's look at the rules for what qualifies as expenses and who can be a beneficiary.

The beneficiary must be under the age of 18 or have special needs when the account is created. The IRS requires that the account be established with a document that states these four conditions:

- The trustee or custodian must be a bank or an entity approved by the IRS. The document must provide that the trustee or custodian can accept only a contribution that is in cash, made before the beneficiary is age 18 (unless the child has special needs), and that contributions will not exceed the maximum of $2,000 in any year.

- Money in the account cannot be invested in life insurance contracts.

- Money in the account cannot be combined with other property, except in a common trust fund or common investment fund.

- The balance in the account generally must be withdrawn within 30 days after the earlier of the following events:

♦ The beneficiary reaches age 30. (Beginning in 2002, this rule no longer applies if the beneficiary is a special-needs beneficiary.)

♦ The beneficiary dies.

Essentially, this account can be used only to pay for your child's education, and you must start it before the child is age 18, although it can be at any age if the child has special needs. The bank, broker, credit union, or mutual fund through which you open your Coverdell ESA will help you with the paperwork.

Audit Alarm!

The special needs designation is new to the Coverdell ESA in 2002 and will be set by Treasury regulations according to the Senate bill. At the time this book went to press, I could find nothing indicating what these regulations are. If you think your child qualifies as a special-needs child, you should research the issue to see if the regulations have been released.

You must withdraw all the funds from the account by the time the child reaches 30, unless he or she has special needs. You must withdraw the money earlier if the child dies, but you have the option to transfer the money to another family member under the age of 30.

If money is left when the child reaches age 30, you can roll over the money to other family members, as long as the new beneficiary is under age 30 and the original beneficiary agrees to the change. Otherwise, the money must be distributed to the original beneficiary, as we'll discuss later in this chapter.

Qualified Education Expenses

For higher education expenses to qualify for the use of ESA funds, they must fall into one of the following categories:

Taxing Terms

With a **qualified state tuition program,** some states and educational institutions allow you to either prepay tuition or save for your child's higher education. We'll take a closer look at these programs in Chapter 13.

♦ Tuition and fees.

♦ The cost of books, supplies, and equipment.

♦ Amounts contributed to a *qualified state tuition program.*

♦ The cost of room and board, as long as the designated beneficiary is at least a half-time student. The cost cannot exceed the school's posted room and board charge for students living on campus, or $2,500 each year for students living off campus and not at home.

You also can use withdrawals from a Coverdell ESA account for certain elementary and secondary education expenses, whether the school is public, private, or religious. These include ...

◆ Tuition, fees, academic tutoring, special-needs services in the case of a special-needs beneficiary, books, supplies, and other equipment.

◆ Room and board, uniforms, transportation, and supplementary items and services (including extended day programs).

◆ The purchase of computer technology or equipment or Internet access and related services, as long as these are used by the beneficiary and the beneficiary's family while the beneficiary is in school (not including expenses for computer software designed for sports, games, or hobbies unless the software is predominantly educational in nature). Sorry, you can't use it to buy that computer game your child has been bugging you to buy!

Eligible Educational Institution

Eligible educational institutions include colleges, universities, vocational schools, or other postsecondary educational institution eligible to participate in a student aid program administered by the Department of Education. Also, virtually all accredited, public, nonprofit, and proprietary (privately owned profit-making) postsecondary institutions are included. Beginning in 2002, private, public, and religious elementary and high schools became eligible institutions. The educational institution you select for your child should have information on whether it is an eligible educational institution.

Contributions and Income Eligibility Limits

If your educational plans for your child meet all these qualifications, you can contribute up to $2,000 per year for each eligible child. You must contribute to the Coverdell ESA by April 15 of the following tax year.

Grandparents, stepparents, in-laws, brothers, and sisters can contribute to a child's ESAs in addition to the child's parents, and more than one ESA can be established in any one year. However, the total contributed for any one child cannot exceed $2,000 each year. Corporations can even contribute, and they have no income limitations.

Anyone contributing to an ESA must meet the modified adjusted gross income (MAGI) limitations. To figure your MAGI for a Coverdell ESA, you must add income excluded from foreign sources, Puerto Rico, or American Samoa, plus any foreign housing costs that were excluded from your 1040 AGI.

You can take advantage of the Coverdell ESAs as long as your MAGI is below $190,000 if you are a married couple filing jointly. Between $190,000 and $220,000, the Coverdell ESA is phased out for married couples filing jointly. Single parents can take advantage of the Coverdell ESA as long as their MAGI is less than $95,000. Phaseout for singles is between MAGIs of $95,000 and $110,000.

Let's look at how the limitations work. If you're married filing a joint return and your MAGI is more than $190,000, the amount you can contribute to a Coverdell ESA is limited. You can figure the Coverdell ESA contribution limit using the following formula if you are married filing a joint return:

1. MAGI – $190,000 = excess income

2. Excess income ÷ $30,000 = percentage reduction

3. Percentage reduction × $2,000 = cash reduction

4. $2,000 – cash reduction = allowable ESA contribution

Let's practice an example. Parents filing jointly have a MAGI of $210,000. How much can they contribute to their child's ESA in 2002?

1. $210,000 – $190,000 = $20,000

2. $20,000 ÷ $30,000 = 66.7%

3. 66.7% × $2,000 = $1,334

4. $666 = Allowable ESA contribution

If you're single, you use the same calculation, but you divide by $15,000 instead of $30,000 to calculate the percentage reduction; then you use $95,000 instead of $190,000 as your MAGI before the phaseout kicks in.

Contributing Too Much

Your beneficiary could get socked with a 6 percent excise tax in any year that excess contributions were made to his or her Coverdell ESA. If you realize the mistake and withdraw the funds before the tax return

> **CAUTION**
>
> **Audit Alarm!** —————
>
> If you and other eligible family members, such as grandparents, are contributing to Coverdell ESAs for your children, be sure to coordinate the amount being contributed in any one year so that you don't exceed the allowable contribution amount of $2,000. Any excess amount is subject to a 6 percent excise tax.

due date, which can include extensions for filing, you can avoid the excise tax. If your beneficiary doesn't have to file a tax return, the excess contributions and any earnings must be withdrawn by April 15, 2002, to avoid an excise tax.

Rollovers and Transfers

You can roll over the assets from one Coverdell ESA to another. As long as money withdrawn is deposited within 60 days into another Coverdell ESA for the same beneficiary or a member of the beneficiary's family who is under the age of 30, you won't have to pay taxes.

Family members can include ...

- The beneficiary's child, grandchild, or stepchild.

- A brother, sister, half brother, half sister, stepbrother, or stepsister of the beneficiary.

- The father, mother, grandfather, grandmother, stepfather, or stepmother of the beneficiary.

- A brother or sister of the beneficiary's father or mother.

- A son or daughter of the beneficiary's brother or sister.

- The beneficiary's son-in-law, daughter-in-law, father-in-law, mother-in-law, brother-in-law, or sister-in-law.

Tax Tips

You can roll over a Coverdell ESA only once during any 12-month period, so be certain that you're moving it to a place you want the money to stay for at least a year.

Using the Coverdell ESA

Now let's take a look at the rules for using the Coverdell ESA. You can withdraw the money from a Coverdell ESA at any time. However, if you want the withdrawals to be tax-free, they must be for qualified education expenses, as discussed earlier in this chapter.

If you take out more than the amount needed for qualified education expenses, you'll have to pay taxes on the amount of the withdrawal that represents earnings, such as *dividends* or *capital gain*. In addition, you'll have to pay a

Taxing Terms

Dividends are a portion of a company's profits paid to shareholders based on the number of shares held.

Capital gains is any profit you make from the sale or exchange of investments.

10 percent tax penalty on your earnings. There are some exceptions to this penalty. These include withdrawals …

◆ Paid to a beneficiary (or to the estate of the designated beneficiary) upon or after the death of the designated beneficiary.

◆ Made because the designated beneficiary is disabled. A person is considered to be disabled if he or she shows proof that he or she cannot do any substantial gainful activity because of a physical or mental condition. A physician must determine that the person's condition can be expected to result in death or will be of long-continued and indefinite duration.

◆ Made because the designated beneficiary received (as long as the withdrawal is not more than the scholarship, allowance, or payment):

 ◆ A qualified scholarship excludable from gross income.

 ◆ An educational assistance allowance.

 ◆ Payment for the designated beneficiary's education expenses that can be excluded from gross income under any law of the United States.

 ◆ You can include the distributions in income, so you will be able to take the Hope or Lifetime Learning credit.

As noted previously, if any assets are left in the Coverdell ESA when the beneficiary reaches the age of 30, they must be either withdrawn or rolled over to another family member under the age of 30. Any funds withdrawn and not used for qualified educational expenses are subject to taxes on the gain in addition to the 10 percent penalty. If the beneficiary dies and there is no family member to whom you want to roll over the Coverdell ESA assets, the money must be withdrawn within 30 days. You'll have to pay taxes on the gain, but you will not have to pay the 10 percent penalty.

To calculate the taxable part of any Coverdell ESA withdrawals not used for qualified education expenses, use the following steps:

1. Calculate the percentage of the account that represents your contributions:

$$\frac{\text{Total contributions left in Coverdell ESA}}{\text{Total account balance}} = \text{Contribution percentage}$$

2. Multiply the contribution percentage by the amount withdrawn to find the amount of contributions withdrawn.

3. Subtract the amount of contributions withdrawn from the total amount withdrawn.

4. The remaining funds are gains and must be reported as taxable income.

If a portion of the money was withdrawn for qualified education and some was not used for qualified education expenses, the withdrawal calculation is a bit more complicated. You need to calculate a second percentage—the percentage of funds used for qualified expenses. You do that using the following equation:

$$\frac{\text{Qualified education expenses paid during the year}}{\text{Total amount of expenses during the year}} = \text{Percentage of qualified expenses}$$

Multiply this percentage by the amount of earnings calculated on the amount withdrawn, to determine how much of the withdrawal was used for qualified expenses. Then subtract the qualified expenses from the earnings. The remaining amount of earnings must be reported as income.

Okay, let's stop talking in the abstract and start doing some actual calculations. We'll assume that your child withdrew $1,200 from his or her Coverdell ESA. Contributions totaled $2,000. The balance in the account before the withdrawal was $2,400. Your child used the money to pay $900 of qualified education expenses for the year; the rest of the money was spent on nonqualified expenses. Here's how you would calculate the taxable portion of the withdrawal:

1. $2,000 ÷ $2,400 = 83.3% (contributions percentage)

2. $1,200 × 83.3% = $1,000 (amount of contributions withdrawn)

3. $1,200 – $1,000 = $200 (Amount of earnings withdrawn—in other words, taxable income)

4. $900 ÷ 1,200 = 75% (percentage used for qualified expenses)

5. $200 × 75% = $150 (amount of earnings used for qualified expenses)

6. $200 – $150 = $50 (amount of earnings that are taxable)

You would need to include $50 in income as withdrawn earnings not used for qualified education expenses. This amount would be taxed at your rate for current income, plus you would need to pay a 10 percent penalty unless the purpose was for one of the permitted exceptions listed previously.

Coverdells and Credits

Before 2002, if you had an ESA for your child, you couldn't claim the Hope Credit or Lifetime Learning Credit (college tuition credits), which we'll talk more about in Chapter 14. Beginning in 2002, families that take advantage of ESAs may still be able to use the credits.

To take advantage of both the Coverdell ESA and the credits, you can't use the money withdrawn from the ESA for the same expenses that you use to get the credit.

Disadvantages of the Coverdell ESA

You never know what your child will decide to do as you save regularly for his or her education. Maybe your child won't want to go for further education after high school, even after you've built up that considerable nest egg just for that purpose. Your child actually owns the assets in a Coverdell ESA, so how the money will ultimately be used can become a major battle if your child decides not to go to college.

Even if your child does go to college, the Coverdell ESA could reduce the amount of financial aid for which he or she may qualify. If you are a lower- or middle-income earner, you may want to think twice before starting a Coverdell ESA for your child. This becomes an issue because of the way parental vs. child assets are considered when calculating financial aid packages.

Tax Tips

You can learn more about federal financial aid rules from the U.S. Department of Education. Visit the Financial Student Aid website at www.ed.gov/offices/OSFAP/ Students/. A coalition of U.S. colleges also has developed an excellent website with information about paying for college, at www.collegeispossible.org/ paying/paying.htm. This website also has great information about calculating college costs, preparing for college, and selecting the right college.

Based on federal methodology, up to 5.7 percent of a parent's assets must be considered when determining whether a child qualifies for financial aid and how much that financial aid will be. But if a child has assets in his or her name (such as a Coverdell ESA), up to 50 percent of those assets must be considered when determining aid amounts. So it is possible that the assets in a Coverdell ESA could lower or possibly eliminate financial aid for your child.

Using Your IRAs

Withdrawing retirement IRA funds before the age of $59\frac{1}{2}$ usually results in a tax penalty of 10 percent—plus, you must pay taxes on any gain. You can avoid the penalty if you withdraw the funds for qualified higher education expenses for yourself, your spouse, your children, or your grandchildren.

When determining the amount of the withdrawal that is not subject to the 10 percent penalty, you must reduce the total qualified higher education expenses by any expenses paid with the following funds before determining whether any retirement IRA funds can be used without the penalty:

◆ Tax-free withdrawals from a Coverdell ESA (formerly known as an education IRA)

◆ Tax-free scholarships, such as a Pell grant

◆ Tax-free employer-provided educational assistance

◆ Any tax-free payment (other than a gift, bequest, or devise) due to enrollment at an eligible educational institution

Although using IRA assets to pay for education might sound like a good idea, remember that you can't replace money taken out of the IRA. You lose the earning power of the principal for your own retirement needs.

Think Bonds

Instead of draining your retirement funds to pay for educational expenses, you may want to consider buying U.S. savings bonds. You have the advantage of maintaining ownership in your name rather than your child's name. You also can avoid having to include some or all of the interest earned on the bonds if the money is used for qualified higher education expenses for yourself, your spouse, or any dependent for whom you claim an exemption on your return. To use bonds to pay for higher education expenses without paying taxes on the interest, your modified adjusted gross income (MAGI) must not exceed $113,650 if filing jointly, or $70,750 if filing separately.

For some reason I'm sure only the IRS can justify, the MAGI for this tax break is figured differently than the MAGI for the Coverdell ESA. You must add back more items to qualify:

◆ Foreign earned income exclusion

◆ Foreign housing exclusion or deduction

◆ Exclusion of income for bona fide residents of American Samoa

◆ Exclusion of income from Puerto Rico

◆ Exclusion for adoption benefits received under an employer's adoption-assistance program

◆ Deduction for student loan interest

Qualifying bonds include the Series EE bond issued after 1989 and the Series I bond. The bond must be issued in either your name or the names of you and your spouse. The bond owner must be at least 24 years old before the bond's issue date, but you don't have to buy a bond on the date it was issued.

You can use the bonds for any of the following reasons and still qualify for this tax break:

- Tuition and fees required to enroll at or attend an eligible educational institution. Qualified expenses do not include expenses for room and board or for courses involving sports, games, or hobbies that are not part of a degree program.

- Contributions to a qualified state tuition program.

- Contributions to a Coverdell ESA.

Now that you know about tax breaks you can use to avoid taxes and save for your child's education, we'll take a look at the another education savings alternative in the next chapter: the qualified state tuition programs, or Section 529s.

The Least You Need to Know

- Coverdell Education Savings Accounts let you save up to $2,000 per child per year totally tax-free, provided that you use the money for qualified education expenses. Your contributions are not tax deductible, but all the money withdrawn—even the gains on your investments—is not taxed as long as you use it right.

- Coverdell ESAs are owned by your child and either must be used by the time your child reaches the age of 30 or must be transferred to another beneficiary in the family under the age of 30.

- Funds in your retirement IRAs can be used for qualified education expenses without incurring tax penalties for early withdrawal, but you will have to pay tax on at least some of the money withdrawn.

- You can avoid paying taxes on U.S. savings bond interest if you use the money for qualified education expenses.

More Tax Savings Options for Your College Savings

In This Chapter

- ◆ Plan rules
- ◆ Saving limits
- ◆ Penalty possibilities
- ◆ Trust alternatives

You may be wondering whether you can save enough for college within the limitations of the Coverdell ESA. You like the idea of tax-free savings for college, but you realize that you need to save more than $2,000 per year toward your children's education costs if you want them to be able to attend the college of their choice.

College costs for the 2001–2002 school year averaged $17,123 for a four-year private school, which was an increase of 5.5 percent over the previous year. Four-year public school costs averaged $3,754, up 7.7 percent from the previous year. Using the 2001–2002 percentage increases, private college costs could be almost $100,000 per year, and public college tuition could increase to about $13,000 per year when your toddler gets ready for college in about 15 years.

Yikes, that's $400,000 if your child chooses a private school (and probably more because tuition will continue to increase during the fours years your child is in school). Even the more than $50,000 for a four-year public college education means that you've got lots of savings to do unless you're sure your child will win a four-year full scholarship.

Even if you start saving $2,000 per year at the time your child is born, the account would grow to only $60,000 if it earned a 6 percent return. That's most likely enough for a four-year public college, but it's definitely not enough if your child chooses a private school.

In this chapter, we'll explore the options for saving considerably more money for your child's education. The tax-advantaged type is the Qualified Tuition Program, but it comes with a lot of strings attached. Wealthy parents might like the greater control of the custodial accounts (UGMA/UTMA) or a Crummey Trust, but they're not tax-free.

Saving Through Your State

You've probably heard the terms Qualified State Tuition Program and Section 529s. Well, beginning in 2002 these programs took on a new name—the Qualified Tuition Program (QTP). The word *State* has been dropped because now these programs can be run by education institutions as well.

Two types of plans fall under the QTP umbrella: prepaid tuition plans and college savings accounts. Prepaid tuition plans let you lock in future tuition at in-state public colleges at current prices. That might sound good to you, but it means that you expect to be living in the same state and that you're sure your child will want to go to one of the schools in the program. I certainly wouldn't want to be choosing a child's college while he or she was still in diapers. Although most states allow you to roll out the money if you change your mind later, your investments are likely to do much better in the more flexible college savings accounts.

Tax Tips

You can compare the QTPs of various states using an online tool at Savingsforcollege.com (www.savingforcollege.com/compare/). This website also has a wealth of information about how these plans work.

SmartMoney.com has an interactive tool you can use for assessing your QTP options, at www.smartmoney.com/college/investing/index.cfm?story=test529.

You can use the funds saved in college savings accounts for any college located in any state, but the investment options are tightly controlled by the state in which you open the account. Most state college savings accounts are managed by professional money managers, and the yearly fees can be as high as 1.5 to 2 percent; be sure you compare the fees for the programs you are considering. Nonetheless, these plans have some great tax advantages:

◆ Withdrawals are tax-free from Federal taxes, as long as they're used for paying qualified education costs. You don't have to pay taxes on the earnings. This exemption ends in 2010 unless Congress acts to keep it. We'll discuss qualification specifics later.

◆ Earnings may be exempt from state taxes if you open the account in the state where you're a resident. Other states may allow you to deduct your contributions on your state tax return. Research your tax advantages within your state, and be sure to consider these additional tax savings as you compare plans. Even if your state's plan doesn't offer the top investment rate, the tax savings might make it a good investment.

◆ You can contribute as much as $250,000 per beneficiary in some states. The maximum contribution limits are set on a state-by-state basis. Contributions are not deductible on federal returns, but gains are tax-free.

◆ Grandparents can use these plans to save for grandchildren. The grandparents maintain control over the funds and their beneficiaries. They can switch beneficiaries without tax consequences as long as they stay within the family. Yearly gifts can be as high as $11,000 per child without having to worry about *gift taxes*.

◆ You may still be eligible for a Hope Credit or Lifetime Learning Credit if you use funds from a QTP, as long as the expenses used to claim the credit were not paid using tax-free funds. We'll be talking more about credits in the next chapter.

Taxing Terms

Gift taxes may be incurred with any gift of more than $11,000 to any individual, including your children. The only exception are gifts between spouses. Parents can give each of their children $11,000, so a couple can actually give each child $22,000 per year without having to worry about the possibility of gift taxes. The first $1 million in gifts received is exempt from the gift tax, but you need to file a special tax form each year that your gifts exceed the $11,000 limit per person. Calculation of the gift tax exemption is cumulative over your lifetime.

This may all sound great. There are catches, though. You can't save more than actually would be needed for college. Earnings on any funds withdrawn for purposes other than education are subject to federal taxes plus a 10 percent penalty. Some states also have tax penalties—in addition to the federal 10 percent penalty—on funds withdrawn for purposes not related to college.

Understanding the Rules

Interested? Now it's time to get down to the nitty gritty of the QTP rules.

Qualifying Programs

A state tuition program qualifies if it was set up to allow you either to prepay a student's tuition or to contribute to an account established for paying a student's qualified higher education expenses at an eligible educational institution. Beginning in 2002, QTPs can also be established and maintained by educational institutions. Your state government or the educational institution can tell you whether a program qualifies as a QTP.

Qualified Higher Education Expenses

Tuition, fees, books, supplies, and equipment required for enrollment or attendance at an eligible educational institution are qualified expenses. You can also pay for room and board costs from QTP withdrawals, but the amount that is qualified will be calculated by the educational institutions based on federal guidelines. You should contact the institution to find out the allowable amounts that meet qualifications. A special-needs student may include additional expenses that are necessary for enrollment or attendance at an eligible institution.

Beneficiary

Any student or future student can be a beneficiary of a QTP. Beneficiaries can be changed after participation in the QTP begins.

Eligible Educational Institution

Any college, university, vocational school, or other postsecondary educational institution eligible to participate in a student aid program administered by the Department of Education is eligible under QTP rules. This includes virtually all accredited public, nonprofit, and proprietary (privately owned profit-making) postsecondary institutions. The educational institution should have information on whether it is an eligible educational institution.

Contributions

Contributions to a QTP on behalf of any beneficiary cannot be more than the amount necessary to provide for the qualified higher education expenses of the beneficiary. You can contribute to both Coverdell ESAs and QTPs for the same beneficiary in the same year, but these contributions cannot exceed what would be considered savings for qualified higher education expenses. This means that you can't put a million dollars away to grow tax sheltered for your child. Don't you wish that you had that much to save?

Withdrawals

When you start taking out the money from a QTP to pay for higher education, you don't have to report the money as income, as long as it's used to pay for qualified higher educational expenses. This bears repeating: If you use the money for unqualified purposes, you may incur a penalty of 10 percent and also have to pay taxes on the money at your current income tax rate. Penalties will not be incurred if …

- The refunded earnings are used to pay qualified higher educational expenses of the beneficiary.

- The refund of earnings is made because of the death or disability of the beneficiary.

- The refund of earnings is made because the beneficiary received a scholarship, a veterans' educational assistance allowance, or another nontaxable payment (other than a gift, bequest, or inheritance) for educational expenses. This applies only to the part of the refund that is not more than the scholarship, allowance, or other payment. It means that you won't be penalized if your child wins a scholarship to attend college.

Withdrawals for any other purpose could be subject to both the penalty and income taxes at your current tax rate.

Changing QTPs

Amounts in a QTP can be transferred tax-free to the QTP of another beneficiary. The transfer must be completed within 60 days of the distribution, and the other beneficiary must be a family member of the beneficiary from whose program the transfer is made.

Starting in 2002, amounts in a QTP of one beneficiary can be transferred tax-free to another QTP for the same beneficiary. You are allowed only one transfer or rollover within any 12-month period for the same beneficiary.

Changing Beneficiaries

You can change beneficiaries, but the new beneficiary must be your spouse or one of the following family members:

- Son or daughter, or descendant of son or daughter
- Stepson or stepdaughter
- Brother, sister, stepbrother, or stepsister
- Father or mother, or ancestor of either
- Stepfather or stepmother
- Son or daughter of a brother or sister
- Brother or sister of father or mother
- The spouse of any individual listed
- First cousins

Trusts for the Wealthy

Now that we've gotten the QTP rules out of the way, let's take a quick look at two other options that wealthy folks use: custodial accounts (UGMA/UTMA) and Crummey Trusts. These aren't tax-free, but they offer much more investment flexibility and have no contribution limits.

The investments are taxed yearly. However, they may be taxed based on the child's earnings, which are usually in a lower tax bracket than the parents, so they offer significant tax savings opportunities. If a child is under the age of 14, he or she is subject to a *kiddie tax*, which doesn't kick in unless investment income and gains exceed $1,500.

You shouldn't try to establish these trusts on your own. Definitely consult a specialist in estate and tax planning before you set one up.

> **Taxing Terms**
>
> A **kiddie tax,** which is not the official name of any tax but a phrase that is commonly used, affects any child's unearned income as long as that child is under the age of 14. The first $750 that a child receives in unearned income, such as income from investments, can be offset by his or her standard deduction. The next $750 is taxed at the child's tax rate. When unearned income exceeds $1,500, all other income is taxed at the parents' rate. If the child works and earns income, that becomes even more complicated, but the earned income can increase the standard deduction that a child can claim.

First let's take a look at custodial accounts. There are two types: the UGMA and the UTMA. UGMA stands for the Uniform Gifts to Minors Act, and UTMA stands for the Uniform Transfers to Minors Act. Although *uniform* may be in the title, they are far from uniform in their rules.

These custodial accounts are controlled by state law, and you'll find differences from state to state. The UGMA first arrived on the scene in 1956 to provide a convenient way to make gifts of money and securities to minors. The UTMA replaced this provision in most states beginning in 1986 because it expands the type of property you can transfer to a minor and permits other types of transfers than just gifts. These accounts are managed by a custodian for the benefit of a minor. They are less expensive, less complicated, and less time consuming than establishing a trust, but the assets transfer to the child's control—usually at age 18, 21, or 25, depending on state law.

For folks who are control freaks and want to manage their children's funds as long as possible, the Crummey Trust is the answer. Each parent can add $11,000 annually without gift tax concerns. Trusts don't generally qualify for the annual tax-free gifts, but Crummey Trusts are designed for this purpose by adding an annual withdrawal possibility (which, of course, your child won't be able to exercise until he or she is no longer a minor).

The trustee makes all financial decisions about the money put into the trust on the child's behalf. You can distribute enough each year to pay the child's taxes, which probably will be at a lower tax rate. These trusts provide more control for parents in case the child decides never to go to college. The trustee can refuse to disburse funds until the age designated in the trust, which can be as high as 40. You will need an attorney to draw up the trust.

Even if you haven't socked away thousands of dollars tax-free for your education or your child's education, you can reduce your taxes as you pay for college. We'll take a look at how you can do this in the next chapter.

The Least You Need to Know

◆ You can contribute as much as $250,000 toward future higher education expenses for each child by using Qualified Tuition Programs (QTPs).

◆ The amount you can save, how you can invest the money, and how you can use the money saved through a QTP are tightly controlled.

◆ If you want to save more than allowed in a QTP, or if you want more invest-ment flexibility, you may want to consider two other options: custodial accounts and Crummey Trusts. Although these don't offer tax-free savings, they still offer tax-avoidance opportunities.

◆ Custodial accounts are less flexible and more tightly controlled by state law. If you want the most flexibility and the greatest amount of control over savings for your child's use, the Crummey Trust is the best option.

14

Getting Your Education Credits

In This Chapter

- ◆ Two ways to get credits
- ◆ Deducting your education
- ◆ When the boss pays

Now that you've learned about tax breaks that help you save for college, we'll move on to the tax credits or deductions you can use as you pay for college. Although tax credits are generally better because they allow you to subtract dollar for dollar from your tax bill, you might earn too much to take advantage of them. However, you may be able to qualify for a College Tax Deduction even if you don't itemize your deductions.

We'll take a look at the rules for the tax-reducing alternatives to help make your education dreams a reality.

Crediting Your Education

Two types of credits are available for postsecondary education: the Hope Credit and the Lifetime Learning Credit. You can't use both of them for the same child in the same year, but you can use the same credit for two children in the same year, as long as you don't exceed the limitations set by law.

The Hope Credit allows a greater reduction in taxes, but it can be used only during the first two years of undergraduate education. There is no similar time limit attached to the Lifetime Learning Credit—it's true to its name and can be used over your lifetime for yourself, your spouse, and your dependents.

In 2002, the Hope Credit lets you reduce your tax bill by up to $1,500, and the Lifetime Learning Credit offers up to a $1,000 reduction. For the Hope Credit, you can subtract up to 100 percent of your first $1,000 in tuition and fees, and 50 percent of the next $1,000, for a total tax bill reduction of $1,500.

The Lifetime Learning Credit in 2002 lets you subtract 20 percent of the first $5,000 in tuition and fees, or a total of $1,000 off your tax bill. Beginning in 2003, the credit will double and you will be able to subtract up to 20 percent of the first $10,000 in tuition and fees, or a total of $2,000 off your tax bill.

Tax Tips

Both education credits will be subject to inflation adjustments, so look carefully at IRS instructions each year to see if the credit amount allowed has been increased because of inflation.

Revenue Ramblings

A loophole exists for some families that earn too much. The law allows your child to take advantage of the credit even if you pay the education costs. To use this loophole, you must give up your dependency exemption. We'll explore this option in greater detail later in the chapter.

If you have more than one child in college, you can use one credit for one child and the other credit for the second child in the same year, but you can't use both credits for the same child in any one year. You can multiply the amount allowed for the Hope Credit by the number of qualified students who are in their first two years of undergraduate programs. The Lifetime Learning Credit is based on the total spent, no matter how many people in your family are attending college. All education credits are limited to your total tax liability—in other words, you can't use them to reduce your tax liability to less than zero (or you can't get more money back then you put in).

The downside of these credits is that you can earn too much to claim them. Income limits are covered later in this chapter.

Most of the rules for the two credits are similar, but there are some significant differences. Since the Hope Credit can be used only during the first two years of college, it makes sense to use that credit first and then switch to the Lifetime Learning Credit.

The Lifetime Learning Credit also allows much more flexibility. There is no limit on the number of years this credit is available. You can claim the credit even if you're not pursuing a degree and even if you're taking only one course. To qualify for the Hope Credit, you must pursue a degree and be at least a half-time student. The Hope Credit can be lost if the student has a felony drug conviction on his or her record. The felony drug conviction rule doesn't apply to the Lifetime Learning Credit.

Hope Credit

We'll take a look at the Hope Credit rules first, and then I'll point out the differences in the Lifetime Learning Credit rules. Generally, you can claim the Hope Credit if you pay qualified tuition and related expenses for higher education for an eligible student. Eligible students can include yourself, your spouse, or a dependent for whom you claim an exemption on your tax return.

Eligible Students

To be eligible for Hope Credit, the student must meet the following four requirements:

- Did not have expenses that were used to figure a Hope Credit in any two earlier years. If academic credit was awarded solely on the basis of the student's performance on proficiency examinations, it is disregarded in determining whether the student has completed two years of postsecondary education.

- Had not completed the first two years of postsecondary education (generally, the freshman and sophomore years of college) before the current tax year.

- Was enrolled at least half time in a program that leads to a degree, certificate, or other recognized educational credential for at least one academic period that began in the current tax year.

- Was free of any federal or state felony conviction for possessing or distributing a controlled substance as of the end of 2001.

Eligible Institutions

Eligible educational institutions include any college, university, vocational school, or other postsecondary educational institution eligible to participate in a student-aid program administered by the Department of Education. This includes virtually all accredited, public, nonprofit, and proprietary (privately owned profit-making) postsecondary institutions. The educational institution should have information on whether it is an eligible educational institution.

Eligible Expenses

Expenses that qualify when calculating the credit include any tuition and related expenses and fees required for enrollment or attendance at an eligible educational institution. Student-activity fees and fees for course-related books, supplies, and equipment can be included only if they must be paid to the institution as a condition of enrollment or attendance. You can prepay expenses for up to the first three months of the next tax year. For example, if the bill for a semester that begins in January of 2003 is paid in December 2002, the fees can be considered when calculating the 2002 tax credit.

If you get tax-free funds to help you pay for higher education expenses, you must reduce your qualified expenses by the amount of this tax-free assistance. This includes …

◆ Scholarships.

◆ Pell grants.

◆ Employer-provided educational assistance.

◆ Veterans' educational assistance.

◆ Any other nontaxable payments (other than gifts, bequests, or inheritances) received for education expenses.

Tax Tips

You can claim the Hope Credit even if you used a loan to pay for qualified tuition and related expenses. You must claim the credit in the year the expenses are paid, not when you pay off the loan.

You don't need to reduce the qualified expenses if you paid them with earnings, loans, gifts, inheritance, or personal savings. Also, if a scholarship was reported as income on the student's return, you don't need to reduce expenses by that amount. Scholarship funds used for items other than qualified expenses for the Hope Credit also do not need to be subtracted.

Audit Alarm!

Expenses that cannot be considered when calculating your Hope Credit include insurance, medical expenses (including student health fees), room and board, transportation, or any similar personal, living, or family expenses. This is true even if the fee must be paid to the institution as a condition of enrollment or attendance. The expenses must be part of the student's degree program to qualify.

Either you or your dependent can claim a Hope Credit, but you can't both claim the credit in the same year. Even if your dependent pays the expenses, you can claim the credit on your tax return rather than on the dependent's return.

If someone other than you, your spouse, or your dependent, such as a relative or former spouse, makes a payment directly to an eligible educational institution, it can be considered as paid by the student. You can use any portion of this payment when calculating the Hope Credit.

Credit Calculations

The credit is relatively easy to calculate, as long as your modified adjusted gross income (MAGI) does not exceed $41,000 if single or $82,000 if filing jointly. You can claim as a credit up to 100 percent of the first $1,000 of eligible expenses, and 50 percent of the next $1,000, for a maximum total tax credit of $1,500.

For purposes of calculating the MAGI for the Hope Credit, you must add back in the following exclusions: foreign earned income, foreign housing costs, and income from American Samoa or Puerto Rico. If the MAGI falls between $41,000 and $51,000, if single, or $82,000 and $102,000, if married, you will have to calculate a partial credit reduction, which is called a phaseout. These income amounts are indexed by inflation and will likely change each year.

To calculate the phaseout of the credit, use these steps:

1. Calculate excess income by subtracting your MAGI from the maximum income allowed without a credit reduction—$51,000 (single) or $102,000 (married filing jointly).

2. Divide the result by $10,000 if single, or $20,000 if married filing jointly.

3. Multiply this amount by $1,500.

Let's practice the calculation with an example. We'll assume that you are married filing jointly and that your MAGI is $90,000. Here's how you calculate your allowable credit:

1. $102,000 − $90,000 = $12,000

2. $12,000 ÷ $20,000 = .60

3. .60 × $1,500 = $900

In this example, the allowable Hope Credit is reduced to $900.

Claiming the Credit

You claim your credit using IRS Form 8863, "Education Credits." Your dependent's educational institution must send you or your dependent a Form 1098-T, "Tuition Payments Statement," or some similar substitute statement, by February 1 of the year after the expenses have been incurred. You can use this information to determine eligible expenses. For example, expenses for the year 2002 must be reported to you by February 1, 2003. You should have this information in the pile you collected in Chapter 1. If not, you may need to dig it up from the pile of papers sent by the educational institution, or contact the institution for a replacement copy. Both the Hope Credit and the Lifetime Learning Credit are claimed using the same form, so you can't try to claim both credits for the same dependent.

You can't claim the Hope Credit if you're married filing a separate return, if you are listed as a dependent in the exemptions section of someone else's return (such as your parents), or if you exceed the allowable income levels. If you or your spouse is a nonresident alien for any part of the tax year and did not elect to be treated as a resident alien, you also will not be eligible to use the Hope Credit.

Lifetime Learning Credit

Many of the rules for the Lifetime Learning Credit are the same as those for the Hope Credit. The only difference related to qualified students is that the Lifetime Learning Credit doesn't have a time limitation, while the Hope Credit is limited to expenses for the first two years of higher education.

Qualified expenses and qualified educational institutions follow the same rules as for the Hope Credit. Also, expenses for students not eligible for the Hope Credit for any reason other the two-year time limitation won't be eligible for the Lifetime Learning Credit. Income limits are also the same for both credits.

The biggest difference is in how the credits are calculated. In figuring the Lifetime Learning Credit, you can take up to 20 percent of the first $5,000 of qualified expenses for all eligible students, for a total of $1,000. The Hope Credit allows you to take the tax credit for each student who is enrolled in an eligible institution for whom you have paid the expenses; the Lifetime Learning Credit is based on total expenses—no matter how many people in your family are taking higher education coursework.

> **Revenue Ramblings**
>
> Expanding educational opportunities has been the centerpiece of the middle class tax cuts. The Department of Education expects that when fully phased in, 13.1 million students—5.9 million claiming the HOPE Scholarship, and 7.2 million claiming the Lifetime Learning Credit—are expected to benefit each year.

If your income is above the allowable limits, you calculate the phaseout amount using a similar method as you did for the Hope Credit. To calculate the phaseout of the credit, use the following steps:

1. Calculate excess income by subtracting your MAGI from the maximum income allowed without a credit reduction—$51,000 (single) or $102,000 (married filing jointly).

2. Divide the result by $10,000 if single, or $20,000 if married filing jointly.

3. Multiply this amount by your allowable credit amount.

Let's practice the calculation with an example. We'll assume that you are married filing jointly and that your MAGI is $90,000. Your eligible expenses total $5,000, so you qualify for a $1,000 credit ($5,000 × 20%). Here's how you calculate your credit:

$102,000 – $90,000 = $12,000

$12,000 ÷ $20,000 = .60

.60 × $1,000 = $600

In this example, the allowable Lifetime Learning Credit is reduced to $600. As noted previously, you claim this credit on the same form as the Hope Credit.

Credit Loophole

Higher-income families may be able to take advantage of these credits even if they earn too much. You can use a loophole that allows a student to claim the credit on his or her tax return as long as he or she isn't claimed as a dependent for exemption on another's tax return, such as a parent. Your child can claim the credit even if you paid the tuition bill. In most cases, even if the student is earning money, he or she will not be earning enough to lose the credit.

The key question you must ask if you decide to use this loophole is whether the tax savings to the family will be greater by allowing the child to claim the tax credit on his or her return or whether the family taxes will be lower by claiming the child as an exemption. Since the credits are limited by the amount of tax owed, your child may not owe enough tax for this credit to be fully used, or a dependency exemption may be worth more to you in tax reduction than the credit your child can deduct. This loophole helps higher earners much more than middle-class folks because the dependency exemption is phased out as income increases. This table shows phaseout levels for the 2002 tax year.

Phaseout of Personal Exemptions in 2002 Tax Year

Filing Status	Phaseout Begins	Phaseout Completed
Joint return	$206,000	$328,500
Head of household	$171,650	$294,150
Single	$137,300	$259,800
Married filing separately	$103,000	$164,250

Remember that the exemption reduces your income by $3,000 per dependent in 2002, while the tax credit reduces your tax bill dollar for dollar. If you're in the 27 percent tax bracket, your tax bill will be reduced by $810 using an exemption. Folks in the 30 percent tax bracket can reduce their tax bill by $900 with the exemption. You can see that being able to use the Hope Credit or the Lifetime Learning Credit fully would reduce taxes more than the exemption.

College Tax Deduction

All is not lost if you earn above the income limits allowed for the credits. You still may qualify for the College Tax Deduction. Although it is not as beneficial as a credit, the deduction will still help reduce your tax bill.

The deduction will see some changes over the next few years. In 2002 and 2003, the maximum deduction is $3,000. Your MAGI can be as high as $65,000 if you are single, or $130,000 if you are married filing a joint return. In 2004 and 2005, there are two tiers for this deduction. Earners with MAGIs up to $65,000 (if single) and $130,000 (if married filing jointly) can deduct up to $4,000 of eligible education expenses. Single earners with MAGIs between $65,001 and $80,000, and married folks filing jointly with MAGIs between $130,001 and $160,000 will be able to deduct up to $2,000. This deduction is set to disappear after 2005 if Congress doesn't act to keep it.

Tax Tips

You can take a College Tax Deduction even if you don't itemize your deductions. You won't be able to use this deduction if you choose to use either of the education tax credits in a given tax year. When making the choice, remember to compare apples to apples. The tax credits are a reduction of your tax bill, while the College Tax Deduction reduces your income. To test the value of the deduction, you must multiply the amount you have to deduct by your tax rate to find its comparable tax-reduction value.

Rules for qualified expenses, eligible institutions, and eligible students are the same as those for the Lifetime Learning Credit.

Employer Education Benefits

You have one other option to help pay for college expenses without increasing your income tax liability. Your employer can provide educational assistance benefits up to $5,250 in any tax year, without your having to report it as income.

Before 2002, these expenses could be used only toward undergraduate-level course, but beginning in 2002, graduate-level courses are eligible as well. Employer assistance is not limited to tuition-related expenses like the credits and deductions.

Eligible expenses paid by your employer can include tuition, fees and similar expenses, books, supplies, and equipment. Also, the assistance doesn't have to be for work-related courses. Your employer will be able to tell you whether the benefits are tax-free.

Your educational-assistance benefits can't include meals, lodging, transportation, tools, or supplies that you keep after completing the course of instruction. The one exception to this rule is textbooks. Courses involving sports, games, or hobbies also aren't eligible unless they have a reasonable relationship to your employer's business or are required as part of a degree program.

> **Audit Alarm!**
>
> You must reduce any education expenses you claim on your taxes by the amount of your employer's education assistance. You can't use funds received tax-free for education expenses as part of your calculation for credits or deductions.

Any educational benefits in excess of $5,250 will be considered as income. Your employer will report the amount of educational assistance on your W-2, if you must include it as part of your income calculations for tax purposes.

Now that we've got your family's educational needs out of the way, it's time to turn to securing your financial future. In the next part, we'll look at ways to use tax breaks to increase your retirement savings, as well as things you can do to reduce your tax bill in retirement.

The Least You Need to Know

◆ You can take up to $1,500 in Hope Credits for eligible education expenses for yourself, your spouse, and your dependents to reduce your tax bill dollar for dollar if you follow the rules and don't earn too much.

◆ You can take up to $1,000 in Lifetime Learning Credits each year based on the total educational expenses of your family, as long as you don't earn too much and follow the rules.

◆ College Tax Deductions of up to $3,000 are allowed even if you don't itemize deductions, as long as you don't earn too much.

◆ Your employer can provide up to $5,250 in educational assistance, and you won't have to include that money as income.

Part **5**

Traveling to Retirement

You may think you'll never be able to make this trip, especially with the losses to your retirement portfolio after the Internet bubble burst in the late 1990s. But don't despair—the tax code offers tax breaks to help you save faster for retirement while paying less in taxes. You will even find a retirement savings alternative that's completely tax-free when you withdraw your retirement money.

Chapter 15

Increasing Your Investments

In This Chapter

- ◆ Tax-advantaged savings
- ◆ Making the most of your employer's account
- ◆ The right saving vehicle for you
- ◆ Saving taxes now or later

Your portfolio is probably looking battered and bruised since the bursting of the Internet/tech stock bubble beginning in the spring of 2000. Many people have run for cover, looking for a safe haven for the savings. Should you put your money under a mattress so you'll be sure it'll be there when you need it at retirement, or are there better alternatives?

Even when you turn to what appears to be the safest place for your money—an insured bank savings account—your earnings potential may not be enough to build your retirement nest egg. Money takes a long time to grow when you can count on interest rates of only 2 to 3 percent. If the earnings on your savings also are being eaten up by taxes, your nest egg cracks even further.

Let's look at the role taxes play in building your retirement savings and how to take advantage of the tax code to build those savings as quickly as possible. We'll start with some basics on how your money grows.

Benefits of Delaying Taxes

First let's look at the impact taxes have on your investments. I'm sure you realize that delaying taxes as long as possible is a goal that makes sense for most people. Do you realize how much tax avoidance can help your long-term savings grow?

Investments held in taxable accounts face two types of taxes. Earnings or gains earned in less than 12 months are taxed at your current tax rate. Gains on a long-term investment held more than one year are taxed at a capital gain tax rate, which is 20 percent for most people.

To show you how taxes can impact the growth of your portfolio, I've developed the following chart showing what happens to a $1,000 investment held over 30 years. I've assumed a growth rate of 10.5 percent, which is the average for a growth stock port-folio over any 30-year period. I've assumed a tax rate of 26 percent.

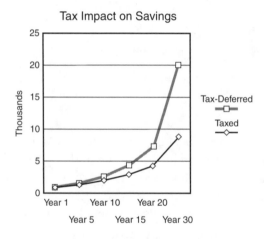

As you can see, initially tax savings are not that significant in a tax-deferred invest-ment. When you get past year 15, though, the earnings start to rise tremendously. By year 30, the tax-deferred account is more than double the portfolio saved without the advantage of avoiding taxes.

Compounding Your Savings

Now let's look at the impact inflation has on your savings. You probably realize that you need to save at a higher rate than *inflation* so that you have more money to cover increasing prices. In other words, your money must grow more than the *inflation rate*.

Here are some historical statistics about inflation from the Federal Reserve:

◆ Since 1960, inflation has averaged 4.5 percent per year.

◆ Since 1982, inflation has averaged 3.5 percent per year.

◆ When inflation averages 3.5 percent per year for 20 years, consumer prices nearly double.

Taxing Terms

Inflation is the increase in prices of goods and services. For consumers, the **inflation rate** is measured using the Consumer Price Index, which reflects the change in the cost of a fixed "basket" of products and services that includes housing, electricity, food, and transportation.

Today inflation levels are lower, but no one can accurately predict that they'll stay there. You can never be certain what the inflation rate will be between now and when you are ready to retire.

So why does this matter when you're considering retirement savings? Well, you want to save your money faster than its value is eaten up by inflation. Even if inflation averages only 3.5 percent, the long-term average of a bank savings account is 2 to 3 percent. In other words, if you put all your retirement funds in an insured account, your money is likely to buy less than it can today because of the increase in consumer prices.

Bonds offer you a better hedge against inflation. Their average earnings have been 5 to 6 percent. Stocks offer your *best* hedge against inflation. Their returns have averaged 10 to 12 percent over any given 20-year period. Seeing these numbers, you might think that you should put all your money in stocks. However, the lessons learned from the recent stock crash show you that may be more risk than you can stomach.

The best portfolio is one that is balanced among these assets based on your time horizon and the amount of risk you want to take. If you have more than 10 years until you need the money, you can invest in riskier options because you have more time to recover any losses. If you need the money in two years or less, cash is definitely your best and safest option.

Tax-Advantaged Retirement Saving Alternatives

Now that we've got the basics of saving and investing out of the way, let's take a look at the tax-advantaged alternatives you can use in retirement. In Chapter 12, I introduced you to the types of IRAs. We'll take a close look at how these work and review the tax-advantaged employer plans that help you save for retirement.

Personal Plans

Everyone should have his or her own Individual Retirement Account (IRA). IRAs were first introduced in 1974 and became so popular so quickly that in the 1980s Congress reduced their tax advantages. They've changed many times since 1974, and I'm sure they will change many more times before you get to use the money. We'll take a look at today's rules and what changes are expected as the 2001 law takes effect over the next 10 years.

Only one of the IRA types allows you to deduct your contributions up front—the tax-deductible traditional IRA, which is primarily for low- and middle-income wage earners or folks who don't have a retirement plan at work. If you don't have an employer-sponsored retirement plan, there are no income limitations for using this IRA. If you do have a retirement plan at work, your 2002 adjusted gross income (AGI) must be less than $44,000 (if single) or $64,000 (if married filing jointly) to contribute. Contributions are phased out between $34,000 and 44,000 for singles, and between $54,000 and $64,000 for married couples.

> ### Revenue Ramblings
>
> If you're a married couple and only one of you is covered by an employer-sponsored plan at work, your rules for a tax-deductible IRA are slightly different. Married couples can deduct the contribution to the traditional IRA of the spouse not covered at work, as long as their AGI is below $150,000. If the couple earns more than that, the person not covered by an employer-sponsored plan can make a partial contribution subject to the phaseout rules between $150,000 to $160,000. If you're married filing separately, almost no IRA deduction is allowed. The deduction phaseout rule begins at $0, and no deduction is allowed if you earn more than $10,000.

If you have a plan at work and earn more than the allowable limits, you can open a Roth IRA or traditional nondeductible IRA. The Roth IRA is the best option because not only can your earnings grow tax-free, but they will also be tax-free when you start taking out the money in retirement. You will have to pay taxes on at least the earnings when you start withdrawing money from traditional IRAs in retirement, whether their contributions were tax deductible or not.

The Roth has income limitations as well. If your earnings are too high, your only option is the non–tax-deductible IRA. But the tax-deferred savings are certainly still valuable in helping your portfolio grow faster.

Roth eligibility is not impacted by your participation in an employee-sponsored retirement plan, but there are maximum earning limits. In fact, its benefits are so good that

Congress made it difficult to figure out whether you can contribute if your earnings are near the contribution limits of $110,000 for singles or $160,000 for married couples.

First, you must determine whether your modified adjusted gross income (MAGI) is within the limits. The IRS rules for calculating your MAGI for Roth purposes are as follows:

1. Subtract any income resulting from the conversion of an IRA (other than a Roth IRA) to a Roth IRA (conversion income). Conversions will be discussed in greater detail later.

2. Add the following deductions and exclusions:

   a. Traditional IRA deduction

   b. Student loan interest deduction

   c. Foreign earned income exclusion

   d. Foreign housing exclusion or deduction

   e. Exclusion of qualified bond interest shown on Form 8815

   f. Exclusion of employer-paid adoption expenses shown on Form 8839

   g. Qualified tuition and related expenses

Now that you know your MAGI, you can use the following rather complicated IRS table to figure out whether you can contribute to a Roth:

Effect of Modified AGI on Roth IRA Contribution

(This table shows whether your contribution to a Roth IRA is affected by the amount of your modified adjusted gross income.)

If You Have Taxable Compensation and Your Filing Status Is …	AND Your Modified AGI Is …	THEN …
Married Filing Jointly	Less than $150,000	You can contribute up to $3,000 if under 50, or $3,500 if 50 or older.
	At least $150,000 but less than $160,000	The amount you can contribute is reduced based on the phaseout rules.
	$160,000 or more	You cannot contribute to a Roth IRA.

continues

Effect of Modified AGI on Roth IRA Contribution (continued)

If You Have Taxable Compensation and Your Filing Status Is ...	AND Your Modified AGI Is ...	THEN ...
Married Filing Separately and you lived with your spouse at any time during the year	Zero ($0)	You can contribute up to $3,000 if under 50, or $3,500 if 50 or older.
	More than zero ($0) but less than $10,000	The amount you can contribute is reduced according to the phaseout rules.
	$10,000 or more	You cannot contribute to a Roth IRA.
Single, Head of Household, Qualifying Widow(er), or Married Filing Separately and you did not live with your spouse at any time during the year	Less than $95,000	You can contribute up to $3,000 if under 50, or $3,500 if 50 or older.
	At least $95,000 but less than $110,000	The amount you can contribute is reduced according to the phaseout rules.
	$110,000 or more	You cannot contribute to a Roth IRA.

Congress sure can make a simple idea confusing!

You can contribute to only one of these IRA types if your earned income at least totals the amount of your contribution. There is one exception to this rule: If your spouse doesn't work outside the home, you can open a Spousal IRA using any of these vehicles, as long as your earnings total more than the amount you put in both your IRA and the IRA of your spouse.

You can earn your income from wages, salaries, tips, bonuses, professional fees, and any other service you provide and report as income to the Internal Revenue Service (IRS).

Revenue Ramblings

You may qualify for other IRAs if you work for a small business—the SEP and SIMPLE IRAs. The SEP-IRA is fully funded by your employer, and the SIMPLE IRA is a type of IRA that both you and your employer can add to. We'll talk about how those work in Chapter 27. We'll also discuss another small business retirement option, a Keogh Plan, which can be the closest to a traditional pension in the small business arena.

The tax advantages of IRAs shift yearly until at least 2008. The good news is that you'll be able to save more tax-deferred or tax-free dollars as the 2001 tax takes effect. Folks 50 and older have even greater savings opportunities, thanks to the catch-up provisions of the new tax law. You'll see from the following table that allowable contributions increase to as high as $5,000 for folks under 50, and $6,000 for folks over 50.

Allowable Contributions for People 50 and Over

Tax Year for Those 50+	Allowable Contribution	Additional Contributions
2002–2004	$3,000	$500
2005	$4,000	$500
2006–2007	$4,000	$1,000
2008	$5,000	$1,000
After 2008	Adjusted for inflation in $500 increments	

Don't let the IRS's complex rules discourage you from considering a Roth IRA. It has the best tax advantages when you get to retirement. All your money withdrawn from a Roth IRA is completely tax-free, as long as you're at least 59½ and the money was deposited in the Roth for at least five years. Another big advantage is that you don't have to start taking out your money at any age; the other types of IRAs require you to start taking out money at age 70½. Your heirs will also appreciate the Roth because they don't have to pay taxes on your contributions that are left in the Roth IRA; they pay tax only on the earnings.

Everything you withdraw from a tax-deductible IRA (as opposed to a Roth IRA or non–tax-deductible IRA) will be taxed as though it were current income. Because your income is usually much lower after you have retired, you'll likely be taxed at a much lower tax bracket, which means significant savings. If you have a traditional non–tax-deductible IRA, only the gains will be taxed; be sure to keep good records of your contributions to avoid paying taxes twice on that money.

The important thing to take into account before socking all your money away in an IRA is that you usually can't take money out of the account before age 59½ without penalties and taxes. Your withdrawal may be taxed at your current tax rate, plus a 10 percent penalty could be tacked on to the bill. You can avoid penalties before age 59½, as long as you are withdrawing funds for one of the following reasons:

◆ You have become disabled.

◆ You're buying your first home and want to withdraw $10,000 or less.

♦ You must pay off significant medical expenses.

♦ You lost your job and must pay for medical insurance.

♦ You want to go back to school and use the money for qualified higher education expenses.

♦ You have reached the age of 55 and retired or were terminated from your job.

Audit Alarm!

If you have a traditional non–tax-deductible IRA, you must be able to prove how much you contributed, or you could get stuck paying taxes on money that has already been taxed. If the financial institution holding your IRA is not tracking these contributions for you, be sure *you* do. The easiest way to build your proof is to file your annual year-end statements for your IRAs. Yep, another good use for that paper pile we built in Chapter 1. It is also important to file Form 8606, "Non Deductible IRAs and Coverdell ESAs," which tracks these contributions.

If you have a Roth IRA and the money has been deposited for at least five years, you can withdraw your own contributions, but not earnings, without any tax or penalty at any time. In most cases, you will have to pay taxes on earnings for early withdrawal if the money has been on deposit for five years. You can withdraw IRA money completely tax-free that has been on deposit for more than five years, even if you are not 59$\frac{1}{2}$, provided that you are using the money to buy a first home or if you become disabled. Remember, that money was put into the Roth IRA after you already paid taxes on it.

When you reach age 70$\frac{1}{2}$, you must start withdrawing from all IRAs except the Roth by April 1 of the next year. If you don't start taking out your money, you could face a 50 percent excise tax on the money you didn't withdraw as required. We'll take a closer look at withdrawal rules in Chapter 17.

Employer Plans

Now let's take a look at the tax advantages of saving through your retirement plan at work. These plans are called salary-reduction plans or defined-contribution plans. Traditional pension plans are called defined-benefit plans.

You may find that these plans at work have several different names, including a 401(k), a 403(b), Tax-Sheltered Annuities (TSAs), Tax-Deferred Annuities (TDAs), or Section 457. The 401(k) is used by for-profit companies. The 403(b), TSA, and TDA are used by nonprofit companies and some state or local agencies. The Section 457 is used by state and local government employers.

> ### Taxing Terms
>
> **Defined-contribution plans** are funded through contributions from you and your employer. Contributions that you make actually reduce your taxable salary and help you build a retirement nest egg. In most employer plans, these contributions work in a similar way to a tax deduction. You don't write off the tax deduction when you file your taxes; instead, your employer reduces your taxable salary before computing your taxes due. You manage the way the money is invested in this retirement nest egg.
>
> **Defined-benefit plans** specify the retirement benefit that the company will pay out when you retire. These plans are fully funded and managed by the employer. The employer must manage the way the funds are invested to be sure he or she can pay benefits promised.

Let's take a closer look at how these plans work. When you decide to participate in one of these plans, you fill out a form giving your employer permission to reduce your salary by a percentage or dollar amount that you set. This amount is deposited in your name. The tax on the dollar amount is tax deferred, and the investment grows tax-free until it comes time to withdraw the money in retirement. Some companies or government agencies will start and contribute to these plans without requiring you to contribute, but that is rare.

Many times you'll find that your employer matches some portion of your contribution. That's just like earning more money. It's a benefit you get only if you make a contribution in most companies. Typically, a company matches 50 percent of the first 6 percent contributed, but that's not required. The amount that companies contribute varies greatly, and the law requires only that the amount of the company match be distributed using the same computations, such as a fixed percentage or dollar amount, among employees.

When you get to retirement, you will be taxed on all withdrawals based on your current income tax rate at that time. A new type of 401(k), tentatively dubbed the Roth 401(k), will debut in 2005. These accounts don't offer the tax deduction for contributions, but contributions grow tax-free and can be taken out tax-free just as with the Roth IRA. Keep your eye on announcements of future tax-free retirement savings plans at work.

IRS Idioms _____

Unquestionably, there is progress. The average American now pays out almost as much in taxes alone as he formerly got in wages.

—H. L. Mencken

Tax Tips _____

If your employer offers a plan at work, you definitely should contribute enough to get your full company match. If you don't contribute enough to get the full match, it's almost like taking a voluntary pay cut. The money is yours, but you must take the first step.

The government limits how much you and your employer can contribute to one of these plans. Just as with the IRAs, contribution amounts are a moving target, thanks to the 2001 tax bill. In 2002, you can contribute up to 15 percent of your salary, with a maximum of $11,000. This will increase by $1,000 per year until it reaches a new maximum of $15,000 in 2006. After that year, the maximum will be indexed to inflation. For a 403(b), the dollar caps are the same, but you and your employer can contribute up to 20 percent of your salary.

Congress also made provisions in the employer plans to let you catch up if you are over 50. After you have made your maximum allowable pretax contribution, you will be able to add additional money. In 2002, you can put in an additional $1,000. That amount will increase by $1,000 a year until it reaches a maximum of $5,000 additional in 2006. After that point the catch-up contribution amount will be indexed for inflation. Employers can match these contributions but are not required to do so.

Choosing Your Alternative

I've talked a lot about the different plans available, so you may be wondering which plan you should choose. That depends on your personal situation, but let me review the alternatives and the types of issues you should consider when selecting your tax-advantaged retirement saving options.

If your employer sponsors a retirement plan and offers a company match, the first thing you should do is deposit enough in your employer's plan to get the match. From this point, it depends on your current and future situations, but here are some scenarios:

◆ Max out the amount you can put into a Roth IRA. This way you'll have the greatest amount of flexibility and the greatest tax savings when you get to retirement. When you max out your Roth contributions, if you still have more money to save toward retirement, then increase your contributions in your employer plan to the maximum allowed by law or the maximum you can afford. Remember, you may be able to afford to contribute more than you think because the amount deposited will reduce your taxable salary and, therefore, your tax bill.

◆ If you earn too much to contribute to a Roth IRA, definitely use the non–tax-deductible IRA to save that extra money after you've maxed out your contributions into your employer's retirement plan.

For folks who have no retirement plan at work, the deductible IRA is probably your best choice; if you don't need the tax break up front, though, you may want to consider using the Roth IRA because of its flexibility in retirement. If you think your tax rate will be higher in retirement, you're certainly better off paying taxes on the money now by choosing to save using the Roth, which can be withdrawn tax-free. If you're certain that your tax rate will be lower, the tax savings that you can get by using a tax-deductible IRA make the most sense if your employer doesn't offer a tax-deferred retirement plan. This way, you can defer paying taxes on your contributions until you take out the money in retirement, when your rates will be lower.

Tax Tips

If money is tight and you can't contribute to both your employer plans and a personal IRA, your first priority should be to contribute enough into your employer plan to get your full company match. You certainly don't want to lose that benefit and the extra retirement savings it can mean for you and your family.

We talked about how to calculate your tax rates in Chapter 1. But those rates are changing between now and 2006. The 10 percent and 15 percent rates will be stay the same, but the other tax rates are going to drop. Here's a table of the rate reduction set in motion by the 2001 tax law:

Future Tax Rates

	2002–2003	2004–2005	2006 and after
28% rate reduced to:	27%	26%	25%
31% rate reduced to:	30%	29%	28%
36% rate reduced to:	35%	34%	33%
39.6% rate reduced to:	38.6%	37.6%	35%

Unfortunately, no one can be sure what his or her tax rate will be in future years. Congress can change its mind any time. You also can't be certain what your income will be at such a distant time in the future. So, unless you're on a fixed income for the rest of your life, the best you can do is guess about your future tax obligations.

Generally, most financial advisors will tell you to avoid paying taxes now with the hopes that your tax obligation will be less in the future. That rule works for most of us, but if you're sure that you are going to have a lot more money when you get to retirement because of an inheritance or any other personal reason, then paying taxes on the money now is your best option for retirement savings.

Next, we'll take a look at another type of retirement income: Social Security. We'll look at current laws and future prospects in the next chapter.

The Least You Need to Know

- ◆ Your retirement savings can grow much faster if you shelter them in one of the tax-advantaged savings vehicles available and defer taxes.

- ◆ Three types of tax-advantaged personal retirement savings plans exist: the tax-deductible IRA, the non–tax-deductible IRA, and the Roth IRA.

- ◆ Numerous types of employer-sponsored plans provide tax-advantaged savings. Some of these plans even offer a mechanism for your employer to match your savings so that your retirement nest egg can grow even faster.

- ◆ You'll have to pay taxes on the withdrawals of most tax-advantaged retirement savings when you finally reach retirement, but one offers totally tax-free withdrawals: the Roth IRA.

Chapter 16

Planning on Social Security

In This Chapter

- ◆ The Social Security tax bite
- ◆ The push for privatization
- ◆ Calculating your benefits
- ◆ How your take is taxed

The politics of Social Security are among the most politically divisive in the country today. The question of whether a part of the contribution should be privatized—in other words, put in personal accounts—is one that will probably be decided by the next Congress. If not decided, it will most likely just be stalled until one side of the fight has a stronger majority than the other.

The stock market collapse has taken the steam out of the calls to privatize Social Security, but it certainly hasn't stopped it completely. And Americans still don't know whether there will be any money left in the Social Security trusts by the time they retire. But before considering these controversial and worrisome issues, let's take a look at how your Social Security taxes work today.

Your Social Security Taxes

If you work in private industry, there really is no legal way to avoid Social Security taxes. Only the lucky few who work for state or local governments in which the state has opted out of the Social Security system can avoid paying Social Security taxes. Others who can avoid the tax include elections workers, college students who work for their academic institution, federal workers who started with the government before 1984, ministers who choose not to be covered, household workers who make less than $1,100 a year, and self-employed folks who make less than $400.

For each working person, 12.4 percent of income up to $84,900 in 2002 must be paid in Social Security taxes. This maximum salary is adjusted upward each year based on national earnings levels. In addition, 2.9 percent is taken from a person's total earnings—with no earnings cap—for Medicare. Even state workers must pay the Medicare portion.

Taxing Terms

Old-Age, Survivors, and Disability Insurance (OASDI) is the largest social insurance program run by the U.S. government. Today more than 95 percent of workers in the United States are covered by Social Security. Note that Social Security is called an insurance program because it not only insures payments at retirement, but it also provides benefits if you become disabled. Your family is insured as well through survivor benefits. In 2001, more than 45 million people were collecting a total of over $400 billion in benefits.

The good news is that, unless you're self-employed, your employer pays half of these taxes for you. So, your actual tax bite is 6.2 percent for Social Security and 1.45 percent for Medicare. You might find these taxes under two different abbreviations on your paycheck—FICA (Federal Insurance Contribution Act) and OASDI (Old-Age, Survivors, and Disability Insurance). Medicare is usually indicated separately. When it isn't, then it's included on the FICA line.

Self-employed workers don't have anyone to pay their employer's share, so they must pay the total taxes for Social Security and Medicare. However, they get to reduce their adjusted gross income by half the amount they pay in Social Security and Medicare taxes.

A Safety Net, Not a Retirement Plan

Social Security was signed into law in 1935 under the Franklin D. Roosevelt administration. As president, FDR saw that many seniors were starving and homeless on the streets after the 1929 stock market crash, and he wanted to be sure that this would never happen again to people who had worked hard all their lives.

Initially, Social Security covered only workers, but gradually other benefits were added to include survivors of deceased workers. Benefits for disabled workers and their families were added later. The system was designed as a progressive system, meaning that lower-income earners get a larger percentage of their income in retirement benefits, even though their actual payout will be considerably less than those who earned the maximum taxable income. Maximum benefits for 2002 were $1,660 per month.

This progressive system is managed using the following formula for calculating benefits:

1. 90 percent of the first $531 of average monthly earnings

2. 32 percent of monthly earnings between $531 and $3,202

3. 15 percent of earnings above $3,202

Let's see how this impacts the benefits of a low-income earner making $2,000 monthly ($24,000 per year) and a high-income earner making the maximum income taxed, $7075 monthly ($84,900).

	Low Income	High Income
1.	$477.90	$477.90
2.	$470.08	$854.72
3.	$0	$580.95
	$947.98	$1,913.57

Since the maximum Social Security benefit is $1,660, the high-income earner's benefits would be even lower than the amount calculated. The low-income earner who worked until full retirement age would get 47.4 percent of his or her earnings as a retirement benefit, while the high-income earner would get only 11.7 percent of his or her earnings at full retirement age.

Tax Tips

Average-income earners can expect about 40 percent of their current income in Social Security benefits.

Social Security was never intended as a person's only retirement income. It was intended to be a safety net so that every retiree could have some guaranteed income. When Social Security was originally crafted, and in all of the more than 100 pieces of legislation that have been passed to tweak the system since it was created, the primary premise of the safety net has been maintained. Higher-income earners have always footed a larger part of the bill, even though their level of benefits collected—based on percentage of their income—is less. The basic assumption is that higher-income earners will have more resources to save additional funds for retirement.

Will There Be Any Money Left for Me?

Now that you understand how benefits are calculated, let's look at why Social Security is facing a crisis, with some folks even saying there won't be any money left by the time you retire.

First, I'll set the record straight. Based on Social Security's own estimates, there's enough money in the combination of current Social Security taxes and *trust funds* to pay full benefits until 2041. After that time, even if no fix is put in place before then, there's enough money to pay 75 percent of benefits. While it's clear that a fix is needed, the emergency is not as great as some people will have you believe. This is a scare tactic to create the political climate to privatize this system.

Why, you may be wondering, are we facing this crisis? The answer is simple: the baby boomers. This generation has wreaked havoc with every system as it has moved through life—first, creating the need for massive spending on new schools, then on medical care, next on housing, and soon on retirement-related benefits. Currently there are 3.4 workers to help pay the benefits of current Social Security beneficiaries, but by 2030, when most baby boomers will be in retirement, there will be only 2.1 workers per beneficiary.

Taxing Terms

Social Security Trust Funds include the Old-Age and Survivors Insurance (OASI) Trust Fund, which pays retirement and survivors benefits, and the Disability Insurance (DI) Trust Fund. The funds can be used only to pay benefits and program administrative costs. By law, the funds must be invested in interest-bearing securities that are guaranteed by the U.S. government.

Eighty-five percent of current Social Security taxes is used to pay current benefits—only about 15 percent is saved in the Social Security trust funds to pay future benefits. Social Security almost ran out of money to pay benefits in the early 1980s. To solve that crisis, Alan Greenspan, who at the time was Chairman and President of Townsend-Greenspan & Co., Inc., an economic consulting firm in New York

City, headed up a presidential commission that recommended a combination of tax increases and benefit reductions so the United States could build up the Social Security trust funds. So, although money is being saved now to pay benefits to the huge numbers of baby boomers who will be entering retirement, not enough is being saved to fully fund the baby boomers' full retirement needs.

A number of fixes are being considered in addition to privatization:

♦ Increasing current Social Security taxes

♦ Decreasing current benefits

♦ Increasing the full retirement age

♦ Investing the trust funds more aggressively than the current mandate of using only treasury bonds

♦ Changing the way cost-of-living adjustments are calculated to increase benefits based on the consumer price index

Most likely some combination of these alternatives will ultimately be used to formulate a plan, but that will happen only once the political posturing turns toward really trying to fix the problem. And there's no question that the problem needs to be fixed. More than 53 percent of the current workforce has no private pension, according to the Social Security administration, and over 35 percent of the workforce has nothing saved for retirement.

Even if the program is fixed and there is no change in future benefits, you still need to save for retirement. Most planners estimate that people will need 70 to 80 percent of their current income during retirement. Social Security is intended to replace only about 40 percent of an average earner's income. You are the one who will need to make up the difference if you want to maintain your current living standards in retirement.

 IRS Idioms

Politics is a jungle—torn between doing the right thing and staying in office.

—John F. Kennedy

Revenue Ramblings

Since Social Security is a pay-as-you-go system—in other words, current beneficiaries are being paid using the taxes of current workers—privatization could create a funding crisis. President George W. Bush's Social Security commission estimates that trillions of dollars would be needed from general tax funds to foot the bill for privatization.

Collecting Your Share

Now let's take a quick look at how you collect your benefits. Basically, you have three choices: retire early (age 62 is the earliest), retire on time, or retire late. Retiring on time, or full retirement age, is a moving target depending on when you were born:

Full Retirement Age Based on Year of Birth

Year of Birth	Full Retirement Age
1937 or earlier	65
1938	65 and 2 months
1939	65 and 4 months
1940	65 and 6 months
1941	65 and 8 months
1942	65 and 10 months
1943–1954	66
1955	66 and 2 months
1956	66 and 4 months
1957	66 and 6 months
1958	66 and 8 months
1959	66 and 10 months
1960 and later	67

So based on the preceding table, if you were born in 1957, your full retirement age is 66 plus 6 months. Right now, the highest retirement age is 67 for folks born in 1960 or later; however, some folks in Congress propose raising that age to 70. Your benefits are based on when you retire, so if you retire early, your benefits are reduced accordingly. Your reduction in benefits will be the same throughout your retirement—it will *not* increase once you reach your full retirement age. The following table shows how the reduction works:

Reduction for Early Retirement

Year of Birth	Full Reduction Retirement	Age 62 Reduction* (in Months)	Monthly % Reduction	Total %
1937 or earlier	65	36	.555	20.00
1938	65 and 2 months	38	.548	20.83
1939	65 and 4 months	40	.541	21.67
1940	65 and 6 months	42	.535	22.50
1941	65 and 8 months	44	.530	23.33
1942	65 and 10 months	46	.525	24.17
1943–1954	66	48	.520	25.00
1955	66 and 2 months	50	.516	25.84
1956	66 and 4 months	52	.512	26.66
1957	66 and 6 months	54	.509	27.50
1958	66 and 8 months	56	.505	28.33
1959	66 and 10 months	58	.502	29.17
1960 and later	67	60	.500	30.00

Percentage monthly and total reductions are approximate due to rounding. The actual reductions are .555, or ⁵/₉, of 1% per month for the first 36 months, and .416, or ⁵/₁₂, of 1% for subsequent months.

This table isn't as confusing as it looks—I promise! Let's practice one calculation together. We'll look at the calculation for someone born in 1950. You can see from the table labeled "Full Retirement Age Based on Year of Birth" that the retirement age would be 66. If this person decided to retire at age 62, that's a reduction of 48 months. The percentage per month is .520. So here is how he would calculate the reduction in benefits for early retirement:

48 months × .520 = 24.96 percent (which is rounded to 25 percent in the table)

So if this person retired at age 62, his benefits would be reduced by 25 percent.

If this person decided to retire at age 63, or three years before full retirement age, he would use 36 months to calculate the reduction:

36 months × .520 = 18.72 percent

So, if you want to figure out whether you can afford to retire early, simply calculate how many months early you want to retire and use the preceding tables to find out your reduction percentage. Once you get that percentage, you can multiply that by the projected full retirement benefit to find out your benefits.

If you're one of those people who just doesn't want to retire, you can get even higher benefits by waiting until the age of 70 to collect your benefits. Once you reach 70, there's no reason to delay any further. Your benefits won't increase any more even if you don't apply for them. You just lose 'em. The following table shows how much your benefits can increase:

Year of Birth	Yearly Rate of Increase	Monthly Rate of Increase
1930	4.5%	$3/8$ of 1%
1931–32	5.0%	$5/12$ of 1%
1933–34	5.5%	$11/24$ of 1%
1934–36	6.0%	$1/2$ of 1%
1937–38	6.5%	$13/24$ of 1%
1939–40	7.0%	$7/12$ of 1%
1941–42	7.5%	$5/8$ of 1%
1943+	8.0%	$2/3$ of 1%

Now that you know the benefit possibilities, let's take a look at how they are taxed.

Taxing the Benefits

Just because you're retired and on Social Security doesn't mean you get to forget about taxes. In fact, your Social Security benefits could be taxed if you earn more than the following limits (called a "base amount" by the IRS):

- ◆ $25,000 if you are single, head of household, or a qualifying widow(er)

- ◆ $25,000 if you are married filing separately and have lived apart from your spouse for all of 2002

- ◆ $32,000 if you are married filing jointly

- ◆ $0 if you are married filing separately and have lived with your spouse at any time during 2002

If you file a joint return, you and your spouse must combine your incomes and your benefits when calculating your earnings. Even if your spouse is not yet retired and not yet collecting benefits, you must add in your spouse's income when trying to determine whether your benefits are taxable. If the only income you receive is from Social Security, your benefits most likely are not taxable. You may not even have to file a tax return. If you do have income in addition to your benefits, you may be stuck filing a return even if you don't have to pay taxes.

To calculate whether your Social Security will be taxable, you'll need an IRS worksheet and one of those forms listed in Chapter 1: an SSA-1099 or an RRB-1099.

Here's a sample of the IRS worksheet you'll need to fill out each year to determine whether your benefits are taxable:

Taxing Terms

SSA-1099 is the form Social Security sends each beneficiary every year. If you are getting benefits on more than one Social Security record, you may get more than one form. The form will include all the benefits you received from the Social Security Administration and adjustments to those benefits. Railroad retirees get an RRB-1099 form instead.

Social Security Tax Worksheet. *You can use the following worksheet to figure the amount of income to compare with your base amount. This is a quick way to check whether some of your benefits may be taxable.*

A. Write in the amount from **box 5** of all your Forms SSA-1099 and RRB-1099. Include the full amount of any lump-sum benefit payments received in 2002, for 2002 and earlier years. (If you received more than one form, combine the amounts from box 5 and write in the total.) A. _____

Note. *If the amount on line A is $0 or less, stop here; none of your benefits are taxable this year.*

B. Enter one half of the amount on line A. B. _____

C. Add your taxable pensions, wages, interest, dividends, and other taxable income, and write in the total. C. _____

D. Write in any tax-exempt interest (such as interest on municipal bonds), plus any exclusions from income (shown in the list under "Exclusions," earlier). D. _____

E. Add lines B, C, and D, and write in the total. E. _____

Note. *Compare the amount on line E to your* ***base amount*** *for your filing status. If the amount on line E equals or is less than the* ***base amount*** *for your filing status, none of your benefits is taxable this year. If the amount on line E is more than your* ***base amount,*** *some of your benefits may be taxable.*

As long as the total on line E is less than your base amount, you won't have to pay taxes. If it's higher than your base amount, the IRS has an 18-step worksheet you will have to complete to find out what portion of your benefits is taxable. Unless you have income above $34,000, or $44,000 if married filing jointly, the most that will be taxable is 50 percent of your Social Security benefits.

If you earn more than $34,000, or $44,000 if married filing jointly, as much as 85 percent of your Social Security income could be taxable. Remember, we're talking about taxable income—not the amount of the actual tax.

Now that you know how Social Security works, we'll turn to other sources of retirement income and how they are taxed once you start using them.

The Least You Need to Know

- Nearly every American pays Social Security taxes.

- The Social Security tax is 12.4 percent of income up to $84,900. Employers pay half of that amount for their employees, but self-employed workers pay the full amount.

- Medicare taxes are 2.9 percent of income. Just like with Social Security taxes, employers pay half.

- If you earn too much in retirement, you could end up paying taxes on your Social Security benefits.

Chapter 17

Withdrawing Time

In This Chapter

- ◆ How pensions are taxed
- ◆ Calculating taxes on retirement savings accounts
- ◆ The beauty of the Roth at retirement time
- ◆ Taking advantage of state exemptions

You've finally made it. After all those years of saving for retirement, you've reached age 59½ and can start taking out some of your retirement savings without having to worry about the possibility of paying tax penalties for early withdrawal. Unfortunately, unless you have all your retirement funds in a Roth IRA, it doesn't mean that you won't pay any taxes—only that the penalties for withdrawal disappear.

Now is the time to look for strategies to minimize your taxes as you withdraw your funds. Taxes are not your only consideration, but since this is a tax book, I'll be concentrating on the tax-related issues. We'll start by looking at the withdrawal rules for the different types of retirement accounts and then review how to balance your options in retirement to minimize taxes.

Tax Impacts of Using Pensions

First, let's look at pensions from your workplace. There are actually two types of pensions:

♦ **Defined-benefit plan.** A retirement pension that is fully funded by your employer. Your benefit is usually calculated based on a complicated formula that takes into consideration your number of years of service and your earnings history and then determines how much you will receive in benefits. You usually have several distribution choices based on your life span, the life spans of you and your spouse, or a set number of years over which you want to receive the benefit.

♦ **Defined-contribution plan.** A plan into which both you and your employer contribute. The amount you will receive from this plan is based on how much you have saved over your work life and how well you have managed the investment of that money. At retirement, the amount you can withdraw is based on the market value of the amount you have saved. You will need to review your balance regularly during retirement and adjust your withdrawals to be sure you won't outlive your money. Plans that fit into this category include 401(k)s, 403(b)s, and Section 457s, which we discussed in Chapter 15. SEP-IRAs, SIMPLE IRAs, and Keoghs also fit in this category; we'll review those in Chapter 27.

We'll look at the rules involving how these pensions are taxed, but it's important to keep in mind that there's a lot more to planning retirement withdrawals than how they are taxed. There is no question that minimizing taxes will help you extend the life of your retirement portfolio. Just don't make beating the taxman your only goal during retirement.

Tax Tips

Your biggest consideration at retirement time will be how to spend down your assets at the proper pace so that you don't outlive them. Be sure to work with a professional financial planner who will review your plans and make sure you won't outlive your assets.

While you might enjoy the game, it won't mean that your funds will necessarily be used in the most effective way to ensure that you'll have enough to fund your full retirement. Sorry to keep beating you over the head with this, but many people run out of funds during retirement just because they didn't draw down the right funds at the right time.

Retirement funds from employer plans will be fully taxable at your current tax rate as you withdraw the money.

Tax Tips

Certain rules of thumb cover withdrawing retirement funds, but in reality each person's situation is unique based on expected life span, health concerns, and family concerns. Only a good financial planner can help you sort these things out. Even if you enjoy managing your own investments, asking a professional to review your plan makes a lot of sense to be sure that it will fully fund your retirement.

One way to find a financial planner is to check with friends you trust who may know a good one. An article that gives great tips on how to pick the right financial planner can be found online at www.cfp-board.org/cons_10qs.html.

If you have a defined-contribution plan, most likely your employer will have you roll out the balance of your portfolio into a personal IRA account or *annuity* at retirement. You can take a lump-sum distribution and deposit it in your local bank account, but I wouldn't recommend it. If you don't roll over the money into an IRA or annuity, you will pay taxes on the entire portfolio immediately. The tax bite would be huge.

Taxing Terms

An **annuity** is a contract sold to you by an insurance company in which the company agrees to provide payments to the holder of the contract at specified intervals.

For example, let's say your 401(k) has a market value of $500,000. If you take out the full amount in the first year of retirement, even if you put it in a bank savings account, you'll have to pay taxes as though you earned the entire $500,000 that year. You would be placed in the highest tax bracket. If instead you rolled the funds into a traditional IRA, you would need to pay taxes only on the amount of money you withdraw each year.

In the distant future, you may actually have a Roth type of 401(k) defined-contribution plan that is tax-free at the time of withdrawal. These plans are still on the drawing board and won't be introduced until 2005.

Revenue Ramblings

Some employers offer the option of purchasing an annuity with your defined-contribution plan. Annuities have substantial fees for managing your funds, but in exchange they offer the advantage of professional management and can guarantee payments over your life span, the life span of you and your spouse, or for a set number of years. An excellent place to learn more about annuities is the learning center at TIAA-CREF (www.tiaa-cref.com/pas/spiawork.html).

If your employer offers the option of keeping your funds in its plan throughout your retirement, you may want to consider it if you think the investment alternatives are good. Whether you slowly take the money out of your employer-based plan throughout your retirement or roll it over to a personal IRA, your tax consequences through the rest of your retirement will be the same as if you had saved the funds in a personal tax-deductible IRA throughout your work life.

Withdrawing from Retirement Savings

First, let's quickly review our discussion from Chapter 15. There are three types of IRAs: tax-deductible traditional IRAs, non–tax-deductible traditional IRAs, and Roth IRAs. All the funds withdrawn from a tax-deductible IRA are taxable at your current tax rate during retirement. If you have contributed to a non–tax-deductible traditional IRA, only your gains are taxable. You will have to use Form 8606 to figure out what part of your distribution is taxable each year. Be sure to keep good records of how much you contributed to the non–tax-deductible IRA. This money was already taxed before you put it into the IRA, and you don't want to have to pay taxes on the money twice.

Audit Alarm!

If you don't take the required minimum distribution (RMD) from a traditional IRA, you can be penalized a 50 percent excise tax on the money not distributed. The Roth IRA has no required distribution schedule.

You must start withdrawing money from a traditional IRA, whether it's taxable or non–tax-deductible, by the time you reach age $70\frac{1}{2}$. If you are over $70\frac{1}{2}$ but you're still working, you can delay your withdrawals until you stop working.

The amount you must withdraw is called the required minimum distribution (RMD). There used to be a complicated series of withdrawal options, but luckily the IRS simplified those beginning in 2002. The following table from the IRS shows you how to figure the RMD based on life expectancy figures.

Age	Life Expectancy Divisor
70	26.2
71	25.3
72	24.4
73	23.5
74	22.7
75	21.8
76	20.9

Age	Life Expectancy Divisor
77	20.1
78	19.2
79	18.4
80	17.6
81	16.8
82	16.0
83	15.3
84	14.5
85	13.8
86	13.1
87	12.4
88	11.8
89	11.1
90	10.5
91	9.9
92	9.4
93	8.8
94	8.3
95	7.8
96	7.3
97	6.9
98	6.5
99	6.1

Using the information on this table, you can calculate your RMD:

$$\frac{\text{Total Assets in Retirement Account}}{\text{Life Expectancy Divisor}} = \text{Required Minimum Distribution}$$

Let's practice to be sure you understand how this works. We'll assume that you are calculating the withdrawal at the age of 75 and that your total remaining assets are $500,000 in your IRAs. Here's what the calculation would look like:

$$\frac{\$500,000}{21.8} = \$22,936$$

This withdrawal would be 4.59 percent of the portfolio. Generally planners recommend that you withdraw no more than 6 percent of your retirement portfolio per year, to be sure you don't outlive the funds. That amount varies, depending upon your life span, your health, your family situation, and the way your funds are invested.

You can calculate the RMD for each IRA individually, but it's not necessary. In fact, you can withdraw all of your RMD from any one of the IRAs or any combination of IRAs you hold.

Roth Benefits at Retirement Time

Retirement time is when the Roth IRA really stands out. There are no required distributions from the Roth IRA at any time in your life. All the funds withdrawn from the Roth IRA are tax-free in retirement, as long as they have been in the IRA for at least five years.

Your heirs also will be happy if you leave them a Roth IRA rather than a traditional IRA. After you die, your beneficiaries can withdraw the money tax-free, or they can decide to leave it in the Roth and take out only the required minimum withdrawal based on their age. The advantage of leaving it in the Roth is that the money can continue to grow tax free. Using this technique, your heirs could have a tax-free annuity for their entire life or withdraw it at some later time tax-free if they need it for a major purchase. The key difference for heirs, other than the spouse, is that they must withdraw some of the money each year to take advantage of this continuing tax-free savings advantage.

If your spouse is the beneficiary, inheritance should be handled differently. Your spouse can transfer the IRA to his or her name; he or she then never is required to take out money and can take money as needed.

Managing Your Distributions

By the time you retire, you'll probably have your savings spread among several different types of tax-deferred accounts, tax-free accounts, and taxable accounts. Generally, a good rule of thumb is to use up your funds in the taxable accounts and let the tax-deferred and tax-free accounts continue to grow without being taxed.

As you draw down funds, be sure to carefully manage your portfolio to keep it balanced for risk among cash, bonds, stocks, and mutual funds. Many financial planners recommend that you keep about 20 to 25 percent of your retirement assets in investments that have growth potential, such as stocks or mutual funds, even in retirement.

Most people live another 15 to 20 years in retirement, so you have to maintain some growth to beat inflation. As you get nearer to the end of your life, you may want to shift more of your portfolio to cash.

Managing retirement distributions so you don't outlive your assets is very complicated, so I'm not going to delve into this topic extensively in this tax book. I've written two books on retirement planning that do take a closer look a this issue: *Teach Yourself Retirement Planning in 24 Hours* (with co-author Alan Feigenbaum) and *Streetwise Retirement Planning: Savvy Strategies and Practical Advice for a Secure Financial Future.*

Don't Forget State Taxes

States tax laws vary greatly when it comes to taxing retirement dollars. Many states lower seniors' property taxes considerably, and some waive them completely. Some states waive income taxes, and others offer additional tax breaks.

Many states offer other tax benefits to seniors, such as exemptions from gasoline taxes or sales taxes, and many do not tax pensions or Social Security benefits. Furthermore, deductions allowed for medical costs and federal taxes can greatly impact your state tax bill. Make sure you research the tax laws for your state to make the most out of your retirement years.

Tax Tips

You can compare state taxes at the website Retirement Living (www. retirementliving.com/ RLtaxes.html).

Now that we've traveled through retirement, we're going to take a look at something that can create a major roadblock in your long-term planning: divorce.

The Least You Need to Know

- ◆ Most of your retirement funds will be taxable as current income when you start to withdraw them at retirement.

- ◆ Withdrawals from employer-based retirement plans and tax-deductible traditional IRAs are fully taxable as current income, while non–tax-deductible IRAs are only partially taxable.

- ◆ Roth IRA withdrawals are tax-free in retirement as long as the funds have been in the account for at least five years.

- ◆ There are minimum distribution requirements for all IRAs at the age of $70^1/_2$ except the Roth IRA. You never have to take out any money from the Roth during retirement.

Part 6

Tripping Through Splitsville

Divorce can be complicated enough—as well as emotionally draining—without having to worry about the tax man. Unfortunately, the IRS doesn't think it has any obligation to make your life any easier just because you are going through rough times. In fact, as you move through the process of separation, tax rules can make things even more costly for you if you aren't careful.

We'll review the deductions you can take and the legal boundaries for these deductions. We'll look closely at the rules for alimony and child support, and we'll examine how to structure your divorce or separation agreements so that you can take advantage of as many credits and deductions as possible.

YOU BETTER CHECK INTO THE TAX CODES BEFORE YOU GET DIVORCED, PARTNER, OR YOU'LL BE PAYING UNTIL THE COWS COME HOME.

Chapter 18

Going Separate Ways

In This Chapter

- ◆ How to file
- ◆ Protecting yourself from liability
- ◆ Dividing write-offs
- ◆ Splitting assets

Deciding to end a marriage creates havoc in many aspects of your life, and taxes are no exception. Frequently, couples don't think about taxes while they're going through divorce, resulting in some ugly tax bills.

Although people going through a divorce often have a hard time being civil to one another, if there is any way to set aside hostility and to carefully plan the division of assets and liabilities, both sides will benefit in the long run. Many financial decisions related to a divorce have significant tax consequences.

We'll take a trip through Splitsville and review the key tax issues that you should consider when negotiating a separation agreement or final divorce decree.

Understanding Your Filing Options

First, let's review filing options because they become so much more complicated when the prospects of divorce enter the picture. Your marital status will depend on whether you are considered legally married. State law governs whether you are married or legally separated under a divorce or separate maintenance decree.

For tax filing purposes, you're considered married for the whole year if on the last day of the tax year you and your spouse meet any one of the following tests:

♦ You are married and living together as husband and wife.

♦ You are living together in a common-law marriage that is recognized in the state where you now live or in the state where the common-law marriage began.

♦ You are married and living apart, but you are not legally separated under a decree of divorce or *separate maintenance*.

♦ You are separated under an interlocutory (not final) decree of divorce. For purposes of filing a joint return, you are not considered divorced.

Taxing Terms

A **separate mainte-nance decree** is used when the parties remain married but seek a court ruling on the rights and liabilities of the couple with respect to child custody, support, visitation, alimony, property, and debts. If the couple decides to divorce at a later date, this decree cannot be converted to divorce decree. A new divorce action would be needed.

Audit Alarm!

If your marriage is annulled, the tax consequences can be extensive. The IRS considers that a marriage never existed if annulled. You will have to file amended returns as a single person or a head of household for all tax years affected by the annulment that fall within the statute of limitations for filing a tax return, which is three years.

If under state law you are considered unmarried or legally separated by December 31 of any tax year, you file as an unmarried person for the entire year even if the divorce was finalized at 11:59 P.M. on December 31. That would certainly be an emotional New Year's Eve party.

As an unmarried person, you would then have the option of filing as single or as head of household. Just to briefly review head of household requirements, you must have paid more than half the cost of keeping up the home for a qualifying child for at least half the year. You can review more about filing status in Chapter 1.

Strangely, some folks have been known to divorce on December 31 and remarry in January just to take advantage of the tax laws. They avoid the marriage penalty by filing as two single individuals or one single and one head of household. However, the IRS could question your motives for the divorce and require you to refile as married individuals.

If you're in the process of separating or divorcing but are still married at the end of the year, you then have two tax-filing options. You can file taxes under the designation of married filing jointly or married filing separately.

If you can get past the anger, your best bet is to look at your financial situation and figure out which filing method would save both of you the most amount of money. Unfortunately, amicable divorce situations are rare, and a lot of people end up filing as married filing separately just to avoid dealing with a spouse.

Married filing separately has lots of special rules that limit your tax breaks. Here's a list of things you lose if you are still married but filing separately:

♦ Both of you must either itemize deductions or file using the standard deduction. One of you can't itemize deductions while the other chooses to use the standard deduction.

♦ You can't deduct interest paid on a student loan.

♦ You usually lose the credit for child- and dependent-care expenses, and the amount you can exclude from income if your employer provides a dependent-care assistance program is limited to $2,500, half of what is allowed for married couples filing jointly.

♦ You can't take the Earned Income Credit.

♦ You can't take advantage of the Credit for the Elderly or the Disabled unless you lived apart from your spouse for the entire year.

♦ You can't exclude interest from qualified U.S. savings bonds that were used for higher-education expenses.

♦ You lose the use of the Hope Credit and the Lifetime Learning Credit.

♦ You most likely will lose the use of the Adoption Credit.

♦ Your use of the Child Tax Credit will be limited.

♦ Limits on itemized deductions and the phaseout of personal exemption deductions are based on income levels that are half those allowed if married filing jointly.

♦ If you're on Social Security or a railroad pension, more of your benefits could be subject to taxes.

- You will not be able to roll over traditional IRAs into Roth IRAs during the year unless you didn't live with your spouse for the entire year.

- Your eligibility to deduct a contribution into a traditional IRA is much more limited.

- Your deduction for capital losses is cut in half, from $3,000 to $1,500.

You can see from this list that the implications of married filing separately can be severe. Your tax advisor can look at your individual situation and figure out what is best for you. If the divorce is hostile, however, you may have no choice but to file separately and suffer the tax consequences. Also, if for any reason you don't trust that your spouse is reporting his or her income to the IRS truthfully, you may not want to sign a joint return.

Tax Tips

When you and your spouse separate, don't forget to file IRS Form 8822, "Change of Address," so that the IRS can contact you. This is particularly important when separating or getting divorced because you don't want to miss a notice about a previous joint return.

Taxing Terms

Understatement of Tax Due means you or your spouse did not report the full amount of taxes due. This is different than underpaying your taxes. If taxes are underpaid, you reported the full amount due just didn't pay the full bill.

Protecting Yourself

Both parties are legally liable for the information filed with the IRS on a joint return. If you sign a joint return and the IRS later determines that more tax is due, you could be liable for that payment even if your ex-spouse is the one who made the error or deliberately tried to avoid taxes.

The IRS Restructuring and Reform Act of 1998 provides some protection for the innocent spouse, but he or she has to jump through a bunch of bureaucratic hoops. There are three types of relief for innocent spouses:

- **Rules for innocent spouse relief.** You may get tax relief if you filed a joint return that had an *understatement of tax due* because your spouse gave erroneous information. You must establish that you had no knowledge of the information and had no reason to know. If you are successful in getting this relief, you may be able to avoid paying additional tax or get a refund if you did pay the tax and are then proven innocent.

- **Rules for separate liability.** You can use this rule for relief if you file a joint return that had an understatement of taxes due, in part because of an item of your spouse. You must be no longer married, be legally separated, or have lived apart from your spouse for the entire year to use this provision. You will have to prove that you had no knowledge of the item in question. No refund is possible with this type of relief.

◆ **Rules for equitable relief.** If you find that a return has an understatement or overpayment of tax and you don't qualify for innocent spouse relief, you can use this rule. The IRS will have to determine that it would be unfair to hold you liable for the underpayment or understatement. Refunds are possible under this rule.

If you think you may qualify for the relief, you must file your request within two years of the time the IRS first notifies you that tax is due. Don't try to do this one alone. Contact an attorney who specializes in these types of cases to be sure you get the protection you deserve.

If you decide to file under the innocent spouse relief rules, you should be aware of the following rules:

◆ You can't transfer assets between spouses so that one spouse owes all the taxes while the other holds all the assets as a means of preventing the IRS from seizing them. It won't work.

◆ The IRS is required to notify your ex-spouse and give him or her the opportunity to object to what you are filing under the innocent spouse rules. If you win your case, your ex-spouse is stuck with the entire tax bill in question, so he or she will certainly try to prove you wrong.

◆ While your application for relief is pending, collection attempts against you by the IRS must be suspended.

◆ If your application for relief is denied, you may make an appeal to the U.S. Tax Court. You have 90 days to file that appeal after you have received the notice of denial.

◆ You are entitled by the Taxpayers' Bill of Rights to know what the IRS is doing regarding collections for a tax bill owed jointly by you and an ex-spouse. You are also entitled to know how much of the bill has been paid.

Now that we've got the filing rules out of the way, let's take a look at how to make the best use of tax breaks once you're legally separated or divorced.

Spelling Out the Tax Breaks

Even after the divorce is legal and you can file as single or head of household, you may face some difficult filing choices if you still have joint assets or if children are in the picture. We'll explore the tax consequences of alimony and child support in the next two chapters.

How you will share tax breaks for things you're sharing, including the costs related to supporting your children, should be carefully spelled out in your divorce or separation maintenance decree. The more detailed your decree is on these issues, the fewer battles you'll be faced with after the divorce.

You can even lose the use of tax breaks if you don't carefully divide them. For example, you both could lose the use of the education tax credits if one of you claims the student as a dependent and the other one actually pays the tuition. You can work around this complication by carefully sorting out who is paying for what and being certain that a tax break is not being lost by the financial structure of the divorce.

Dividing Assets

How you divide assets can also have tremendous tax consequences, particularly when a home, rental property, and retirement assets are involved. Let's take a look at some of the issues you must consider as you work out the terms of your divorce or separation decree.

Tax Tips _____

Generally, the IRS doesn't consider the transfer of assets between spouses a taxable event. So, transferring ownership from one spouse to the other will not likely create the need to pay additional taxes.

Home

When it comes to dealing with your home, you have several options:

♦ Sell the house and split the proceeds.

♦ Have one spouse buy out the interest of the other spouse in the property.

♦ Continue to hold the property jointly, with the intention of selling the house in the future.

If you choose to sell the house and split the proceeds, you will be entitled to exclude up to $500,000 in gain on the sale. If one spouse buys the house from the other spouse, the spouse who continues to own the property will be able to exclude only up to $250,000 in gain on the property when it is later sold.

If one of the spouses decides to stay in the house and the divorced couple continues to hold the property jointly, part of the decree should include a very detailed arrangement about how the expenses will be paid, how much of the deductions each will be able to use, and how the proceeds will be split at the time of sale.

Couples who own two homes may be able to exclude up to $500,000 gain on the primary residence and $250,000 gain exclusion on the second home. To take advantage of this, one spouse must remain in the primary residence, while the other spouse moves into the second home or rental property. For this to be successful, the primary residence would have to be sold within three years because both spouses would need to have lived in the home for two of the last five years. The spouse who moves into the second home or rental property would have to live there at least two years before selling the property to take advantage of the gain exclusion. You can't use the exclusion more than once every two years.

> **IRS Idioms**
>
> I've been married and divorced so many times—I won't do it again. Next time, I'll just find a woman I don't like and give her my house.
>
> —Lewis Grizzard

If the second home was a rental property, any depreciation claimed after May 6, 1997, would have to be recaptured upon the sale. The depreciation would be subject to a 25 percent federal tax rate. Your divorce decree should spell out who will be responsible for what taxes and how any profits from these sales should be divided.

Retirement

Dividing up profits and taxes generated by homes sales can be complicated, but retirement assets can create even more complications. Retirement assets in an employer-sponsored defined-benefit or divided-contribution plan should be divided using a *Qualified Domestic Relations Order*, or *QDRO*. This primarily protects the spouse who is not employed by the employer that manages the funds, but it also helps the employed spouse to avoid tax penalties.

> **Taxing Terms**
>
> A **Qualified Domestic Relations Order (QDRO)** is a divorce order that instructs the administrator of a traditional pension plan or defined-contribution plan on how the assets of that plan will be divided between spouses. It's critical to have the order on file with administrators of any retirement plans that are in place at the time of divorce, to protect the ex-spouse who is not part of the plan.

Retirement assets can be left in the plan to be divided later or rolled out. When making this decision, you should consider which option will result in the lowest tax hit and the greatest benefit at retirement.

If retirement assets divided at divorce are not rolled over into an IRA, the money withdrawn will be taxed as current income. There are no tax penalties for withdrawals made from a defined-benefit or defined-contribution plan to satisfy a QDRO. Any funds withdrawn from an IRA because of a divorce may face a 10 percent tax penalty in addition to being taxed as current income.

Other Assets

Other assets can also create battles at divorce time. These include dividing stock options, stocks or bonds, and any other assets with significant market value. As it stands now, any stock options that are transferred to an ex-spouse based on a divorce decree are taxed as income at the time of transfer. Interest from savings bonds is also taxed at the time the ownership is transferred.

Jointly held stocks or assets that may have appreciated in value could result in a huge tax hit if they need to be sold or transferred to a different owner at the time of divorce to divide assets. The tax consequences of the sale should definitely be taken into consideration when dividing assets. Capital gain taxes for assets held more than 12 months are generally 20 percent.

Couples who own a small business face very tricky issues at the time of divorce. The greatest problem usually centers on valuing the business. Sometimes the couple will decide to maintain a joint interest in the business, but more commonly one spouse will buy out the interest of the other. Fortunately, the purchase of a business by a spouse or divorced spouse is tax-free.

Making Payments

Another major consideration is whether alimony or child support will be paid. Alimony is usually tax deductible for the spouse making the payments and is treated as taxable income for the spouse receiving them. Child support is nontaxable and nondeductible.

We'll look more closely at alimony in the next chapter and child support in Chapter 20.

The Least You Need to Know

♦ You must be considered legally separated or divorced under the laws of the state in which you reside to file as single or head of household (HOH) for federal tax purposes.

♦ If your separation or divorce is final on December 31, you can file as single or HOH for that entire year.

♦ If your divorce or separation is not yet legally final on December 31, you have the option of filing jointly or as married filing separately for that year. The tax consequences are tremendous, so make this decision carefully.

♦ How you plan to split assets, tax credits, and deductions must be carefully planned and spelled out in your separate maintenance or divorce decree to be certain you can use them in a way that best benefits both parties.

Chapter 19

Paying Your Ex

In This Chapter

- ◆ Alimony payment options
- ◆ Avoiding front loading and recapture
- ◆ Keeping payment records
- ◆ The pros and cons of lump sum payments

Paying your ex's living expenses can be an emotionally grating experience, but if you are an ex who stayed at home to take care of the kids during the marriage, those payments can be your lifeline. There is no question that the most contentious part of any divorce agreement is determining whether there will be alimony payments, how much they will be, and whether they will be tax deductible.

If you're able to get past the anger, there are ways of structuring alimony to minimize the tax bill for both sides, depending on your individual circumstances. Medical bills, insurance policies, homes, business assets, and other individual financial aspects of your married life can all play a role in the proper financial structure of alimony payments to minimize both spouses' tax bills and the pain of making those payments.

We'll take a look at the key issues that drive a decision of how to characterize alimony payments and how they can be paid. We'll review payments that can result in tax traps and even larger-than-expected tax bills.

Defining the Payments

Alimony is also known as spousal support, maintenance, or rehabilitative support—your state's laws determine the name for it. Before the 1970s, alimony was automatic with the dissolution of a marriage. Today, with a majority of families having two-income earners, alimony is no longer an automatic payment to the soon-to-be ex-wife. Instead, the following key factors help determine who will get alimony and how much he or she will get:

- Recipient's need

- Payer's ability to pay

- Age, health, and living standard of the couple

- Length of the marriage

- Each spouse's earning ability

- Recipient's nonmonetary contribution to the marriage

- Tax advantages and disadvantages

Revenue Ramblings

The number of men being awarded alimony is increasing. It is hard to find statistics, but according to the Virginia National Organization of Women website, between 5 and 10 percent of men in divorce cases are being awarded alimony. This is up from 3 percent just five years ago. Alimony is based on earned income levels and need. If the wife makes more than the husband, he can seek alimony at least temporarily.

If you and your soon-to-be ex-spouse can get along amicably enough to negotiate, you can determine the amount and length of the alimony payments; if you can't reach an agreement, the courts can order one. Some states have established financial schedules that judges can use to determine support, and others allow their judges full discretion. Whichever is the case, you probably won't be happy with what someone else determines is a fair arrangement, so it's best to try to work it out.

You could end up with no alimony at all if you leave it to the courts. Here are some general guidelines that today's courts follow when determining alimony payments:

- If the couple is married less than five years and has no children, alimony will probably be denied but could be given on a temporary basis.

- If there are children under school age, alimony will probably be ordered.

- If the marriage lasted at least eight years, alimony is likely to be awarded to ensure some continuity of living standard for both spouses.

- If the marriage lasted more than 10 years, alimony is likely to be ordered indefinitely or until the recipient dies, remarries, cohabitates, or no longer needs alimony.

Tax Tips

Legal fees paid to get a divorce generally aren't tax deductible. The one exception is legal fees paid to obtain alimony; these are deductible because they are spent to generate future income. If you are battling to get alimony, be sure your attorney separates out the fees related to the alimony fight so that you can deduct them.

Alimony is tax deductible for the person who pays it and is taxed as income for the person who receives it. However, the couple has the option to state in the divorce or separate maintenance decree that alimony will be non–tax deductible and, therefore, not taxable as income. We'll look at why a couple may chose to make payments non–tax-deductible later in this chapter. First, let's look at what type of payments are deductible as alimony and what ones are not.

Learning What's Deductible

Before you can start deducting alimony payments on your tax form, you must be sure that they are properly structured to satisfy the IRS. Alimony must be ordered under a divorce or separate maintenance decree. If a written decree does not exist, the payments will not be tax deductible. Here are some other key rules you must abide by to maintain the tax deductibility of the payments:

- Payments must end at the death of the recipient. There can't be any obligation to make payments to the recipient's estate.

- Payer and recipient cannot continue to file a joint return. (I can't imagine why anyone would want to do so.)

◆ Payments must be in cash for a definite period. Cash used to pay rent, mortgage, taxes, tuition, health insurance, or medical expenses of the recipient can qualify as part or all of the alimony payment.

◆ If you continue to live together, payments will not qualify as tax-deductible alimony.

◆ Payment is not designated as child support.

Alimony payments don't have to be in the form of direct cash payments to the ex-spouse. Other types of cash disbursements can also count toward alimony and be deductible:

◆ Premium payments on term or whole-life insurance policies provided the recipient owns the policy.

◆ Payments of the recipient's attorney's fees.

◆ Payments of rent or half the upkeep of a home co-owned by the payer and recipient. Upkeep costs can include the principal and interest payments of the mortgage, taxes, utilities, and insurance.

◆ Military allotments, in some cases. If you're in the military, check with a military advisor for more information.

Tax Tips

If you want to make additional payments into your IRA, you can consider alimony payments you receive as eligible compensation. Remember that you must have at least as much income as you contribute to an IRA.

If the marriage was annulled, payments may or may not be deductible. This depends on how your state treats alimony after an annulment. In some states, alimony is treated the same whether a marriage is dissolved by annulment or divorce, but others treat the two situations differently.

Some types of payments to an ex-spouse don't qualify as tax-deductible payments:

◆ Payments not required by the decree.

◆ Fair rental value of property owned by the payer and used by the recipient.

◆ Mortgage payments on property owned by the payer and used by the recipient. The payer may be able to use these payments as an itemized deduction, though.

◆ Payments made to the recipient as a beneficiary of the estate if the payer dies. The recipient must report the payments as income.

◆ Repayments of loans to your ex-spouse.

◆ Payments made before the written decree or agreement was in place, even if the payments become part of the decree.

◆ Payments made to your ex after he or she remarries.

◆ Payments made after your ex dies, even if required by the decree.

◆ Payments made as part of a property settlement.

Nothing is easy when it comes to divorce. As you can see, you must be very careful in structuring payments to be sure they are going to be tax deductible if you want them to be.

Splitting Year

The year your divorce or separation decree was put in place must also be taken into account. Decrees executed after 1984 have different rules than those executed before 1985.

These differences primarily affect whether a payment is treated as alimony or child support for tax purposes. While alimony is tax deductible, child support is not. Agreements before 1985 frequently grouped alimony and child support as one payment. If there is no designation of what amount is for child support and what amount is for alimony, the entire payment is tax deductible if the agreement was put in place before 1985.

This gives the payer a nice deduction, but it hurts the recipient because he or she would have to report the entire payment as income.

In decrees executed after 1984, child support can be inferred as part of the payments, even if not specifically designated; therefore, that part will not be tax deductible. In these cases, the recipient does not have to report the child support portion as income. For part of the payment to qualify as child support, there must be some contingency based on the child. These can include a change in payment when the child reaches a certain age or income level or when the child dies, marries, gets a job, or finishes school.

Decrees put in place before 1985 can be revised to reflect a split between alimony and child support.

Audit Alarm!

Child support payments are fixed, and any downward adjustment to support payments is considered a reduction in alimony rather than child support. Child support payments can be modified only by court order.

Avoiding the Tax Traps

You can go merrily along making payments and taking deductions, only to find out you are caught in a tax trap and will have to pay back taxes. Let's take a quick look at how that can happen and what you'll have to do to correct the situation.

Property Settlement

If you are giving your spouse property as part of the divorce decree, you cannot include that property as part of a tax-deductible alimony payment. For example, if you are giving your spouse the car, you can't write that off as alimony. This also includes assets such as trust transfers and business property.

Payments are considered property if any of the following pertain:

◆ The sum is fixed.

◆ They are not based on the payer's income.

◆ They continue after the recipient's death or remarriage.

◆ Property rights were given up in exchange for the payment.

> **Audit Alarm!**
>
> If the payer transfers an annuity contract to the recipient as part of an alimony payment, it will not be tax deductible. The recipient would need to report as income only the part of the payment that is higher than the original cost. To avoid this, the payer can keep the annuity and use the money to make alimony payments.

Front Loading

You might also find yourself in a tax trap if you pay a large part of the alimony in the first year and then reduce it greatly in subsequent years. This is a no-no, and it could result in the IRS declaring it *front loading*. For example, if your agreement specifies that you will give your spouse $50,000 in the first year to help him or her buy a house and then $20,000 for the next three years, that would be considered front loading. Your alimony payments must be in equal amounts over a set number of years to avoid the possibility of the IRS ruling it front loading.

Any payment that is reduced by more than $15,000 in subsequent years runs the risk of being called front loading by the IRS during the first three years of alimony payments.

> **Taxing Terms**
>
> **Front loading** may be determined by the IRS if a large portion of alimony payments is paid in the first year or two and later payments are reduced by more than $15,000 per year.

Recapture Rule

What happens if the IRS decides your payments were front loaded? You will be subject to the recapture rule, and the IRS will require you to report deducted alimony as income. The recipient who previously reported the income will be able to deduct the recaptured amount. Recapture might be required in the following instances:

♦ Change in divorce or separation decree or agreement

♦ Failure to make timely payments

♦ Reduction in your ability to provide support

♦ Reduction in your spouse's support needs

You can avoid the recapture trap in the following cases:

♦ Payments end because the payer or recipient dies

♦ Payments were made as part of a temporary support order

♦ Payments are based on a fixed portion or portions of income for three or more years

When determining alimony, be certain that you structure it carefully to avoid the risks of recapture if you plan to deduct the alimony.

Keeping Records

Both the payer and the recipient should keep careful records of the payments. As payer, you should keep a log that lists each payment and keep copies of the checks. If you make the payments by cash, be sure to get receipts. You'll need to keep these records for at least three years.

Recipients also need to carefully track payments because they will have to be reported as income. A log should be kept that includes the date and amount of payment, along with copies of the checks or money order. If the payment was made with cash, be sure to keep a copy of the receipt you signed.

Audit Alarm!

If you are receiving taxable alimony payments, be sure you are setting aside money to pay taxes on them. You should file quarterly estimated taxes because you will have to report the payments as income.

Getting a Lump

Some folks decide they don't want the continued contact that alimony requires and instead settle up using a lump-sum alimony payment. Choosing the lump-sum payment option involves advantages and disadvantages for both parties.

The advantages for the recipient includes the reduction of the risk that the payer will default on alimony payments in the future. Furthermore, the money can be used as a down payment on a new home or other big-ticket items. Plus, if the lump sum is designated as nontaxable alimony, it doesn't have to be reported as income.

The possible disadvantages of a lump-sum payment for recipients include these:

- You can't change your mind if you need more money later.
- You may end up taking less than you would have gotten in monthly payments.
- You won't have a regularly monthly income.
- You may invest the money badly and lose some or all of it.

The advantages for payers are primarily emotional. The lump sum means that they won't have to make monthly payments, which can grate on their nerves. They can make a clean break from the ex, provided there are no children. The total amount that needs to be paid will likely be less than the total monthly payments because it will be discounted to reflect the current day value of future payments and also will be adjusted for taxes.

The disadvantages, for payers, include these:

- They need to shell out a large sum of cash.
- If they pay the lump sum based on 10 years and their ex-spouse remarries or dies in two years, they will have paid more than if they had chosen the monthly alimony option.
- If the recipient gets a higher-paying job and the payer gets laid off or his salary is reduced, the lump sum could have been higher than necessary. While monthly payments can be adjusted based on income changes, lumps are not.

If you plan to deduct the payment, be certain that it's carefully structured to avoid being interpreted by the IRS as a property settlement or front-loading. If a lump sum payment is less than $15,000, there is no problem, but higher lump-sum payments are at risk of losing deductibility.

Non–Tax-Deductible Alimony

You may decide that you don't want to deduct the alimony payment. Let's take a quick look at some situations in which this might make sense.

If the tax bracket of the payer is lower than the tax bracket of the recipient, it might be to your advantage to consider non–tax-deductible alimony. For example, if the payer runs a business and has significant loses, he or she can choose not to make alimony deductible and save the recipient taxes.

Another situation that might make non–tax-deductible alimony a good solution arises when the recipient has large medical bills. By having to report alimony as income, the recipient's adjusted gross income could reduce the value of medical expense deductions because 7.5 percent of the AGI is subtracted from these expenses as an itemized deduction limit.

A third situation that might make non–deductible-alimony attractive occurs when the payer is a higher earner and has already lost most of his deductions because of itemized deduction limitations, while the recipient's earnings do not yet require a phaseout of itemized deductions. If the recipient must report alimony as income, itemized deductions could be phased out because the AGI would then be too high.

Tax Tips

Negotiating alimony payments that make sense for both you and your ex-spouse is much better than waiting for the court to settle the dispute. You could end up with a court ruling that satisfies neither you nor your ex-spouse.

In all these situations, non–tax-deductible alimony might make sense. If the couple carefully considers the tax advantages, both people may realize that it is better to agree that the alimony won't be deducted. They could instead agree to a lower alimony payment because of future tax savings.

As you can see, careful structuring of alimony in the divorce or separate maintenance decree can significantly improve your tax situation, while careless structuring can result in an ugly bill at tax time. Divorce is certainly an emotional time, and people often aren't in the mood to be conciliatory. If you can get past that, you can both reduce your tax bills and end up with more money in your pockets.

In the next chapter, we'll move on to tax issues involving child support. Unfortunately, this can get even more complicated than alimony because deductions, credits, and exemptions are all impacted by how child support is structured.

The Least You Need to Know

◆ Alimony is generally tax deductible for the payer and is reported as income by the recipient.

◆ Alimony doesn't have to be direct cash payments. Payments such as rent or mortgage can also count toward alimony.

◆ The structure of alimony must be carefully written out in a divorce or separate maintenance decree to make sure it will qualify as tax deductible.

◆ In some situations, the divorcing couple may decide to forego tax-deductible alimony.

20

Supporting Your Children

In This Chapter

- ◆ Custodial arrangements
- ◆ Claiming child exemptions
- ◆ How to make the most of medical deductions
- ◆ Maximizing your credits

When getting a separation or divorce, all the terms of the agreement *except child support* can be negotiated between the parties without court intervention. A judge will need to approve the child support arrangements, taking into consideration the needs of the child, each parent's earning and support ability, and the amount of time each parent spends with the child.

In this chapter, we'll take a look at the issues determining custody and its impact on filing status. We'll also review how you can share both the costs and the tax benefits in ways that will help you minimize your tax bill while doing what's best for your children.

Determining Custody

Custody used to be a simple arrangement. One parent had physical custody and the other parent had visitation rights. Parents were known as custodial parents or noncustodial parents.

Revenue Ramblings

States were required to establish statewide child support formulas when Congress passed the Family Support Act of 1988. The act was a welfare-reform bill that emphasized the enforcement of child support orders against delinquent parents. The bill also expanded job training and educational opportunities to reduce parents' reliance on welfare. In most cases, states must include automatic wage attachments in new or modified child support orders. The act also encourages the use of paternity tests to establish responsibility for child support. It requires the use of uniform guidelines in making support awards.

Today, as more parents share custody, the legal terminology is changing. Terms such as *joint custody*, *primary custody*, and *secondary custody* are becoming more common. Custody also has two additional components: legal custody and physical custody. Courts are commonly awarding joint custody, which allows parents to share legal or physical custody or both.

Taxing Terms

Legal custody gives the parent the right to make decisions about medical, educational, health, and welfare needs of the children.

Physical custody gives the parent physical control over the child.

Tax Tips

Both parents may be able to claim head of household status if they have more than one child, provided that they carefully structure their joint custody arrangements. Both parents would need to prove to the IRS that at least one child lives with them 51 percent of the time.

There's no question that keeping up two households will be much more expensive, making less money available to pay for expenses involved in raising a child. However, you can increase the amount of money that's available if you and your ex-spouse work together to find ways to minimize taxes and take advantage of all the deductions and credits available to both of you.

Filing Status

One of the first things you need to establish is the filing status of each party. The parent who has the child for 51 percent of the time can claim head of household, while the other parent must file as a single person.

Why is this such a big issue? For starters, the standard deduction for a head of household is $6,650, while a single taxpayer's standard deduction is only $4,550. Besides the more than $2,000 deduction advantage, head of household filers have fewer limits on their abilities to take advantage of various tax breaks than single filers.

If you have two or more children, rather than fight for primary custody of all children, think about sharing the arrangements in a way that allows both of you to file as heads of household.

Making Claims

Once you get filing status out of the way, you'll need to determine who gets to claim exemptions for each child. Sometimes the noncustodial parent will pay higher child support so that he or she can claim the child or children at tax time. In these cases, the custodial parent must sign IRS Form 8332, "Release of Claim to Exemption for Child of Divorced or Separated Parents."

Parents who share custody can alternate years that they claim exemptions for the children. This can be based on a preset agreement or can be flexible so that the parent who will get the greatest tax benefit claims the children in any one year.

The flexible arrangement can be particularly helpful if one parent has widely fluctuating income because of commissions or other business earning arrangements. In some years he or she may need the exemption, while in other years income is lower and the exemption won't truly provide a tax savings.

Whatever you decide to do, you will have to make some kind of yearly report to the IRS when you file taxes. If your divorce or separate maintenance decree specifies that one parent will always be able to claim the exemption, then you don't have to file Form 8332. Instead, you can provide a copy of the decree's cover page, the page that states that you can claim the child, and the signature page with the other spouse's signature and date of the agreement.

If a parent gives up the rights to use the exemption for a number of years on a Form 8332, the person taking the exemption must file only the original Form 8332 the first year of the agreement. After that, copies of the form can be filed for every year in which agreement stands.

Deducting Medical Care

Medical expenses can be claimed by either parent and must be based on who actually paid the expenses. Remember that medical expenses can be deducted only if they exceed 7.5 percent of the adjusted gross income.

If medical expenses are high enough, you can decide to allocate them to the parent with the lower income so that a greater percentage of the medical expenses can be written off.

Let's take a look at how this works for a divorced couple. We'll assume that one person has an AGI of $60,000 and that the other's AGI is $30,000. One of their children had extensive medical expenses totaling $10,000. The person earning $60,000 would have to subtract $4,500, which represents 7.5 percent of income. The allowable deduction would be $5,500. The person earning less would need to subtract only $2,250 and could deduct $7,750.

> **Tax Tips**
>
> Both parents can take deductions for medical expenses that they actually paid. Remember the limits, though. You can deduct only medical expenses that exceed 7.5 percent of your AGI.

A divorced couple who works together to maximize tax breaks could allocate medical expenses differently in that tax year so that the greater tax deduction can be used. They can then shift other expenses so that the share of overall child support remains the same.

Credit Problems

Tax credits are another area in which parents who work together to maximize tax breaks will do much better after a divorce than parents who don't. Let's take a look at how the tax rules impact child-related credits after divorce or separation.

Earned Income Credit

The Earned Income Credit, which we discussed in Chapter 11, is primarily for people with low incomes. If you have one qualifying child and are single, your 2002 income must be less than $29,201 to claim the credit. If you have two or more qualifying children, income cannot exceed $33,178. Income levels are adjusted each year for inflation.

You may think that you can just let the lower-earning parent claim the child to get the credit. Well, it's not that easy. The 2001 tax law requires divorced parents to meet different criteria:

- The credit can be used by the parent with whom the child lived the longest during the year.

- If the child lives 50 percent of the time with each parent, the parent with the highest AGI must get the credit.

Sharing custody can certainly complicate things if one parent earns less and could take advantage of the credit. If parents share the child 50/50, the parent who earns the most would have to be the one to take the test for the credit—and most likely would fail to get it. If the Earned Income Credit is a possibility for the parent with the lower income, you may want to be sure that this parent has custody 51 percent of the time.

Of course, this will also mean that the higher earner can't claim the child as an exemption, so you shouldn't make a tax decision based on any single aspect of the tax code. Negotiating a good agreement means looking at your entire financial picture and figuring out what combination of exemptions, deductions, and credits will net both of you the lowest tax bill. Tax savings can be offset within provisions of alimony or child support agreements.

Child Care Credit

The Child and Dependent Care Credit is another tax credit that's available only to the custodial parent (read Chapter 9 for more details about this credit). Employed custodial parents of a dependent child under the age of 13 can take this credit for child-care expenses that were incurred so that the parent could earn an income. The credit begins to phase out if your adjusted gross income exceeds $75,000 as a single parent.

If you are divorced, you may still qualify for the credit even if you aren't the custodial parent, provided that the following conditions are satisfied:

◆ One or both parents had custody of the child for more than half of the year.

◆ One or both parents provided more than half of the child's support for the year.

Finally, one of these two situations must also exist for the noncustodial parent to claim the credit:

◆ The custodial parent signed Form 8332 agreeing not to claim the child's exemption for the year.

◆ The noncustodial parent provided at least $600 for the child's support and can claim the child's exemption under a pre-1985 decree.

As you sort out who will pay what child expenses, be sure to remember the child-care tax credit and what expenses are allowed. You can maximize the use of this tax credit by carefully allocating allowable expenses to the parent who will use this credit.

Child Tax Credit

Only the parent who claims the child as a dependent can take advantage of the Child Tax Credit. Don't forget that the credit isn't available for people whose modified AGI is over $75,000 as a single person or head of household. You can learn more about this credit in Chapter 9.

Education Credits

Divorced couples have a bit more flexibility when it comes to who gets to take the Hope Credit or the Lifetime Learning Credit for the children's tuition. (You can learn more about these credits in Chapter 14.) Only the parent who claims the child as a dependent can use this credit.

But you must actually pay the tuition to make use of this tax break.

You may be able to get your ex to pay more tuition if you offer to waive your rights to the dependent exemption using Form 8332 during the college years. Another way to handle this is to adjust spousal support or another deduction so that the spouse with the exemption can actually pay the tuition.

Basically, taking advantage of tax breaks and deductions related to your children after separation or divorce comes down to working together to figure out your best tax-savings options while still doing the things you want to do for your children. Rather than fight each other and risk losing some tax advantages, sit down with a tax specialist as you work out your child support arrangements, and be certain you are not paying more to the tax man just so you can satisfy some need for revenge.

Now that we've finished our trip through Splitsville, we'll journey to a more positive aspect of life: your own business. The last part of the book reviews the tax breaks and deductions available to small business owners.

The Least You Need to Know

- Custody goes by many names, including physical custody, legal custody, joint custody, primary custody, and secondary custody.

- Custodial arrangements can impact your ability to take various tax credits and deductions.

- Be sure that filing status is considered when drawing up your divorce or separation agreements.

- Most tax breaks can be used only by the parent who has the right to claim the child as a dependent. This right doesn't have to be the same each year. Parents can share the right in any way they determine, as long as they file the right form.

Part 7

Taking a Business Trip

You've taken the plunge and started a new business working from your home. We'll take a trip through the tax code to find out what you can deduct and how you go about doing it.

We'll review rules for using your home, using your car, buying new equipment, insuring your business assets, and handling other operating expenses. We'll even look at your options for organizing the business.

Chapter **21**

Structuring Your Business

In This Chapter

- ◆ Going solo with sole proprietorships
- ◆ Working with a business partner
- ◆ Limiting your business liability
- ◆ Incorporating strategies
- ◆ Deciding which option is best for you

Your first act as a small business owner will be to decide how to structure your business. Don't worry—this decision isn't cast in stone, but it's necessary so you know how to keep records and file taxes.

We'll take a look at the various legal structures for small businesses—sole proprietorships, limited liability partnerships, and S and C corporations—and then compare the tax implications of each. However you decide to structure your business, though, be sure to seek legal and tax advice so you know that you've made the right choice for your individual circumstances.

Sole Proprietor

If you are just starting up a new business and are a single owner, a sole proprietorship is the easiest form of business for both tax purposes and record keeping. As a matter of fact, the IRS will assume a sole proprietorship if your business has only one owner unless you've actually incorporated the business under state law. In other words, you don't have to do anything legally or financially to get started as a sole proprietor in the eyes of the federal government.

Revenue Ramblings

Self-employed people are a major economic force in the United States today, with more than 70 percent of all businesses now in these ranks, according to the U.S. Department of Commerce. Most self-employed folks who don't hire others are sole proprietors, with about 6 percent incorporated and 5 percent set up as partnerships. The American Association of Home-Based Businesses reports that more than 24 million Americans run home-based small businesses.

In fact, the sole proprietorship isn't a taxable entity. All your business assets and liabilities belong directly to you—the business owner. You report the business on a Schedule C, "Profit or Loss from Business," or Schedule C-EZ, "Net Profit from Business." Both forms actually become part of your individual tax return. The net profit or loss is reported on the first page of your 1040, and you pay taxes on the income based on your current individual tax rate.

You also must complete Schedule SE, "Self-Employment Tax." You use this form to calculate your Social Security and Medicare taxes. Social Security and Medicare taxes total 15.3 percent. If you work for someone else, half is paid by you and half by your employer. As a self-employed person, you must foot the entire bill, but you can write off half of it as an adjustment to income. Because you don't have an employer to pull taxes out of your payroll, you'll need to pay quarterly estimated taxes. These quarterly payments include your anticipated income tax and self-employment tax with Form 1040-ES. If you have employees, you'll also need to file periodic forms to pay their payroll taxes.

Audit Alarm!

The greatest downside of sole proprietorship is that it isn't a separate legal entity and all debts or claims are made against the individual who owns the business. To protect your personal assets, you may want to get business liability insurance. I discuss insurance options in Chapter 25.

Other tax forms that could come into play for sole proprietors in specific types of businesses include Schedule F, "Profit and Loss from Farming," and Schedule E, "Supplemental Income and Loss." It's obvious who needs to use Schedule F: farmers. Schedule E is for people who own real estate rentals but otherwise are not running a real estate business.

Partnerships

If you are starting a small business with one or more additional people, you would more than likely want to set up the business as a partnership. The IRS considers any business with more than one owner a partnership unless you have it incorporated under state law or you elect to be taxed as a corporation by filing IRS Form 8832, "Entity Classification Election." We'll be talking more about corporate tax issues later in this chapter.

Partnerships file their own tax returns using IRS Form 1065, "Partnership Return." These forms are actually information returns that show income, deductions, and other tax-related business information. This return must also include the names and addresses of each partner and each partner's distributive share of taxable income. The return must be signed by a *general partner.* If the partnership receives no income and doesn't pay or incur any expenses in any particular tax year, Form 1065 does not have to be filed.

> **Taxing Terms**
>
> **General partners,** who actively run the business, are subject to the same personal liability for partnership debts and claims as sole proprietors, even if the act that caused the claim to be filed was carried out by one of the other partners. Be careful who you partner with, especially if you plan to be the general partner with all others being limited partners.
>
> **Limited partners** don't take an active role in the management of the partnership. Their liability is limited to their investment in the business and any obligations they may have to make additional investments.

In addition to filing the information Form 1065, partnerships must file a Schedule K-1, "Shareholder's Share of Income, Credits, Deductions, etc.," for each partner. This form is used to report the income or loss of each of the partners, which will then be taxed as part of each partner's individual tax return. Like a sole proprietorship, the partnership itself is not a tax entity. Even if the partnership doesn't actually distribute the cash and decides to hold some of the money for future company needs, the individual partners—not the partnership—will still have to pay taxes on the income.

Partnerships are the most flexible form of ownership if more than one person is involved in the business because income and losses can be distributed as determined by the owners, such as 40 percent to one owner and 60 percent to the second owner. Any split is okay, as long as it is based on a business purpose and not solely for the purpose of tax avoidance. Other business entities, such as corporations, must distribute their income and losses based on the percentage of ownership or investment in the business. We'll talk more about this later when we explore the other types of business entities.

Partnerships offer a major tax advantage for new businesses because you can write off losses. Generally, new businesses have losses rather than net profits due to start-up expenses and the time it takes to build a client or customer base. Partnerships provide a mechanism to write off these losses against other income. There is one catch, though: You can't write off a loss that exceeds your personal investment in the business; however, if you increase your investment in future years, you can then write off the loss.

> **Tax Tips** _____
>
> Tax issues are only one small part of what needs to be considered when you form a partnership. You must also consider major legal issues, including how the partnership will be sold, if necessary; what happens if one of the partners dies or wants out of the business; and other key operating and insurance issues. You should set up a partnership only with the assistance of an attorney and financial advisor, to be sure you are protecting your interests as well as the interests of the business and your other partners.

Sometimes families establish partnerships for their business. This can be a great way to minimize a family's tax burden by paying some of the income as salaries to children partners. However, the IRS is acutely aware of the potential tax-avoidance schemes that such partnerships can provide and has set up some strict rules for families who go into business together.

Family members are recognized as partners by the IRS only if one of the two following situations applies:

♦ **Capital is a material income-producing factor and the partners all got their ownership interest by buying into the business, even if it was as a gift from another family member. The family member must also have a controlling interest in the business.** Basically, this means that you can't make your toddlers business partners unless they truly can make business decisions. And you certainly don't want a five-year-old deciding what products to buy— you'd probably end up with lots of candy.

♦ **Capital is not a material income-producing factor and the partners joined together in good faith to conduct a business.** This condition covers partnerships that are primarily service businesses whose income is in the form of fees, commissions, or other compensation for personal services. Again, it precludes you from setting up a business with your 3-year-old as a partner because each partner has to actively participate in the business.

Partnerships face the same liability issues as sole proprietorships because the managing owners can be fully liable for any debt or claims. The rest of the business structures limit the liability of the owners.

Limited Liability Companies

A partnership or sole proprietorship can be set up as a limited liability company (LLC). This is actually a hybrid somewhere between a corporation and a partnership or sole proprietorship. An LLC is a state entity organized under state laws, so any protections against liabilities depend on the state in which the company is formed. However, generally an LLC is given the same protection from liability given to traditional corporations.

LLCs are treated as partnerships or sole proprietorships (if only one person owns and runs the company) when it comes to filing federal income tax forms, unless a Form 8832 is filed to classify them as corporations. State laws for filing tax forms vary on a state-by-state basis.

While limited liability may sound great because they protect individuals from many business liabilities, when it comes to borrowing money, sole proprietors or partners may still be required to give personal guarantees to get the money, especially if the business is first getting started. Few financial institutions will make loans to new businesses that don't have much in the way of business assets.

> **Revenue Ramblings**
>
> In 1994, all the big accounting firms, including Arthur Anderson, changed from general partnerships to limited liability partnerships (LLPs). Anderson partners will soon find out how well this structure protects them as Enron shareholders and creditors who seek some relief from their losses file lawsuits against them.

Liability limitation may be helpful when it comes to protecting yourself or your partners from claims of malpractice or other related issues. Again, this will depend on your state and how it sets up its LLCs.

Corporations—C and S

Your greatest liability protection as a small business owner comes from using the business structure known as a corporation. A corporation is a separate legal entity, and individuals are protected from getting sued for the corporation's actions or facing collections from the corporation's creditors.

Many legal advisors recommend that a sole proprietor or partners incorporate if the business is particularly "risky"—in other words, if it faces a strong possibility of being sued. Corporate structures can also make it easier to raise needed investment capital to grow the business.

There are actually two types of corporations for tax purposes—C and S. The C corporation is the standard kind of corporation that most large business are structured as, and it is subject to corporate income tax. A small company just getting started can avoid corporate taxation by filing with the IRS as an S corporation. The S corporation is strictly an IRS designation that you elect and isn't a unique legal entity. Whether you file as a C corporation or seek the special IRS designation as an S corporation, it is still the same legal entity.

All corporations have a board of directors (even if it's just you, your wife, and your children) and shares of stock that represent ownership. Most small businesses have privately held stock that is not traded on any public exchange.

To qualify as an S corporation you must meet all of the following conditions:

♦ Your corporation must be organized under the laws of the United States or one of its states or territories that is taxed as a corporation under local law.

♦ All shareholders must agree to the S corporation election.

♦ Your corporation may have only one class of stock. Larger corporations may have *common and preferred stock* for example.

♦ Your corporation may not have more than 75 shareholders (corporations formed before 1997 were limited to 35 shareholders). So S corporations are only for small business entities.

♦ Shareholders may not include a nonresident alien or a nonhuman entity, such as another corporation or partnership. There are some

> **Taxing Terms**
>
> **Common stock** is a portion of ownership in a corporation that includes the right to vote on key corporation issues and entitles the owner to share in the company's success, usually through dividends or increase in stock value.

> **Taxing Terms**
>
> **Preferred stock** usually has a specific dividend that must be paid prior to the dividends paid to common stock holders. This type of stock usually has no voting rights. If the company fails, these shareholders will get their share of the assets before common stock holders.

exceptions to this. A shareholder can be a trust or estate authorized as an S corporation under tax laws. Also, certain tax-exempt organizations, such as qualified pension plans, profit-sharing plans, or stock bonus plans, can be shareholders.

The S corporation is treated similarly to partnerships for tax purposes. Profits and losses are passed through to the owners and taxed at their individual income tax rates. The key difference when it comes to taxes is that the profits and losses of an S corporation must be allocated based on actual stock ownership. Remember, partnerships have more flexibility because their distributions can be done by any formula the business owners decide makes business sense. For example, if one partner has a lot of cash to put up front while the other partner is primarily offering his or her unique knowledge, a partnership could more easily adjust for this difference.

Audit Alarm!

The biggest disadvantage for a C corporation is that income is taxed twice, once at the corporate level and again at the individual level for any distributions to the corporation's stockholders. In other words, if you are a small business owner, you could end up paying taxes twice on the same money. That's certainly not a good tax strategy!

C corporation income is taxed twice: once at the corporate level and again at the individual level for any distributions to stockholders. Business write-offs and salaries may offset the negative of double taxation, though. Business owners are allowed to pay themselves a reasonable salary (reasonable based on industry standards within the industry that the company operates) and avoid the corporate tax level on the money paid as salary.

I'm not going to delve deeply into C corporations because their tax rules are very complicated and go beyond the scope of this book. If you're thinking of establishing your business as a C corporation, you definitely should seek good legal and financial advice—don't try to go it alone!

Just so that you have an idea of corporate tax rates, here's a table that shows the current rates:

2002 C Corporation Tax Rates

Taxable Income Over	But Not Over	Tax Rate
$0	$50,000	15%
$50,000	$75,000	25%
$75,000	$100,000	34%

continues

2002 C Corporation Tax Rates   (continued)

Taxable Income Over	But Not Over	Tax Rate
$100,000	$335,000	39%
$335,000	$10,000,000	34%
$10,000,000	$15,000,000	35%
$15,000,000	$18,333,333	38%
$18,333,333	—	35%

Making Your Choice

Now that you know the choices for structuring your business, let's look at what might make sense for you. Of course, every situation is unique, and I strongly suggest that you seek guidance from a legal and financial advisor to figure out what is best for your company.

Most small business structures are taxed at your individual tax rates, even S corporations, but they offer different levels of liability protection. The key differences as you move from sole proprietor to partnership or corporation is how earnings and distributions are treated for tax purposes. Also, when you get to the highest level, a traditional C corporation, you must pay both corporate and individual taxes on dividends paid to shareholders.

Basically, if you're a sole proprietor and want to keep things as simple as possible, there are very few tax advantages to organizing as anything other than a sole proprietor. Your lawyer may see some reasons to incorporate from a legal perspective if you are subject to frequent lawsuits. If that's the case, a limited liability company might be the best solution for you, but be sure you consider your state laws and state tax provisions for LLCs before going that route.

> **IRS Idioms**
>
> The difference between getting somewhere and nowhere is the courage to make an early start. The fellow who sits still and does just what he is told will never be told to do big things.
>
> —Charles M. Schwab

A sole proprietor may consider establishing an S corporation as a way to limit liability, but taxes will never be simple to file again; be certain that you understand the liability advantages before taking that step. Although you may be able to pay yourself a salary and avoid employment taxes on your share of corporate income above a reasonable wage, you need to be certain that the tax savings are worth the additional legal, tax, and other financial expenses of maintaining corporate status. Perhaps business liability insurance, which is discussed in Chapter 25, would be more cost-effective and offer the protection you need.

If you have partners, setting up as a limited liability partnership (LLP) probably makes the most sense. It provides the maximum amount of flexibility, allows a single level of taxation, and gives you liability protection as well. Organizing as a corporation is a good choice if you plan to produce or manufacture a product and want to build the company into a major nationwide or worldwide business. You don't have to make the decision right away. You can wait a year or two or elect S corporation status initially before taking the plunge into the more complicated tax structure that requires you to pay taxes twice.

This overview of business structures is intended solely for the purpose of explaining various tax strategies. You definitely should seek advice from an attorney or tax advisor before making major business decisions, and take it slow. You might think that it sounds exciting to be incorporated or that you'll look more professional, but that's not necessarily the case. Before making a decision, make sure you know not only the legal costs of setting one up, but also the continuing annual costs, both legally and financially.

> **Tax Tips**
>
> The government runs two excellent websites for small business owners. One is the main site for the Small Business Administration (www.sba.gov), and the second is a website for women business owners (www.sbaonline. sba.gov/ womeninbusiness). Both websites offer a wealth of information about starting up and running a small business.

The Least You Need to Know

- The first order of business when you start your own company is to figure out what business structure you want to use.

- If you are planning to run your business alone, you can choose one of three business structures: sole proprietorship, limited liability company, or corporation. Be sure you understand the legal, financial, and tax ramifications before taking the plunge.

- If you plan to start the business with one or more additional people, you can select a partnership, limited liability company, or corporation.

- There are two types of corporations: S and C. A C corporation is the only type of business structure whose income is taxed twice, once at the corporate level and a second time on the money distributed to its shareholders. The income of an S corporation is passed through to its owners and taxed based on their individual income tax rates.

Chapter 22

Home-Based Business Deductions

In This Chapter

- ◆ Determining whether your home qualifies
- ◆ Calculating what part of your home is used for business purposes
- ◆ Deducting home expenses
- ◆ Avoiding capital gain tax when you sell your house

You may be able to cut your tax bill considerably if you write off a portion of your home as a business expense. However, because your home is a potentially substantial write-off, the IRS requires taxpayers to jump some pretty high bars to qualify for it.

Don't be afraid to attempt this jump, but be careful that you do meet the qualifications. If the IRS questions you, the onus is on you to prove that your home office or home-based business passes the test.

Let's first take a look at the strict rules, and then we'll review how you go about figuring your deduction. We'll also discuss the impact on the future sale of your home if you choose to deduct a portion of it for use in your home-based business.

Meeting the Qualifications

It's test time again! For your home office to qualify as a business expense, it must pass the following tests:

1. Your use of the business part of your home must be:

    ♦ Exclusive (we'll discuss exceptions shortly)

    ♦ Regular

    ♦ For your trade or business

AND

2. The business part of your home must be *one* of the following:

    ♦ Your principal place of business

    ♦ A place where you meet or deal with patients, clients, or customers in the normal course of your trade or business

    ♦ A separate structure (not attached to your home) that you use in connection with your trade or business

Tax Tips

Employees can use part of their home for business, but to qualify for a deduction as a business expense, you must pass additional tests. See Chapter 8 for more information about how to qualify for this tax break.

Tax Tips

Your home office does not have to be a separate room. You can even use part of a room that is not even marked off by a permanent partition, but it does have to be identifiable as only for business use. Permanent furnishings and equipment can certainly help make that case for you.

Now that you know the official rules, we'll break each of them down one by one.

Exclusive Use

This is the hardest test to pass. You must use a specific part of your home only for your trade or business. You can't use the room or area even for a short time to do personal finances or allow your kids to play on your computer. Yup, that's right. No games allowed. Buy yourself a second computer for personal use if you want to be sure your home office will pass the test.

You will fail the test if you use the area in question for both business and personal purposes, even if the personal purposes are at night after your normal business hours. That's right, it's not very fair. If you ran a business outside the home and used the office for parties at night, the costs of operating the office would still be a business expense. And everyone who works outside the home takes care of some personal business at their office, but the IRS doesn't give a hoot about any of these excuses—if you want to claim a portion of your home for business, it must be exclusively used for your business.

Exclusion Exceptions

Okay, now that I've said how strict the IRS is, it's time come clean and admit that it allows two exceptions to the exclusive use rule:

 ◆ You use part of your home for the storage of inventory or product samples.

 ◆ You use part of your home as a day-care facility. Day-care facilities can claim all the rooms used during the time the facility is in operation. This can include a kitchen or living room that is used for personal purposes when the facility is closed. To determine the home business use, you calculate the deduction based on the number of hours per day and the number of days per year the rooms are used for the business. We'll take a closer look at how to do that later in this chapter.

You can use part of your home for the storage of inventory or product samples and claim expenses for the business use of your home even if the room in which you store these things is not exclusively used for business. To qualify, you must pass these four tests:

 ◆ You keep the inventory or product samples for use in your trade or business.

 ◆ Your trade or business is the wholesale or retail selling of products.

 ◆ Your home is the only fixed location of your trade or business.

 ◆ You use the storage space on a regular basis.

 ◆ The space you use is an identifiably separate space suitable for storage.

Exclusive use is the strictest test; now let's look at some of the others.

Regular Use

The Regular Use Test requires that you use a specific area of your home for business on a continuing basis. If you use the business area of your home only occasionally or incidentally, you will not pass this part of the test.

Trade or Business Use

You must actually be using part of your home in relation to a trade or business to pass this test. You can't use the space for other profit-seeking activity, such as managing your portfolio, unless you are actually a broker or dealer.

Principal Place of Business

Your home office must also be your principal place of business. To pass this test, you must consider the following factors:

- The relative importance of the activities performed at each location. For example, if you are a doctor who works at several hospital locations and a clinic, you would need to determine which location has the greatest importance to the business operation.

- If the relative importance factor does not determine your principal place of business, you can also consider the time spent at each location. If more than one place has the same relative importance, then time spent at each location is considered to pick the place of business.

Revenue Ramblings

Believe it or not, the current tests for determining principal place of business are easier to pass than they were before 1999, in part because Congress had not carefully defined "principal place of business." In a 1983 case, the Supreme Court ruled that a doctor who spent 80 percent of his time at hospitals, even though the hospitals did not provide him an office, could not write off the home office because his primary business activities were done outside the home. This ruled out home office deductions for many people, including those in sales and trades, such as plumbers and electricians.

You can declare your home office as a "principal place of business," provided that it is the primary place to perform administrative and management activities for your trade or business. To qualify, however, there must be no other fixed location where you perform these same functions. If you do some of these things in your car or at a hotel when away from home, that's okay, as long as it isn't substantial.

Administrative or Management Activities

Many activities qualify as administrative or management functions. Here are some key examples:

- ◆ Billing customers, clients, or patients

- ◆ Keeping books and records

- ◆ Ordering supplies

- ◆ Setting up appointments

- ◆ Forwarding orders or writing reports

You don't have to do all administrative and management activities at home. Some of these activities can be done by you or others outside the home, and you can still take the home office deduction. The IRS allows the following exceptions:

- ◆ You have others conduct your administrative or management activities at locations other than your home. (For example, another company does your billing from its place of business.)

- ◆ You conduct administrative or management activities at places that are not fixed locations of your business, such as in a car or a hotel room.

- ◆ You occasionally conduct minimal administrative or management activities at a fixed location outside your home.

- ◆ You conduct substantial nonadministrative or nonmanagement business activities at a fixed location outside your home. (For example, you meet with or provide services to customers, clients, or patients at a fixed location of the business outside your home.)

- ◆ You have suitable space to conduct administrative or management activities outside your home, but you choose to use your home office for those activities instead.

Running More Than One Trade or Business

If you run more than one trade or business, you must test for the home office deduction separately for each trade or business activity. Your home office may be the principal place of business for more than one activity. But you could lose the home office deduction if the room is used for one business that qualifies and another that does not. For example, if you are a full-time teacher who grades tests at home in your home office, that office does not qualify for a deduction even if you are running a second business from that office and the second business does qualify.

Place to Meet Patients, Clients, or Customers

If you meet or deal with patients, clients, or customers in your home in the normal course of your business, even though you also carry on business at another location, you can deduct your expenses for the part of your home used exclusively and regularly for business if you meet the following tests:

- ◆ You physically meet with patients, clients, or customers on your premises. Phone calls, occasional meetings, e-mails, and faxes don't count to help you meet this test.

- ◆ Your use of your home is substantial and integral to the conduct of your business.

Doctors, dentists, attorneys, and other professionals who maintain offices in their homes usually can meet this requirement. You must meet the rules for exclusive and regular use, but your home does not have to be your principal place of business to write off a home business if you use a part of it to meet patients, clients, or customers.

Separate Structure

You can deduct expenses for a separate free-standing structure, such as a studio, garage, or barn, if you use it exclusively and regularly for your business. The structure does not have to be your principal place of business or a place where you meet patients, clients, or customers.

If you believe you have passed all these tests and want to deduct your home office, let's look at how you compute your deductions. First, I'll show you how to calculate the business share; then we'll explore the expenses you can deduct.

Computing Your Business Share

You can use two different methods to calculate the business share of your home expenses. Either is acceptable, so your best bet is to figure your share using both methods and then choose the one that will give you the greatest tax break.

One method is to total the number of rooms in the house and then total the number of rooms used exclusively for the business. You then divide the number of rooms used by the total number of rooms to find your business use percentage. You can only use this method if all the rooms in your house are similar in size.

For example, if you have a nine-room home, all rooms are of similar size, and you use one for business purposes, here's how you figure out the deductible percentage:

$$\frac{1}{9} \; = \; 11.1\%$$

You then multiply this percentage by your total home office expenses.

The second acceptable method is to calculate the usage based on square footage devoted to your office. You calculate this by adding up the space used for the office and then dividing it by the total square footage of the house. For example, if you use 150 square feet for your office and your house totals 1,500 square feet, you figure out your deductible portion this way:

$$\frac{150}{1,500} \; = \; 10\%$$

Again, you then multiply the percentage by your total home office expenses. Whichever gives you a higher tax break is the one you should choose.

Day-care providers have to perform a more complicated calculation. Not only must they calculate the portion of the home used, but they also must calculate the percentage of time it is used. The extra work is worth it, however, because they can use the rooms for personal purposes when the day-care facility is not in operation.

Let's practice with an example. We'll assume that Sally keeps her day-care facility open 10 hours per day for 5 days a week, or 50 hours. The total number of hours in a week is 168 (7×24). Sally has 10 rooms in her house (4 bedrooms, 2 bathrooms, a living room, a kitchen, a dining room, and a den), and she uses 5 of them for day care (the living room, the kitchen, a bathroom, the dining room, and a bedroom), or 50 percent of the house. She has a total of $10,000 in expenses for her home office. Here's the calculations she'll need to do to figure out her deduction:

Multiply 50% (percentage of use) $\times$ $10,000 (total home office expenses) = $5,000

Calculate the percentage of use like this:

$$\frac{50}{168} \; = \; 29.7\%$$

Multiply 29.7% $\times$ $5,000 = $1,485

Now that you know how to calculate your home office percentage, let's look at what qualifies as deductible home office expenses.

Deducting Home Office Expenses

A lot of expenses qualify for home office use. Expenses directly related to the business can be written off 100 percent. Other expenses are subject to the eligible percentage calculation you decide to use. These include your mortgage interest or rent, real estate taxes, home insurance, utilities, services, repairs, and decorating. There are limits to these costs, though.

The principal payment of your mortgage does not qualify as a home office expense. Your principal is written off through depreciation of the cost of your home. Taxes or assessments collected for the purpose of local benefits such as streets, sidewalks, or water and sewers systems cannot be deducted as expenses, but they may qualify as part of your depreciation calculation, which is discussed shortly.

If you have a second mortgage or home equity line of credit, this interest may be deductible, but there are limitations. Your mortgage interest is deductible only up to a mortgage amount of $1 million. Any interest on a loan over that amount is not deductible. Interest on a home equity line of credit is eligible only up to a loan amount of $100,000.

Taxing Terms

Depreciation is an expense that allows you to deduct for the wear and tear of using the property. We'll take a closer look at how to figure depreciation on the home later in this chapter.

Tax Tips

High-income earners get a special benefit here. If your income is high enough that all your itemized deductions have been phased out, you can still use your mortgage interest to calculate your home office deduction.

Although home mortgage interest is deductible as an itemized expense, using a portion of the interest as a deduction when calculating your home office expenses can offer more tax savings. You'll be reducing not only your adjusted gross income, but also all the net income that will be taxed for self-employment taxes toward Social Security and Medicare.

You can't write off the cost of your first phone line because it is assumed that you will use it for personal purposes. However, if you pay for a second phone line or use a cell phone for your business, you can write off those expenses. In either case you can always write off long distance calls for business purposes.

You can write off 100 percent of any of the eligible expenses that can be directly tied to the business. All other expenses must be determined using one of the methods for figuring business proportion.

Repairs

Repairs to the home may or may not be deductible in the year paid. A major improvement, such as a new roof or new heating system, would need to be added to your depreciation calculations and deducted as part of that calculation. Minor repairs such as patching a roof leak can be added to the total home office expenses that will be used in the proportion calculation. If you must repair something that is specific to your home office and does not benefit the rest of the home, you can write off 100 percent of that repair.

Decorating

Decorating a room for home office purposes is also a deductible expense that can be written off 100 percent as a business expense. So, if you need to paint the room, put up window dresses, or put up drywall, all costs could be deductible, provided that the work is directly related to the home office use.

Insurance

Insurance that you take directly for the business is 100 percent deductible, but you can deduct only a portion of your homeowner's or renters insurance. Just add the cost of your homeowner's or renters insurance to the total home office expenses that will be subject to eligible percentage calculation.

Utilities

If you think your business uses a greater percentage of some utilities than the room usage or space usage calculation method you choose, you may be able to justify a higher percentage for those utilities. You may need to show the IRS why you believe that your business uses more of the utility, such as electricity, so be sure you can prove that you have used a reasonable estimate of your deductible expense.

Depreciation

Now that we've got the easiest ones out of the way, let's take a look at depreciation. This allows you to deduct for the wear and tear on your home. Your first step is to calculate the tax basis of your home. This will be the lower of two possible numbers:

- The fair market value of your home when you started using it as a home business.

- The cost of the home (not including the land) plus the value of any improvements you made before using the home office. You'll need to subtract any casualty losses you deducted.

Most times the second calculation is lower, unless your area of the country has experienced a major drop in housing prices. When figuring your home cost, you can include the actual amount paid, commissions, loan costs, legal and tax fees, utility installations, title insurance, and any other costs that you incurred to buy the home. If you take out your home closing documents, you can quickly find these numbers. You can then add on the costs for any major improvements to find your total basis. Also any tax assessments for major improvements can be added to the basis.

For most years, you will use what is called straight-line depreciation, or an equal share of the costs over the life of the property. You figure this by using the IRS determination for the life of the property, which for nonresidential use is 39 years. You then multiply $1/39$ by the cost basis of your home office. For example, if the cost basis of your home is $390,000 and your home office use percentage is 10 percent, the calculation would look like this:

$390,000 \times 10\% = \$39,000$ basis $\div$ 39 years = $1,000 depreciation per year

Your depreciation would be $1,000 annually for 39 years. The first year that you put the property in use and the last year that you use the property, you would take only a portion of that deduction based on how long you used the property that year. Here is the IRS table for how to figure that portion depending on the number of months the home office was used:

Percentage Table for 39-Year Nonresidential Real Property

Month First Used for Business	Percentage to Use
1	2.461%
2	2.247%
3	2.033%
4	1.819%
5	1.605%
6	1.391%
7	1.177%
8	0.963%
9	0.749%
10	0.535%
11	0.321%
12	0.107%

In a year in which you have only partial use of the home, you would multiply the allowable depreciation expense by the percentage of use that matches the month you started to use the office.

Let's practice. We'll assume that your depreciation deduction is $1,000 and that you started using the office in June (the sixth month). You would multiply the basis of $39,000 by 1.391 percent to find the amount by which you must reduce your deduction. This equals $542, which makes sense since it is a little more than half of the $1,000 annual deduction and the office was used a little more than half the year.

Selling Your Home

Deciding whether to depreciate the value of your home can be a major decision because, when it comes to selling the home, you could get stuck with a huge capital gain bill. Although up to $500,000 of the gain on a home owned jointly by husband and wife, or $250,000 for home owned by a single person, is exempt from capital gain taxes, any depreciation that you took for a home office is not exempt. You will have to pay capital gain on the depreciated portion of your home.

Recouping Loses

If you experience a casualty loss on your home such as major damage from a fire, you can write off any expenses that were not reimbursed by your insurance company if they are directly related to your business as a business expense. The major advantage to this tax break is that casualty loses that are not business related are subject to limits, while business-related items can be written off 100 percent. The first $100 of a personal loss is not deductible, and you must subtract 10 percent of your adjusted gross income from the remaining expenses.

Partnership or Corporation Differences

If your home business is a partnership or corporation, writing off your home office gets a bit more complicated. If you are involved in a partnership, your partners will have to agree to the expense because it must be added to the partnership return, which could reduce everyone's income. If you have incorporated the business, you must write off your home office as an employee expense on Schedule A. You could consider allowing the corporation to rent the space, but then any rental would have to be reported as personal income.

Finally, you could have the corporation buy your residence, but I wouldn't recommend it. You would then have to "rent" the portion of the home that you use for personal purposes. If you don't do that, the IRS will likely consider the personal use of the home as the underpayment of a dividend or unreported compensation. You would then have to pay income taxes on this money.

By now, you realize how complicated taking a home office deduction can be, but it's still usually worth going through the trouble of making sure you meet all the IRS's criteria. You can get more details in IRS Publication 587, "Business Use of Your Home."

If you plan to deduct your home office, you may want to review your plans at least the first year with a tax advisor to be sure you've got it right so that you don't risk the IRS questioning your decisions. The IRS can make you go back up to three years to correct any problems with your calculations and charge you back taxes, interest, and possibly penalties.

The Least You Need to Know

- You must use your home exclusively for business to take a home office deduction, unless you operate a day-care facility or use a part of your home for storage.

- You can calculate your office deduction using any reasonable method, but two different methods are most commonly accepted—one based on the number of rooms used if all rooms are similar in size, and the second on square footage.

- You can write off a lot of expenses related to your home, including mortgage interest, taxes, insurance, and utilities.

23

Making the Most of Business Travel

In This Chapter

- ◆ Taking business trips
- ◆ Deducting T&E expenses
- ◆ Depreciating your car
- ◆ Mixing business and pleasure

Unless you're a computer nerd who does his or her job entirely by using the Internet, you probably have to leave your house at some point to do business-related activities. You may just need to do things near your home, or you may have to travel outside the city in which your principal place of business is located.

Whether traveling around town or around the world, you can take advantage of some nifty tax breaks to lower your tax bill. In this chapter, we'll take a look at what's deductible and how you determine those deductions.

Traveling or Using Transportation?

First, you have to figure out whether you are traveling or using transportation. Traveling for IRS tax purposes involves any time you need to be away from your *tax home* for longer than an ordinary day's work and you need time to sleep while you are away. You don't necessarily need to be away for 24 hours for the trip to qualify as travel. We'll take a closer look at the expenses you can deduct for travel later, but first let's see how the IRS defines transportation.

No surprise here: Transportation is what you use to get around in the city or general area where your business is located. Transportation expenses can include the ordinary and necessary costs of any of the following activities:

◆ Getting from one workplace to another in the course of your business or profession when you are traveling within the city or general area that is your tax home.

◆ Visiting clients or customers.

◆ Going to a business meeting away from your regular workplace.

◆ Getting from your home to a temporary workplace when you have one or more regular places of work. These temporary workplaces can be either within the area of your tax home or outside that area.

> **Taxing Terms**
>
> Your **tax home** is your regular place of business, regardless of where you maintain your family home. It includes the entire city or general area in which your business or work is located.

You may have some questions about what is your regular place of business if you are not always located in the same city for work. You could have a temporary work location, no regular work location, or two places of work. There are also special rules for Armed Forces reservists. Let's take a quick look at how the IRS defines each of these work locations before we start discussing transportation expenses.

Temporary Work Location

If you have one or more regular places of business away from your home (and also sometimes work at a temporary location), you can deduct the expenses of the daily round-trip transportation between your home and the temporary location. The temporary work must be in the same trade or business. For IRS purposes, the work is temporary if it is expected to last for less than one year and actually *does* last less than one year—for example, if you are a computer consultant and you take a six month project at a temporary location to install a new system. Normally, you cannot deduct commuting expenses to and from your regular place of work, so a temporary designation can be major tax break. But as soon as you find out that the work assignment will last for more than one year, you have to consider it a regular work location even if it is not where your family lives.

No Regular Place of Work

If you have no regular place of work but ordinarily work in the metropolitan area where you live, you can deduct daily transportation costs between home and a temporary work site outside that metropolitan area—for example, a construction contract worker, such as a plumber or an electrician, may not have a regular place of work. A metropolitan area includes the area within the city limits and the suburbs that is considered part of that metropolitan area. You cannot deduct daily transportation costs between your home and temporary work sites within your metropolitan area. These are nondeductible commuting costs. This is when setting up and meeting the criteria of a home office can be a major benefit. You then will be able to write off your costs of traveling between your home office and your work sites.

Two Places of Work

If you work at two places in one day, whether or not for the same employer, you can deduct the expense of getting from one workplace to the other. You can't make a stop in between for personal reasons and write off the transportation costs involved in that stop. You can include only costs related to going from one place of work to the other. Transportation expenses that you incur while traveling between home and a part-time job on a day off from your main job are commuting expenses—you cannot deduct them.

Armed Forces Reservists

If you serve in the Armed Forces reserve, you can consider attending a meeting of an Armed Forces reserve unit as a second place of business if the meeting is held on a day on which you work at your regular job. You can deduct the expense of getting from one workplace to the other as though it is a second place of work. You usually cannot deduct the expense if the reserve meeting is held on a day on which you do not work at your regular job. In this case, your transportation generally is a nondeductible commuting cost. However, you can deduct your transportation expenses if the location of the meeting is temporary and you have one or more regular places of work. If you ordinarily work in a particular metropolitan area but not at any specific location and the reserve meeting is held at a temporary location outside that metropolitan area, you can deduct your transportation expenses. If you travel away from home overnight to attend a guard or reserve meeting, you can deduct your travel expenses.

Now that we've explored the types of workplaces, let's look at the expenses that can be written off.

Writing Off Transportation

Your modes of transportation to get from your regular place of work to other places where you do business can include the cost of air, rail, bus, taxi, or any other means of getting around, in addition to the cost of driving and maintaining your car. Commuting expenses are not deductible when you go from your home to your regular place of work, even if you work while you are commuting.

Let's review all the things that can be written off as transportation expenses:

- **Parking fees.** You can deduct business-related parking fees when visiting a customer or client, but you can't deduct them to park your car at your regular place of work.

- **Advertising display on car.** Putting display material that advertises your business on your car does not change the use of your car from personal use to business use. If you use this car for commuting or other personal reasons, you still cannot deduct your expenses for those uses. However, you can deduct them if you travel from your regular place of work for other business-related activities.

- **Carpools.** If you operate a carpool for a profit, you must include payments from passengers as part of your income. You can then deduct your car expenses, (discussed in detail later in this chapter). You cannot deduct the cost of using your car in a nonprofit carpool. In this case, you don't include payments you receive from the passengers in your income because such payments are considered reimbursements for your expenses.

- **Hauling tools or instruments.** Hauling tools or instruments in your car while commuting to and from work doesn't make your car expenses deductible if they weren't already deductible. But you can deduct any additional costs you have for hauling tools or instruments. For example, if you need to rent a trailer and tow it with your car, the rental would be deductible.

- **Union members' trips from a union hall.** If you get your work assignments at a union hall and then go to your place of work, the costs of getting from the union hall to your place of work are nondeductible commuting expenses. Although you need the union to get your work assignments, you are employed where you work, not where the union hall is located.

♦ **Office in the home.** If you assignments have an office in your home that qualifies as a principal place of business (remember, we talked about that in the last chapter), you can deduct your daily transportation costs between your home and another work location in the same trade or business.

Deducting Car Expenses

Writing off your car expenses can be your biggest transportation tax break. Let's take a look at all the expenses you can deduct.

Car expenses can be deducted using one of two methods: Actual expenses and standard mileage.

Standard Mileage Rate

Using the standard mileage rate (SMR) is the simpler method. You don't need to collect all those receipts for car expenses; instead, you calculate your transportation costs by multiplying a standard mileage rate by the number of business miles you drive. The rate for 2002 is 36.5 cents. This rate is adjusted periodically for inflation.

If you choose to use the standard mileage rate, you cannot deduct your actual car expenses, including repairs, maintenance, gasoline, oil, vehicle registration fees, lease payments, insurance, and depreciation, for that year. Furthermore, if you want to use the SMR at any time during the life of the car, you must use it in the first year your car is used for business. In later years, you can choose between the SMR and actual expenses, depending on which provides the greater tax savings or is easier for you to do. One catch to switching back and forth between methods is that you must use straight-line depreciation in the actual expense years.

Rules for cars you lease are different. Once you choose to use the SMR for a car you lease, you must use it throughout the term of the lease.

> **CAUTION**
>
> **Audit Alarm!**
>
> Why not choose the SMR? The key factor is depreciation on the wear and tear of the car. The SMR already includes a write-off for depreciation as part of the rate. If you think you will get a higher write-off using depreciation, you may want to use the actual expenses method.

You cannot use the SMR rate, if you …

◆ Use the car for hire (such as a taxi).

◆ Use two or more cars at the same time (as in fleet operations). You can use two or more cars or trucks for your business and still qualify for the SMR. The key to qualifying is that you can't use both vehicles at the same time. For example, if you run a landscaping business and use a car yourself while your crew uses a truck, you won't be able to use the SMR. If you run the same business by using the car occasionally for sales calls and use the truck for servicing your customers along with your crew, then you can use the SMR for both vehicles.

◆ Claimed actual car expenses after 1997 for a car you leased.

◆ Are a rural mail carrier who received a qualified reimbursement.

Even if you use the SMR, you can deduct some additional expenses related to your car, including interest and parking fees or tolls. For interest to be deductible, you must be self-employed and use your car for business. The interest expense deduction be depends on how much you use your car for business. For example, if 60 percent of your mileage is for business, then 60 percent of your interest cost is deductible.

You can also deduct any parking tolls and fees incurred during business-related activities. You can't deduct any parking fees paid at your regular workplace; they are non-deductible commuting expenses.

Actual Car Expenses

Actual car expenses can include registration fees, licenses, insurance, repairs, gas, oil, tires, garage rent, parking fees, tolls, lease payments, and depreciation. Even if your car is fully depreciated, you can continue to claim your other actual car expenses. Sorry, you can't deduct fines you pay for traffic violations!

If you use your car for business and personal purposes, you need to calculate what percentage of your car is used for business purposes. You must track the mileage of business trips and then divide your business mileage by your total mileage to calculate your business use.

Let's practice with an example. We'll assume that you use your car for a total of 15,000 miles per year and that 10,000 of those miles are for business purposes. Your business percentage in this case would be this:

$$\frac{10,000}{15,000} = 66.7\%$$

You would then total your expenses on the car and multiply them by this percentage to figure out your write-off for the car. The expenses you need to total are pretty straightforward. The key exceptions are how to handle lease payments and depreciation. Also, if you buy a new vehicle, you have the option of a *Section 179* deduction.

Taxing Terms

Section 179 lets you recover the costs of a major capital expense more quickly than depreciation. This deduction allows you to treat the first year of the car expense as a current expense rather than depreciation. To be eligible for the Section 179 deduction, you must use your car more than 50 percent for business or work in the year you acquired it. Also, there are limits. The maximum you can take in any one year for a car using Section 179 or depreciation is $3,060 in the first year of use. There is a different amount allowed for each year of use. This amount is further reduced if you use your car for work less than 100 percent of the time.

In 2002, Congress passed a new tax law called the Job Creation and Worker Assistance Act of 2002 that allows an even greater deduction than the Section 179 deduction. This law lets you deduct up to 30 percent of the cost of a new car purchased after September 10, 2001. If you choose to use this new special deduction instead of the Section 179 deduction, you can deduct up to $7,660 for a car ($23,080 for an electric car), including the new deduction plus depreciation. You are limited to $3,060 ($9,280 for an electric car) if you choose to use the Section 179 deduction or depreciation without the new deduction. Of course, these limits are reduced based on your business use percentage if you use the car less than 100 percent for business. Oddly enough, if you don't want to use this deduction you must attach a statement to your return saying that you elect *not* to take it. If you don't include such a statement, the IRS will require you to reduce your basis in the vehicle when you sell it as if you had taken the deduction, and you could end up with a greater gain at the time you sell the car.

Taxing Terms

The **Modified Accelerated Cost Recovery System (MACRS)** is the name given to the tax rules for getting back (recovering) through depreciation deductions the cost of property used in a trade or business or to produce income. The maximum amount you can deduct is limited depending on the year you place your car in service. Under the MACRS, cars are classified as five-year property. You actually depreciate the cost of a car or truck in six calendar years because you usually place the vehicle in service in the middle of the first year. You then use a partial-year calculation for the first and last years.

Basically, depreciation lets you write off the wear and tear on your car. Generally, you figure depreciation on cars using the *Modified Accelerated Cost Recovery System (MACRS)*.

Three possible methods exist for calculating depreciation on your car, and I've listed them below. But please note, no one actually does these calculations; instead, they use the MACRS charts provided by the IRS:

- The 200 percent declining balance method over a five-year recovery period that switches to the straight-line method when that method provides an equal or greater deduction

- The 150 percent declining balance method over a five-year recovery period that switches to the straight-line method when that method provides an equal or greater deduction

- The straight-line method (SL) over a five-year recovery period

The percentages you use to determine your depreciation expense vary depending upon when the vehicle is put in service. Once you figure out your percentage, you multiply that by the market value of the car. But there is a limit. You can't use the full market value of a luxury car to calculate depreciation. The maximum market value allowed is $15,300.

Luckily you never have to do these calculations. The IRS provides a MACRS Depreciation Chart each year that you can use in Publication 946, "How to Depreciate Property."

Just to give you an idea of how the MACRS works, here's a chart showing the percentages for a car put in service halfway through a year using the 200 percent declining balance method:

Year	Depreciation Percentage
1	20%
2	32%
3	19.2%
4	11.52%
5	11.52%
6	5.76%

As you can see, you can use a much higher percentage in the early years. If you choose straight-line depreciation on a car over five years, you deduct 20 percent each year. The first and sixth years are only 10 percent because they are partial years and a midyear convention is used.

As I noted previously, if you use the SMR in the first year of business use, you must depreciate your car using the straight-line method. Before determining the method you want to use, consider that the straight-line method provides equal yearly deductions throughout the recovery period, while the other two methods allow greater deductions in the earlier years. If you are starting up a new business and think you'll be operating initially with losses, the straight-line method probably will be the better choice.

To figure out the depreciation on your car, you need to know its basis (total cost of acquiring the car) and the date you placed it in service for use in your business or to produce income. You'll also need to choose your depreciation method. If you use your car for business less than 50 percent of the time, you must use the straight-line depreciation method. If in the first year of the business you used the car for 50 percent of the time and after that year your usage dropped, you must switch to the straight-line depreciation method.

Tax Tips

In Chapter 11, we talked about the special tax breaks you get if you buy an electric car. Those benefits can be used for business vehicles as well. The depreciation amount allowed for an electric car used for business purposes increases to $9,280 in the first year of service from only $3,060. If you elect to use the new special depreciation allowance, first-year depreciation on an electric car could be as high as $23,080.

Leasing a Car

If you lease a car for business, you can use either the SMR or the actual expenses calculation to figure your car expense. If you choose actual expenses, you can deduct the part of your lease payment that is for business use. You'll need to adjust the lease payment based the fair market value of the car. This is similar to the reduction you would need to take related to the depreciation limits discussed previously, which is known as the inclusion amount. The IRS provides tables you can use in Publication 463, "Travel, Entertainment, Gift, and Car Expenses," to calculate the inclusion amount.

Selling Your Car

When you sell a car that you depreciated for business purposes, you might have to pay a taxable gain or you might get to take a deductible loss, depending on whether you made a profit or sold the car at a loss. Your car's basis (or cost) will be reduced by the amount you took as depreciation or a Section 179 deduction. If you are able to sell the car for more than the remaining value, you will have to report a gain and it will be treated as ordinary income. The one exception to this rule is if the car was lost because of theft or casualty. If you get less out of the car than its remaining value, you will have a deductible loss.

You also can avoid the gain if you replace the car with a new one. When you trade in the car toward a new one, it's considered a *like-kind exchange*. You avoid having to recognize a gain or loss in most trade-in situations.

Taxing Terms

A **like-kind exchange** occurs when similar business or investment assets are exchanged. Gain can be tax deferred until a later actual sale.

If you used the SMR to figure your business use of the car, you must adjust the cost basis of the car to reflect the depreciation that was part of this deduction. To do this, you multiply the total number of business miles deducted in years you did not use the actual expenses method by 15 cents. This amount is adjusted periodically for inflation. Each year IRS Publication 463, "Travel, Entertainment, Gift and Car Expenses" will have current rates for depreciation and SMR.

Time for Travel

When you are temporarily away from your tax home for business purposes, you can write off expenses in addition to transportation, as long as you must be away from the home for a period long enough to require sleep. Members of the Armed Forces who are on a permanent duty assignment are not considered traveling away from home, so they cannot deduct expenses for meals and lodging.

Travel expenses can include the following:

◆ Fifty percent of your meal costs

◆ Air, rail, and bus fares

◆ Baggage charges

◆ Cleaning and laundry expenses

- Computer rental fees

- Car expenses

- Hotel expenses

- Telephone or fax expenses

- Public stenographer or clerical fees

- Tips on eligible expenses

- Transportation costs for sample or display materials

If you don't want to collect lots of receipts for meals, laundry, cleaning, and tips, you can choose to use the government's standard meal allowance, which is $30 a day. In some higher-cost cities, the government allows as much as $45 per day. You can find these per diem rates at www.policyworks.gov/perdiem.

If your trip is partially business and partially personal, the amount you can deduct will depend on how much time you actually spend on business. You can deduct the cost of traveling to and from the location only if your trip was primarily for business. Otherwise, you can deduct only the travel expenses directly related to business activities.

Bringing Friends or Family

If you take your spouse, other family members, or friends along with you on a business trip, you can't deduct their travel costs unless the person traveling with you meets all three of the following criteria:

- Is your employee

- Has a bona fide business purpose for the travel

- Would otherwise be allowed to deduct the travel expenses

Business associates can also qualify if the person is a current or prospective (likely to become) customer, client, supplier, employee, agent, partner, or professional advisor. To qualify as a bona fide business purpose, the person traveling with you must have a true business purpose and not be there just to type notes or assist with entertaining customers. In other words, you can't take your spouse or kids on a vacation and say they are taking notes just so you can write off their costs.

Foreign Travel

If you travel outside the United States, the rules are slightly different. If the trip is 100 percent business related, you can deduct the expenses as listed previously.

If the trip is partially for business and partially for pleasure, you must calculate the number of days actually spent directly on business and prorate the costs of getting there and back based on the percentage actually business related. Any day that your presence is required for business purposes can count, even if you don't spend the entire day on business. You can use the federal per diem rates at www.state.gov/m/a/als/prdm.

Going Cruising

If you travel by ocean liner, cruise ship, or other form of luxury water transportation for business purposes, there is a daily limit on the amount you can deduct. The limit is twice the highest federal per diem rate allowable at the time of your travel.

Just to give you an idea of these rates, here is how they were calculated for luxury water travel in 2001:

2001 Dates	Highest Federal Per Diem	Daily Limit on Luxury Water Travel
January 1 to June 14	$244	$488
June 15 to September 15	253	506
September 16 to December 31	244	448

Conventions

You can deduct your travel expenses when you attend a convention if you can show that your attendance benefits your trade or business. You cannot deduct the travel expenses for your family. If the convention is for investment, political, social, or other purposes unrelated to your trade or business, you cannot deduct the expenses.

If the convention is on a cruise ship, you can deduct up to $2,000 per year of your expenses attending conventions on cruise ships. What a nice way to go on a working vacation! However, you must meet these five requirements:

♦ The convention, seminar, or meeting is directly related to your trade or business.

♦ The cruise ship is a vessel registered in the United States.

- All of the cruise ship's ports of call are in the United States or in possessions of the United States. Nope, that Caribbean cruise won't do it. Shucks!

- You attach to your return a written statement signed by you that includes information about:

    a. The total days of the trip (not including the days of transportation to and from the cruise ship port)

    b. The number of hours each day that you devoted to scheduled business activities

    c. A program of the scheduled business activities of the meeting

- You attach to your return a written statement signed by an officer of the organization or group sponsoring the meeting that includes:

    a. A schedule of the business activities of each day of the meeting

    b. The number of hours you attended the scheduled business activities

Now that you know what you can deduct when you take a business trip, our next stop looks at what you can deduct for business equipment.

The Least You Need to Know

- You can deduct all your transportation costs from your home office to any of your business activities outside the home.

- There are two possible methods for calculating car expenses—standard mileage rate and actual expenses methods.

- When choosing the actual expense method you can use straight line depreciation or one of several accelerated depreciation options—150% declining balance, 200% declining balance, Section 179 deduction, and the new Special Depreciation Allowance.

- To qualify for travel expenses, you must be away from your tax home for longer than a day's work and need a time period for sleep.

Chapter 24

Equipping Your Business

In This Chapter

- ◆ Getting equipped
- ◆ Writing off equipment expenses
- ◆ Depreciating equipment
- ◆ Keeping a lease a lease—*not* a sale

All businesses use equipment, and when you buy new equipment you have a number of tax breaks to consider for writing off the cost. In many cases, you may even be able to write off the full cost of the new equipment in the first year.

Qualifying Equipment

Before I explain your write-off options, let's look at what qualifies as business equipment. Equipment qualifies if it meets all these conditions ...

- ◆ Has been used in a trade or business, or has been held for the production of income (such as rental real estate).

◆ Has a finite period of usefulness in your business that is longer than one year.

◆ Wears out, decays or gets used up, becomes obsolete, or loses value from natural causes.

Can you think of any equipment you use for your business that doesn't qualify here? I can't. Basically, this includes cars (which we discussed in Chapter 23), computers, office furniture, machines, buildings, and significant additions or improvements in these kinds of property or equipment. You can write off these assets by depreciating (accounting for the wear and tear of normal use) them over a number of years. You may even have the option of deducting the full cost in the first year.

Some things you use in your business are not depreciable. Land is a biggie. When you buy a building for your business, you must subtract the cost of the land before determining your write-off options. Also, any costs involved with clearing, grading, planting, landscaping, or demolishing buildings are not depreciated. Instead, these costs are added to the basis (original cost of buying the land or buildings) and reduce any future capital gain.

You can't depreciate personal property, either. So if you use business equipment for personal reasons as well, the portion of the cost of the equipment used for personal reasons is not deductible. You also can't depreciate property that you rent or lease from others, but if you make permanent improvements to rented or leased property, you may be able to depreciate those additions.

Fastest Write-Off Option

Before we delve more deeply into depreciation options, let's first look at the law that allows you to expense the total cost of equipment in the first year you buy it. Yep, you read that right: You may be able to deduct 100 percent of what you spent in the first year!

This special law, called Section 179, is intended to help small businesses. You can write off the total cost of up to $24,000 in new equipment in the year you buy it (this amount will increase to $25,000 in 2003). You must use the equipment for business purposes more than 50 percent of the time. You will have to reduce the amount of the up-front deduction if you use it less than 100 percent of the time. To calculate that reduction, you must multiply the cost of the equipment by the percentage actually used for business. For example, if you use a $1,000 computer 75 percent of the time for business, you can deduct $750 in the first year.

Audit Alarm!

If you sell or stop using property at least 50 percent of the time for your business, you may need to repay some of the Section 179 expense deduction. You calculate this repayment by determining how much you could have depreciated under the fastest depreciation method available, and you pay the difference between what could have been depreciated and what you actually wrote off as an expense. If you think you'll use this equipment for your business for only a year or two, you may not want to take advantage of the Section 179 deduction.

Congress is serious about the Section 179 deduction being for small business. If a business spends more than $200,000 on equipment, the allowable Section 179 is reduced by the amount over $200,000 that you spend. For example, if you purchased $210,000 of equipment in one year, you must reduce the Section 179 deduction by the amount you spent over $200,000. You would calculate that reduction like this:

$24,000 – $10,000 [$210,000 – $200,000] = $14,000

In this situation, only $14,000 would be eligible for a Section 179 deduction. The amount that could not be deducted in the first year could then be written off using depreciation options available for the equipment.

If you are at risk of exceeding the deduction limit, you may want to put off some purchases until the next year. If you need everything in the current year, you're probably better off expensing the equipment that has the longest depreciation periods. I'll give you a chart later that you can use to determine how long you must depreciate different types of equipment.

To qualify for the Section 179 expense deduction, the new property must be *tangible* but cannot include real estate. It also must be something that you actually use in your business and that would qualify for depreciation otherwise. You can include equipment that you need for

Revenue Ramblings

Having a hard time keeping expensing and depreciating straight? Expensing a piece of equipment means that you write it off immediately. Depreciating means that you write off the wear and tear of equipment over a number of years. Both of these are types of tax deductions. Section 179 is a hybrid that allows people to expense their depreciation up front.

Taxing Terms

Tangible property is physical property that can be moved.

Intangible property is property that consists of rights rather than physical attributes. In a business setting, examples of this include notes, accounts receivable, patents, or goodwill.

Taxing Terms

Goodwill is used to account for a business's competitive advantage, such as a strong brand, reputation, or high employee morale.

manufacturing, production, or extraction. Equipment for providing transportation, communication, electricity, gas, water, research, storage, or waste-disposal services qualifies. Furniture, computers, cars, and other basic office equipment pass the test, too.

You can't use Section 179 for *intangible property*, such as patents, contract rights, or *goodwill*. You may be able to amortize intangible property; I'll tell you more about that later in this chapter.

You can even use the 100 percent Section 179 expense deduction if you bought the equipment as late as December 31 in that tax year, as long as you used it on December 31 for business purposes. The equipment must be put in service before you can take the expense deduction.

The Section 179 deduction can be written off only against your business income, but if your business is a sole proprietorship, you can include salary or wages from other jobs that you or your spouse may have when determining how much you can write off. If you don't have enough taxable income to take the full deduction in one year, you can carry it forward and write it off in future years.

If you are involved in more than one business that is an S Corporation or a partnership, the $24,000 limit is tested twice. Once at the corporate level and a second time when it is passed on to the shareholders for their personal returns. If your Section 179 deductions from more than one business total over $24,000, then you would need to carry forward the excess to future tax years.

Depreciation Types and Rules

We've danced around the topic of depreciation. Now it's time to take a look at the rules. In Chapter 23, we talked about the depreciation methods in the Modified Accelerated Cost Recovery System (MACRS). Remember, there were three methods for calculating depreciation:

- The 200 percent declining balance method over the IRS determined recovery period that switches to the straight-line method when that method provides an equal or greater deduction

- The 150 percent declining balance method over the IRS determined recovery period that switches to the straight-line method when that method provides an equal or greater deduction

- The straight-line (SL) method over the IRS determined recovery period

When we discussed these calculations for cars, we used a five-year recovery period. Recovery periods are not the same for all types of business equipment. The following table shows the recovery period for common equipment types.

Depreciation Recovery Periods for Business Equipment

Property Class Recovery Period	Business Equipment
3-year property	Tractor units and horses over two years old
5-year property	Cars, taxis, buses, trucks, computers, office machines (faxes, copiers, calculators, and so on), research equipment, and cattle
7-year property	Office furniture and fixtures
10-year property	Water transportation equipment, single-purpose agricultural or horticultural structures, and fruit- or nut-bearing vines and trees
15-year property	Land improvements, such as shrubbery, fences, roads, and bridges
20-year property	Farm buildings that are not agricultural or horticultural structures
27.5-year property	Residential rental property
39-year property	Nonresidential real estate, including a home office but not including the value of the land

In addition to figuring out the recovery period, you must determine the convention based on when the equipment was put into service. There are three possible conventions:

- **Midmonth convention.** This is used for nonresidential real estate. The IRS assumes that the first month you put nonresidential real estate into service it is midmonth, and you deduct half the allowable depreciation for that month plus a monthly amount for the rest of the year.

- **Half-year convention.** All non–real estate business property falls under this convention for the first year. The IRS assumes that you put the property in use midyear, no matter which month you started to use the equipment. You can deduct half of the first year's depreciation.

- **Midquarter convention.** You can't buy all your equipment at the end of the year and take the half-year convention, though. If you place more than 40 percent of your equipment in service in the last quarter of the year, the IRS uses this convention. You must go back and calculate your allowable percentage of the year's depreciation based on when you actually put the equipment in service, using these percentages:

- First quarter: 87.5%

- Second quarter: 62.5%

- Third quarter: 37.5%

- Fourth quarter: 12.5%

Fortunately, you don't have to actually calculate your depreciation percentage under MACRS. The IRS provides tables each tax year that you can use to find the percentage based on the date put in service and the recovery period.

Tax Tips

If you place more than one asset of the same type in service during the year, you can group the assets, but you are probably better off keeping them separate. You might need depreciation records on each piece of equipment if you sell or scrap them at different times. For example, if you buy three computers for your new office and sell one a couple of years later, you must include the entire proceeds from the sale as income, but you continue to depreciate the asset as part of the group. Eventually, the entire cost is written off.

Property that you put in service before 1987 may use other depreciation methods. IRS Publication 534, "Depreciated Property Placed in Service Before 1987," can give you more details on older methods.

Some types of property fit into a group called listed property. Primarily, these are the kinds of business property that are frequently used personally as well. Listed property must exceed 50 percent use to use any of the depreciation methods that are faster than straight-line depreciation. Listed property includes the following:

- Cars and other vehicles

- Cell phones

- Equipment normally used for entertainment or recreation, such as photographic, audio, communication, or video-recording equipment

- Computers and their peripheral equipment

- Significant additions or improvements to any type of listed property

You can continue depreciating the property until you write off the entire basis of the property, sell it, scrap it, or lose it by theft, fire, or other casualty. If you sell it or receive an insurance reimbursement for its loss, you may have to pay a capital gain tax or get to take a capital loss on the difference between the amount of money received and the depreciated value. If you replace it with like equipment, you will not have to pay a gain and won't be able to take a loss. The cost basis of the new property will be adjusted by any gain or loss on the disposal of the old property. You essentially are delaying any capital gains until the new property is sold.

Any gain for equipment held over a year is taxed at the capital gain rate of 20 percent (10 percent for people in the 15 percent tax bracket). If you held the property for more than five years and it was put in service after 2000, you are eligible for the longer capital gain rate of 18 percent (8 percent for people in the 15 percent tax bracket). Property used for both business and personal purposes must be allocated based on its proportionate use at the time of sale to calculate any capital gain tax.

Amortizing Assets

I mentioned previously that intangible assets must be amortized rather than depreciated. Examples of amortized assets include franchise rights, business licenses, patents, copyrights, trademarks, trade names, and goodwill. All are amortized over 15 years. The calculation is similar to straight-line depreciation, with equal amounts deducted each year. For example, let's say you purchased franchise rights to open a fast food restaurant for $150,000. You would amortize that cost over 15 years or $10,000 per year.

Leasing Options

You might decide to lease a piece of equipment rather than buy it. In those situations, you can write off the lease payment as a business expense. But beware: If the IRS determines that your lease is actually a financial agreement to purchase the equipment, you may have to account for it differently.

If the IRS recharacterizes your lease as a sale, your rental payments will not be deductible. You will instead have to depreciate the equipment as other owned property. Here are some situations that look suspicious to the IRS:

◆ Part of the rental payments establishes equity for you in the property.

◆ You get the title to the property after you pay the rent.

- Rental payments are for a short period of time and are large in comparison to the actual purchase of the property.

- Your rental payments greatly exceed the amount for the fair rent of the property in your area.

- You can buy the property for a nominal amount at the end of the lease.

- Part of your rent is assumed to be interest or is recognized as being the equivalent of interest.

CAUTION

Audit Alarm!

Lease payments are not always fully tax deductible. If the IRS determines that your lease does not qualify, it can be recharacterized as a sale and your payments will not be deductible as rent.

We discussed in Chapter 23 how leases are handled for property that must be depreciated. Essentially, the IRS has charts that you can use to calculate a depreciation adjustment for your lease payments.

Now that we've covered all your business assets—your house, your car, and your equipment—it's time to talk about protecting those assets and taking advantages of the tax breaks you can get for that protection.

The Least You Need to Know

- You can write off up to $24,000 as part of Section 179 in the first year that you purchase equipment for your small business.

- There are three different methods for calculating the depreciation deduction for business equipment. Key factors in determining that amount include the type of equipment, the amount paid, and the date the equipment was put in service.

- You can amortize the value of intangible business property, which is similar to a straight-line depreciation deduction.

Chapter 25

Insuring Yourself and Your Assets

In This Chapter

- ◆ Lessening your liabilities
- ◆ Covering your losses
- ◆ Insuring your health

We've talked a lot about building your business and the assets you acquire for it. Now it's time to make sure you protect all that you have built—and take advantage of tax savings at the same time. Business insurance falls in three categories: business liability, business property and casualty, and workers' compensation (if you have employees). All your expenses for insurance are fully deductible as a business expense—with one major exception: health insurance.

We'll take a tour of the various types of business insurance you may want to consider based on your individual circumstances. Then we'll look at several health insurance options.

Business Liability

You certainly wouldn't go without liability insurance for your house in case someone were injured on your property, and definitely not for your car in case of accident. So why do people think they don't need liability insurance for their business?

I'll briefly review the various types of liability insurance available, but your best bet is to sit down with an insurance advisor whom you trust and determine what makes sense given your business and its liability risks.

First, there is general liability insurance. This covers a business against accidents or injury that might happen on its premises. If you are operating a business out of your home, your homeowner's policy may offer sufficient coverage, but don't take that for granted. You may need to add a rider that specifies that you run a business out of the home, so check with your insurance agent to see if you're covered, especially if you see clients or customers in your home.

Professional liability insurance protects you against claims arising from your business activities, including errors or omissions when providing professional services. No matter what kind of business you run—from advertising to medical care or engineering—you should protect yourself in case you are sued because of an error or omission when providing your services.

Tax Tips

If your company has a board of directors, you may want to consider purchasing directors' and officers' liability coverage. This protects your top executives and board members from personal liability in case the company is sued.

You can top off all your liability insurance with an umbrella policy if you think you need more coverage than is provided in your existing policies. Umbrella policies take over when general insurance policies fall short. In fact, many individuals carry a $1 million umbrella policy so they are protected against major accidents involving a car or home.

Business Property and Casualty

Business property and casualty insurance protects you from loss if your property is lost, damaged, or stolen. Two kinds of business property and casualty insurance are available:

◆ **Named-peril.** This protects against losses that are specifically named.

◆ **All-risk.** This is much broader and protects against all perils.

Named-peril insurance is cheaper because the coverage isn't as broad, but if a loss occurs because of something not named in your coverage, you get nothing. There are also three forms of coverage:

- **Basic form.** Covers damage from common perils, such as fire, lightning, windstorm, vehicles, aircraft, and civil commotion.

- **Broad form.** Covers all the basic perils plus others such as water damage; collapse; glass breakage; weight of snow, ice, or sleet; and sprinkler leakage.

- **Special form.** Covers all perils except those specifically excluded. Exclusions can include flood, earth movement, war, wear and tear, insects, and vermin.

When you buy insurance—whether it is for your business or home—make sure you know what perils are covered. You certainly don't want to find out that you don't have coverage after a major catastrophe happens.

You also can select two different reimbursement options:

- **Replacement cost reimbursement.** This pays you the cost of actually replacing the lost property.

- **Actual cash value reimbursement.** This pays you based on the replacement cost minus the physical depreciation of the property.

The actual cash value reimbursement option might cost you less up front, but you'll also collect a lot less if you have a loss.

Special named perils that you may want to consider, depending on your specific business situation, include the following:

- **Crime.** This protects you against burglary, robbery, embezzlement, employee theft, and disappearance or destruction of property because of criminal acts. The cost of this coverage depends on the size of your company and its risks of needing to file claims.

- **Cargo.** This protects you against loss of inventory or goods while on a company truck.

- **Business interruption insurance.** This covers losses incurred because your business operations are interrupted by an act beyond your control. It provides resources so that you can continue to pay utilities, payroll, loans, and other obligations until your business is up and running again.

- **Product liability insurance.** If you produce and sell a product, this insurance covers you if you are sued related to a problem with the product's performance.

Service business can also be covered under this type of insurance for services performed.

♦ **Inland marine insurance.** This insurance covers high-risk, mobile items that have a high stated value not covered by your other commercial property policies. This can include valuable tools, artwork, or jeweler's inventory.

♦ **Fire and extended coverage policies.** This covers losses from hail, windstorm, vandalism, or fire beyond the normal coverages of commercial liability. This can include protection for your accounts receivable records, computer files, currency, securities, and valuable papers.

♦ **Flood.** If your business or home is in a flood zone, you will need flood insurance policy to be sure your assets are protected.

Workers' Compensation

If you have employees, you might need workers' compensation insurance. This insurance pays benefits to your employees if they are hurt on the job. Coverage includes medical bills, a part of lost wages, vocational rehabilitation, and death benefits.

Whether you need to carry this coverage depends on state law. If you fail to carry it when state law requires you to, not only will you be subject to covering an employee's costs after an accident or injury, but you also may face severe fines and even jail time for violating the law. You can usually purchase this insurance from your state or through various private companies.

Audit Alarm!

Five states require that you purchase workers' compensation insurance from them: North Dakota, Ohio, Washington, West Virginia, and Wyoming.

Premiums for workers' compensation are based on the size of your payroll. The higher your payroll is, the more you pay.

Health Insurance

Self-employed folks get far fewer tax advantages when it comes to health insurance than people who are insured through their employers. While employees' health insurance costs are deducted before taxes are taken out, self-employed folks can take only a portion of their health insurance deduction on their Form 1040.

This is changing, though. In 2002, up to 70 percent of health insurance premiums will be deductible; beginning in 2003, they will be 100 percent deductible. The 30 percent that is not deductible on Form 1040 in 2002 can be deducted on Schedule A if you itemize your deductions, but it's subject to the medical deduction limitations. (Remember, when we talked about medical deductions in Chapter 4, you can deduct only costs above 7.5 percent of your adjusted gross income.)

Medical Savings Accounts

In 1997, Congress decided to experiment with a new insurance option for small business with fewer than 50 employees and created a new creature called medical savings accounts (MSAs). Basically, self-employed people or small business owners can buy health insurance with a high deductible. Participants can then save money in tax-deductible savings accounts. These accounts can continue to build throughout their lifetime.

To qualify as a high-deductible plan, the annual deductibles must be between $1,600 and $2,550 for individuals, and $3,200 and $4,050 for families. Officially, this program is ending in 2002, but self-employed folks already participating can continue to contribute to their MSAs.

Congress is making an attempt to continue the program. The House of Representatives passed legislation in August 2001, but the Senate has not yet passed similar legislation. The House bill makes MSAs permanent and opens them up to all taxpayers. The House bill also lowers the deductible requirements to $1,000 for individual coverage and $2,000 for family coverage.

Tax Tips

You can learn more about medical savings accounts online at www.msa.net/index.html.

Participants who open MSAs now can contribute up to 65 percent of their medical deductible amount each year if they have individual coverage, or 75 percent if they have family coverage. These contributions are tax deductible and can be withdrawn tax-free when used for eligible medical expenses. The House proposes to raise allowable MSA contributions to 100 percent of the deductible. Money is withdrawn tax-free for medical expenses.

I have no predictions about whether the MSAs will continue to be an option or whether they

Revenue Ramblings

MSAs are primarily a Republican cause. Democrats fear that healthy and wealthy folks will shift to MSAs and drive up the cost of traditional health coverage for everyone else. Supporters of MSAs believe the opposite is true. Their theory is that individuals will be more cost-conscious when spending their MSA savings and will drive prices down. Which do you believe?

will gradually disappear as no new accounts can be opened. If they are of interest to you as a self-employed person or a small business owner, closely watch legislation regarding patient's rights because that is where the MSA is hidden right now. It could change stripes and become a separate bill or a health insurance bill as well.

Now that you've got a good handle on your insurance options and what's deductible against your business income, let's take a look at other small business operating expenses that are deductible.

The Least You Need to Know

- ◆ Businesses need a variety of business liability insurance coverage, depending on the types of risk the business may incur.

- ◆ Just as you must protect your personal assets from various casualties, business assets need insurance protection. Business property and casualty insurance can be structured to meet the exact needs of your business.

- ◆ Health insurance is not fully deductible for owners of a small business and their families in 2002, but it will be in 2003.

Chapter 26

The Costs of Doing Business

In This Chapter

◆ Eligible business expenses

◆ Taking advantage of business credits

◆ Deducting employee expenses

"Can I deduct this?" is probably the most frequent question asked of any accountant preparing tax returns. Business returns can be even more complex as folks try to place as many expenses as possible on the business side rather than the personal side to lower their net income and, ultimately, the taxes that must be paid.

In this chapter, I'll explain how the IRS views business expenses. Then I'll describe the ones that easily qualify and, in most cases, that have specific rules. The rest is up to your imagination—if you can justify them to the satisfaction of the IRS that it was a business expense, then it's a business expense!

Defining Business Expenses

Let's start with the part of the tax code known as Section 162, which allows for trade or business expenses. Here's how it starts:

(a) In General—there shall be allowed as a deduction all the ordinary and necessary expenses paid or incurred during the taxable year in carrying on any trade or business.

Several phrases in the passage are key for making sure your expenses qualify. Those words are "expenses," "paid or incurred," "ordinary and necessary," and "carrying on any trade or business." We'll take a look at each separately.

Expenses

To qualify as a business expense, it must be a cost for an item that will be used up in the same tax year. Items that benefit the business for more than one year are capital expenses; these include a car, furniture, or other items, and they must be depreciated rather than expensed. Of course, there are exceptions to rule, such as Section 179 deductions, which we discussed in Chapter 24.

Paid or Incurred

This relates to the type of accounting you choose to do in your business. There are basically two types—*cash method* and *accrual method*.

If you use the cash method, you write off the expense in the year you actually paid for it. If you use the accrual method of accounting, you write off the expense in the year that it is incurred.

Taxing Terms

Cash method is the type of accounting in which income is reported when it is actually received and expenses are reported when they are actually paid.

Accrual method is the type of accounting in which income is reported when it is actually earned and expenses are reported when they are actually incurred.

Most home-based small businesses operate using the cash method of accounting. This is much easier for bookkeeping purposes. Also, a key problem of the accrual method for a small business can be that income is reported when it is earned, not when it is received.

This can create a problem, for example, if you complete a major project in December and have officially "earned" a huge payment but won't "receive" it until the next year. You would have to report that income using the accrual method but would not have to do so until it was received in the next tax year using the cash method. This could cause a major cash crisis, when you have to pay estimated tax on January 15, until the money is actually received.

Ordinary and Necessary

The words *ordinary* and *necessary* haven't been clearly defined in the tax code, so you have to look to court rulings for their definitions. The Supreme Court has determined that *ordinary* means "normal, usual, or customary." If the IRS raised a question about your expense being ordinary, your best defense would be to show that it is a normal, usual, or customary cost of doing business in your particular trade or business.

Now back to the Supreme Court on the meaning of *necessary*—"appropriate and helpful." That leaves a lot of room for creativity on your part if you must justify an expense to an IRS auditor. If you are unsure about a major expense, however, check with a tax advisor.

Carrying on Any Trade or Business

By IRS rules, you actually must be conducting a trade or business—not *preparing* to do so—to write off business expenses. However, you can deduct start-up business costs as long as the business gets off the ground, so keep track of them. You can amortize start-up costs (remember amortization—we talked about that in the last chapter) over the first 60 months once the business is started.

Now that you know the IRS's primary ground rules, let's look at some of the common business expenses and their rules.

Meals and Entertainment

You'll probably want to entertain clients and customers as part of your normal business operations. Those costs can add up and, luckily, can also be deducted. You are limited to 50 percent of the costs, though. The costs must have a necessary relationship to your business, and you must keep adequate records to prove your expenses.

You can deduct meal and entertainment expenses, provided that they were for the purpose of …

♦ Entertaining business guests at either your place of business, your home, a restaurant, or some other location.

♦ Attending a business convention, reception, meeting, or luncheon at a club.

Tax Tips

You must be able to prove the business purpose of all meals and entertainment expenses. A good practice is to keep your receipts and note on the back of them the date, the people who were there, and the business purpose.

◆ Traveling away from home on business, whether you are eating alone or with others. If you pay for others, it must be business related.

If you entertain guests by getting some hot tickets, you can write off only half of the face value of the ticket even if you paid more to get them through a broker, agency, or scalper. Sorry! It might have been a great concert and worth the extra price, but you won't be able to write off that extra cost.

Giving Gifts

It's standard practice for businesses to give gifts to customers, clients, and employees, especially around the holidays. The IRS doesn't let you be too generous, though—the most you can give to one person in any tax year is $25 if you want to deduct the cost of the gift. This limit doesn't include expenses that are incidental to giving the gift, such as engraving, mailing, packaging, or insuring the gift.

Getting Business Credits

We talked a lot about credits in Part 3, but some credits are related specifically to business activities. Remember that credits are better than deductions because they are subtracted from your tax bill rather than from your net income. I've listed the key business credits that might fit a home-based small business.

Gasoline Tax Credit

If you use gas for business purposes, you may be able to write off the federal excise taxes that are charged for diesel and motor fuels. Business purposes that qualify for this deduction include:

◆ Operating vehicles for farming

◆ Operations vehicles for nonhighway purposes of your trade or business, such as a golf course that uses vehicles to maintain its property

◆ Operating vehicles for inner city transportation

◆ Operating a business that provides local or school bus services

◆ Operating vehicles for export or foreign trade

Use Form 4136, "Credit for Federal Tax Paid on Fuels" to get a credit for applicable federal excise taxes on fuel.

Welfare to Work Credit

If you hire someone who is qualified for long-term family assistance, you can get a credit of 35 percent of up to $10,000 in wages (or $3,500) in the first year, and up to 50 percent of $10,000 ($5,000) in the second year of employment. As the current law stands, this credit is scheduled to end, although Congress could decide to extend the credit in some future tax legislation. To qualify for this credit, you must hire the person before January 2004.

Work Opportunity Credit

The Work Opportunity Credit was enacted to encourage employers to hire people from certain disadvantaged groups:

- ◆ Families who receive cash welfare benefits for at least nine months

- ◆ Veterans who are members of families receiving assistance or food stamps

- ◆ High-risk youth aged 18 to 24

- ◆ Vocational rehabilitation referrals certified to have a physical or mental disability

- ◆ Ex-felons who are hired within one year of their conviction or release from prison who are members of low-income families

- ◆ Youth aged 18 to 24 who are in families that have been receiving food stamps for six months

If you hire someone who fits in one of these categories, you can get a credit of 40 percent of the first $6,000 (up to $2,400) of wages paid during the employee's first year of employment, provided that the person works at least 400 hours in that year. You can get a smaller credit of 25 percent if the employee works less than 400 hours but at least 120 hours. To qualify for this credit, you must hire the person before January 2004. Congress could decide to extend this in some future tax legislation.

Employer-Provided Child Care Credit

If you offer child-care benefits to your employees, you can get a credit of 25 percent of the qualified child-care expenses you provide, plus 10 percent of the cost of child-care resources or referral services you offer. This credit is capped at $150,000 per tax year. We discussed qualifications in Chapter 9 when we talked about the Child and Dependent Care Credit.

Learning More

You can deduct the cost of seminars, training sessions, and vocational, technical, or academic classes that you pay for yourself or your employees, as long as the courses are related to your business activity.

Paying Employees

If you have employees, you can deduct the salary, wages, commissions, bonuses, and other compensation you pay them, as well as any federal or state taxes you must pay on that income. To qualify as a deduction, the expenses must be ordinary and necessary (as defined previously), and reasonable in amount. (This means that you can't pay your spouse most of your business income if he or she wouldn't normally make that amount doing the same job in another trade or business.)

The wages must also be for services rendered and actually paid or incurred in the year you are claiming the deduction. Sound familiar? This is another pair of words we discussed previously.

You can deduct the amount you give in awards or bonuses, as long as the payment is based on services rather than a gift. If you make a loan or advance for which you don't expect to be paid, you can deduct the amount as compensation.

Sole proprietors can deduct wages paid to employees, but not their own salary. Their income is counted as net profits of the business.

Employee Benefits

You can deduct the cost of benefits you provide to your employees, including accident and health plans, group term life insurance, adoption assistance, dependent care assistance, educational assistance, retirement benefits, and welfare benefits funds.

Retirement benefits are another big item you can offer employees. Let's take a quick look at the types of plans small businesses can offer.

The 401(k), which we discussed in Part 5, is still the most popular plan, with 58 percent of all small businesses offering that type of plan in 2001. Most companies that do offer a 401(k) have more than 20 employees, and it's usually not cost-effective for smaller companies. Fortunately, more cost-effective plans are available for small home-based businesses that have only a few employees.

SEP-IRA

The Simplified Employee Pension (SEP) is actually a type of Individual Retirement Account (IRA). The SEP-IRA is the most flexible of small business retirement alternatives. This makes SEP-IRAs very popular for small businesses, especially those with 10 employees or fewer. As a small business owner, you are not required to make mandatory contributions; in fact, if business is bad, you can skip a year completely. You can offset a skipped year by putting in the maximum when business is good.

You can contribute up to 25 percent of salary per employee, but no more than $40,000 per year in a SEP. The key to the plan is equality. You must contribute the same percentage of earning for every eligible employee.

The SEP-IRA is also a good choice if you are self-employed. Your maximum contribution is only 13.04 percent of your net income, up to the maximum of $40,000, rather than 15 percent. This percentage is lower for self-employed folks because of the complicated way the SEP contribution is calculated. First, as a self-employed person, you must figure net earnings on a Schedule C by subtracting business expenses and 50 percent of the self-employment tax. The computation is complicated further because you then subtract your SEP contribution to arrive at your eligible net income figure, which ends up reducing your 15 percent contribution to 13.04 percent.

You get a tax benefit by offering a SEP-IRA. Your contributions are fully tax deductible. Folks who are self-employed also can deduct their SEP-IRA contribution and reduce their adjusted gross income (AGI).

You can hold off making your SEP contribution until your taxes are actually filed as long as you have asked the IRS for an extended filing deadline. This can be a particularly nice benefit if your cash is tight at the end of the year. You don't need to rush to make a contribution to your retirement plan, especially if you know that a major payment is coming in at the beginning of the next year. You can even delay adding to a SEP until as late as August 15 of the next year, which is the last day for requesting a tax filing extension.

Tax Tips

Contributions for self-employed folks can be logistically difficult to plan. Frequently, you do not know what your net income will be until the end of the year. This can make it difficult to fund a SEP-IRA until after you have completed calculating your tax return. There are tax penalties if too much is invested and some funds need to be withdrawn.

SIMPLE IRA

The new kid on the retirement block is the SIMPLE IRA. This plan was designed by Congress to give small businesses an alternative that would be easier and less costly to administer than the 401(k). The SIMPLE IRA was born in 1996 but took a while to catch on. Its growth tripled between 1998 and 1999.

Revenue Ramblings

You as the employer must match the employee contribution, which is tax deductible. You have a choice of matching the employee contribution dollar for dollar up to 3 percent of the employee's compensation or fund all employees' SIMPLE IRAs with a 2 percent of compensation contribution up to a maximum of $3,400 (or 2 percent of the maximum compensation of $170,000).

The SIMPLE IRA gives you as a small business owner the opportunity to offer a tax-deferred salary-reduction plan similar to a 401(k), but without the extensive administrative costs that a 401(k) plan can incur. Your employees can elect to make contributions up to $7,000 in 2002, which will increase by $1,000 per year until 2005, when it maxes out at $10,000. After that year, the maximum will be indexed to inflation.

You must deposit any employee salary-reduction contributions to the SIMPLE IRA within 30 days after the end of each month. Your employer-matching contributions do not have to be made until the due date of filing your tax returns, which can include filing extensions.

Keoghs

Keoghs are the granddaddy of retirement plans for small businesses and self-employed folks. Congress first established them in 1962. These plans are used primarily by businesses that operate as sole proprietorships or partnerships. Eligibility is limited to people who own their own business and file a Schedule C, have a Subchapter S corporation, are self-employed, are a partner in a business that files a Schedule K, or do freelance work. You may also use a Keogh if you are part of a limited liability company (LLC), provided that you are actively involved and not just a passive investor. Other types of corporations cannot use a Keogh.

Keoghs offer structures that come closest to traditional pension plans found in major corporations. They are also the most complex type of retirement plan that a small business can establish, but they offer the highest level of tax-sheltered investing you can find as a small business owner. They also provide you with greater flexibility in establishing criteria for employee participation and eligibility.

You can set up the Keogh as a defined-benefit or defined-contribution plan (remember, we talked about those differences in Part 5), while all other small business retirement options are defined-contribution plans. Another benefit of Keoghs is that you can make provisions to borrow from them, which is not allowed in other small business retirement plans.

CAUTION

Audit Alarm!

If your business fails, you can no longer contribute to a Keogh. You can roll the money into an IRA, but there could be penalties depending on the type of Keogh you set up. Obviously, this complicated alternative requires professional assistance to establish and has much higher costs to maintain. While Keoghs were popular when first introduced because they finally gave small business owners and self-employed folks a better way to save for retirement, their complexity has now rendered these plans almost extinct except for folks who established them many years ago. The SEP-IRA or SIMPLE IRA is most likely a better choice for you, but the Keogh does offer some aggressive savings options that you might want to consider if you have a lot of catching up to do with your retirement savings.

The Keogh is a maze of regulations. It has three sets of regulations: one for the self-employed, one for small business owners, and one for employees of a company that has a plan.

Financial institutions have standardized plans that a small business can use to establish its Keogh plan, but to take advantage of the Keogh's full flexibility, it's best to seek the help of a lawyer or CPA who is a Keogh specialist, to be certain you are setting up the type of plan that best matches your specific situation. The first thing you must do is name a plan administrator, even it that person is yourself.

Tax Tips

You can shelter the highest percentage of your income using a defined-benefit Keogh, which permits contributions of up to $135,000 annually and can be even 100 percent of your income. The maximum contribution allowed in a defined-contribution Keogh is $50,000, which is permitted in the money-purchase defined-contribution plan.

The four types of Keogh plan structures include a profit-sharing defined-contribution plan, a money-purchase defined-contribution plan, a paired plan, and a defined-benefit plan. There are numerous ways to structure these plans, but the catch is that if you cannot make the contribution set out in your original documents, you can be penalized in taxes for as much as 100 percent of the amount that should have been contributed. That's quite a penalty!

The least complicated structure, and the safest if your business income is uncertain each year, is the profit-sharing defined-contribution plan. You can contribute as much as 15 percent (before adjustments) of your business income or $40,000, whichever is less.

The money-purchase defined-contribution plan may offer you the largest tax shelter opportunities, but it comes with the greatest risk of penalties. You are allowed to shelter as much as 25 percent of your income, up to $200,000 ($50,000), but if you are unable to contribute that amount in any one year, you will owe up to 100 percent in penalties of the amount you should have contributed—and it won't be counted as a contribution. You must select a percentage at the time the plan is set. The percentage can be as low as 3 percent of earnings.

If you are looking for flexibility in a Keogh, the best choice is the paired plan, which combines key provisions of the profit-sharing and money-purchase defined-contribution plans. You are locked into making a contribution each year even if your business hasn't made much money, but you can set the percentage low and still contribute up to 25 percent in the good years.

Defined-benefit Keogh plans offer you the greatest chance to shelter the largest portion of your small business income. When you establish this type of plan, you decide on a specific annual benefit that you want to receive at age 65, which cannot top 100 percent of your highest three earnings years or a maximum of $135,000. You fund the plan so that you will be able to receive your desired payout, even if it means that you contribute 100 of your earnings each year. You will need to work with an actuary to determine how much your annual contribution should be to meet your goals. You have to submit the actuary's report each year with your tax return. The defined-benefit plan could be just right for you if you are trying to catch up late in your career.

While the tax shelter may sound great, Keoghs are an unpopular option. In 2001, only about 1 percent of small businesses chose this option. Essentially, people avoid Keoghs because of the huge amount of paperwork required. In most cases, you will need a Keogh expert to help with the annual paperwork. You also may need an annual actuarially report to justify the annual contribution. Before you take the plunge, be sure that you not only understand the initial paperwork, but also that you have a good understanding of the yearly requirements for managing this retirement savings alternative.

Profit-Sharing Plans

As a small business employer, you can supplement any of your retirement plans with a deferred profit-sharing plan (DPSP). In fact, in 2001, 22 percent of small businesses did offer this type of plan. Employers can contribute up to 18 percent of an employee's compensation.

Employers who offer this type of plan do so primarily to give employees a stake in the business by sharing company profits. This is considered a good way to encourage higher efficiency, increase morale, and ultimately result in higher profits. These plans can also help you retain employees.

These type of plans offer you a lot of flexibility in how to plan your contributions so that you can better match business conditions each year. Your contributions are exempt from federal payroll taxes, which helps to offset plan costs. You don't have to provide a definite formula for figuring the profits to be shared, but if there isn't a formula, you must make systematic and substantial contributions.

I've just introduced you to the basics of small business retirement options. Smart-money (www.smartmoney.com/tax/workbusiness/index.cfm?story=smallbiz), a website jointly operated by Dow Jones & Co. and the Hearst Company, is a great place to find more information on the topic.

Happy Hunting

By now you should have a pretty good handle on how to take advantage of the existing tax law to save tax dollars while also doing what you want to do—whether that means going to college, buying your dream house, or starting a business. Although you'll probably still have to pay taxes, hopefully you'll be paying a lot less in the future!

The Least You Need to Know

- ◆ Business expenses that can be written off are up to your imagination, as long as you can justify them to the IRS.
- ◆ You can write off 50 percent of meals and entertainment if there is a business relationship to the expense.
- ◆ Business gifts are strictly limited. You can't give a gift with a value of more than $25 per year to clients and customers.
- ◆ If you have employees, you can write off the cost of most wages and benefits.

Tax Calendar

I've listed some key tax dates for your reference. Whenever a date falls on the weekend, you can assume that the next Monday is the due date.

January 15

Estimated Tax Deadline   If you pay estimated taxes for the previous tax year, the fourth installment is due to the IRS.

January 31

W-2s, 1099s   Employers, banks, brokers, and other financial institutions usually have until January 31 to provide employees and customers with W-2s, Form 1099s, and other year-end tax statements.

February 15

Withholding Exemption   If you claimed exemption from withholding last year on the W-4 form you gave your employer, you must file a new W-4 by this date to continue your exemption for another year.

February 28 or 29

Household Employers If you provided your household employees with W-2s and paid a portion of their Social Security taxes, you must send copies of the W-2s to the Social Security Administration.

March 15

Corporate Filing Deadline Corporations and S Corporations that file on a calendar-year basis must file by this date.

Partnership K-1 If you manage a large partnership, this is the deadline for providing your partners with a Schedule K-1.

April 1

Retirement Account Withdrawals If you reached age 70½ in the previous year, you must start making withdrawals from your Individual Retirement Accounts (except for Roth IRAs) and other tax-favored retirement plans.

April 15

Estimated Tax Deadline If you make estimated tax payments, the first-quarter installment is due.

IRA Contribution Deadline If you want to make IRA contributions for the previous year, they must be made by this date.

Tax-Filing Deadline Individuals must either file their taxes by this date or request a four-month filing extension. If you request an extension, you should pay any estimated taxes or risk interest and penalties when you finally do pay. Taxpayers in Maine, Massachusetts, Michigan, Rhode Island, and upstate New York may have one more day for filing in the years that the tax-filing deadline falls on Patriot's Day, a state holiday in Massachusetts. (The states that get the delay are the ones whose returns are processed in Andover, Massachusetts.)

June 15

Estimated Tax Deadline If you pay estimated taxes, this is the payment deadline for the second-quarter installment.

August 15

Extended Filing Deadline   If you got a filing extension on April 15, you must file your taxes by this date or request a further extension.

September 15

Estimated Tax Deadline   If you pay estimated taxes, this is the payment deadline for the third-quarter installment.

October 15

Final Filing Deadline   If you've requested the two previous extensions, you can't delay filing any longer. This is tax day for you.

Roth IRA 2001 Conversions   If you want to undo a Roth IRA conversion made in the previous tax year, this is the deadline for that possibility.

December 31

Keogh Plan   This is the last day to establish a Keogh plan for the current tax year.

Retirement Account Withdrawals   If you must make a withdrawal from your retirement account in the current tax year, this is the last day you can make that withdrawal.

Roth IRA Conversion   This is the last day you can convert your retirement savings to a Roth IRA for the current tax year.

Taxing Terms: A Glossary

accrual method   The type of accounting by which income is reported when it is actually earned and expenses are reported when they are actually incurred.

adjusted basis   The original cost of an item at the time of purchase, increased by any improvements and decreased by any depreciation or tax credits.

adjusted gross income (AGI)   The calculation of your income after adjustments for things such as retirement contributions, but before standard or itemized deductions and personal exemptions are made. This is the number at the bottom of the first page of IRS Form 1040.

amortization   The way you can recover an investment cost for an intangible asset. This is similar to depreciation for a tangible asset.

annuity   A contract sold to you by an insurance company in which the company agrees to provide payments to the holder of the contract at specified intervals.

capital gain   Any profit you make from the sale or exchange of investments.

cash method   The type of accounting by which income is reported when it is actually received and expenses are reported when they are actually paid.

charitable remainder annuity trust   A trust that usually is funded with a gift of cash, property, or marketable securities. The trust pays fixed income to one or more persons for life or for a selected term of up to 20 years. The annuity amount, which is set when the trust is established, does not change. The amount must be at least 5 percent of the initial trust value. After the income interest ends, the trust assets go to the qualified charitable institution to be used as directed in the trust document.

custodial parent   The person who has primary care, custody, and control of a minor child or children.

defined-benefit plans   Retirement plans that specify the retirement benefit that the company will pay out when you retire. These plans are fully funded and managed by the employer. The employer must manage the way the funds are invested, to be sure he or she can pay benefits promised.

defined-contribution plans   Retirement plans funded through contributions from you and your employer. Contributions that you make actually reduce your taxable salary and help you build a retirement nest egg. In most employer plans, these contributions work in a similar way to a tax deduction. You don't write off the tax deduction when you file your taxes; instead, your employer reduces your taxable salary before he or she computes your taxes due. You manage the way the money is invested in this retirement nest egg.

dependent exemption   The amount you can subtract annually from your adjusted gross income before calculating your taxes. Your spouse is never considered a dependent.

depreciation   A deductible expense through which you write off a portion of the wear and tear on property over the life of the property. A portion of the initial cost of the property is written off each year. There are many different methods for depreciating property.

dividend reinvestment plans   Plans that allow you to choose to use your dividends to buy additional stocks instead of getting the dividends in cash. They can be bought through a broker or directly from the company.

dividends   A portion of a company's profits paid to shareholders based on the number of shares held.

dual-status alien   An individual who was both a nonresident alien and a resident alien in the same year.

earned income   Salaries, wages, tips, professional fees, and other amounts you were paid for work you actually performed.

501(c)3   Part of the United States Federal Internal Revenue Code that exempts organizations from federal income tax if they are organized and operate exclusively for religious, charitable, scientific, testing for public safety, literary, or educational purposes; to foster national or international amateur sports competition; or for the prevention of cruelty to children or animals.

fair market value   The price for which you could sell your property to a willing buyer when neither of you is under any duress to buy or sell.

front loading   May be determined by the IRS if large portions of alimony payments are paid in the first year or two and later payments are reduced by more than $15,000 per year.

general partners   Business partners who are subject to the same personal liability for partnership debts and claims as sole proprietors, even if the act that caused the claim to be filed was carried out by one of the other partners. Be careful who you partner with, especially if you plan to be the general partner, with all others being limited partners.

gift taxes   Taxes that may be incurred on any gift of more than $11,000 to any individual, including your children. The only exception are gifts between spouses. Parents can give each of their children $11,000, so a couple can actually give each child $22,000 per year without having to worry about the possibility of gift taxes. The first $1 million in gifts is exempt from the gift tax, but you do need to file a special tax form each year that your gifts exceed the annual limit. Calculation of the gift tax exemption is cumulative over your lifetime.

goodwill   Used to account for a business's competitive advantage, such as a strong brand, reputation, or high employee morale.

gross income   Any money, property, or services that are not exempt from tax. Rental receipts, gross business income, gross partnership income, unemployment claims, and some scholarship and fellowship grants count as gross income. Scholarships or grants that are only for tuition, fees, supplies, books, and equipment for specific courses are not considered gross income.

head of household   Someone who is not married but who has a dependent child or parent. To qualify, you must have paid more than half the cost of keeping up the home, as well as half the costs of the dependent person or persons.

inflation   The increase in prices of goods and services. For consumers, the inflation rate is measured using the Consumer Price Index, which reflects the change in the cost of a fixed basket of products and services that includes housing, electricity, food, and transportation.

intangible property   Property that consists of rights rather than physical attributes. In a business setting, examples of this are notes, accounts receivable, patents, or goodwill.

kiddie tax   Not the official name of any tax, but a phrase that is commonly used to refer to any tax that affects a child's unearned income, as long as the child is under the age of 14. The first $750 that a child receives in unearned income, such as income from investments, can be offset by the standard deduction. The next $750 is taxed at the child's tax rate. Once unearned income exceeds $1,500, all other income is taxed at the parents' rate.

legal custody   Gives the parent the right to make decisions about medical, educational, health, and welfare needs of the children.

like-kind exchange   When similar business or investment assets are exchanged. Gains can be tax-deferred until a later actual sale.

limited partners   People who don't take an active role in the management of the partnership. Their liability is limited to their investment in the business and any obligations they may have to make additional investments.

Medicare   The health insurance provided to people once they reach the age of 65. Most people have paid into the system all their lives as a deduction from their paychecks. The government does allow people who have not paid into the system or who haven't paid enough to purchase this insurance.

Modified Accelerated Cost Recovery System (MACRS)   The name given to the tax rules for getting back (recovering) through depreciation deductions the cost of property used in a trade or business or to produce income. The maximum amount you can deduct is limited depending on the year you place your property in service.

mortgage credit certificates   Certificates issued by state or local government entities that are usually related to a new mortgage for the purchase of your main home, but that occasionally include funds for qualified rehabilitation or home improvement. The MCC shows the certificate credit rate you will use to figure your credit. It also shows the certified indebtedness amount. Only the interest on that amount qualifies for the credit.

nonresident alien   An individual who is not a citizen or a permanent resident of the United States.

Old-Age, Survivors, and Disability Insurance (OASDI)   Generally referred to as Social Security, it's the largest social insurance program run by the U.S. government. Today more than 95 percent of workers in the United States are covered by Social Security. Note that Social Security is called an insurance program because it not only insures payments at retirement, but it also provides benefits if you become disabled. Your family is insured as well through survivor benefits.

permanently and totally disabled   To be considered permanently and totally disabled according to the IRS, you must be unable to "engage in any substantial gainful activity because of your physical and mental activity." You will also need to provide certification from a physician stating your condition and also stating that it is expected to last for 12 months or more, or that the condition will result in your death.

personal exemption   The amount you can subtract annually from your adjusted gross income before calculating your taxes due for yourself and your spouse. This is in addition to your standard or itemized deductions.

physical custody   Gives a parent physical control over the child.

principal place of business   Where you conduct your substantial business activities or substantial administrative and management activities of your trade or business. If you use a part of your home regularly and exclusively for administrative or management activities of your trade or business. To consider it your principal place of business, you must have no other fixed location where you conduct substantial administrative or management activities.

private foundation   A foundation operated by a company or family that does not get money from the general public. A foundation that engages in charitable activities is called an operating foundation. Nonoperating foundations give money but don't run their own charitable activities.

progressive tax system   Requires wealthier citizens to pay higher tax rates than those who are less well off.

qualified domestic relations order (QDRO)   A divorce order that instructs the administrator of a traditional pension plan or defined-contribution plan how the assets of that plan will be divided between spouses. It is critical to have the order on file with administrators of any retirement plans that are in place at the time of divorce, to protect the ex-spouse who is not part of the plan.

qualified state tuition program   Program provided by many states and some educational institutions to allow you to either prepay tuition or save for your child's higher education.

real estate investment trusts (REIT)   Trusts that invest in real estate property and mortgages. The REIT pools the capital of many investors and purchases income property or mortgage loans. REITs are traded on major exchanges just like stocks. Their primary advantage is that they are much more liquid than investing in real estate property directly. You know that it can take a while to sell your home, while a REIT can be traded rather quickly on a major exchange.

resident alien   An individual who is a permanent resident of the United States but is not a citizen.

Schedule A   The form used to calculate your itemized deductions. There are sections for medical and dental expenses, taxes, interest, gifts to charity, casualty and theft losses, job expenses, and miscellaneous deductions.

Section 179   A tax rule that allows businesspeople to deduct up to $24,000 for new property in the year this property was put into service rather than having to depreciate the property over a number of years. In 2003, the amount increases to $25,000.

secured loan   A loan in which the loan assets are backed by property that belongs to the borrower, which decreases the risk for the lender. The assets may be forfeited to the lender if you cannot afford to make the payments. This is why you should always be cautious when you take out additional loans, such as a second mortgage or an equity line, against your home. You could lose the property if you can't make the payments.

securities   Any investment instrument that is issued by a corporation, government, or other organization. The only exceptions to this are insurance policies or a fixed annuity. Publicly traded securities are available on the open market. Privately traded securities are not available for general sale to the public.

separate maintenance decree   Used when two people remain married but seek a court ruling on the rights and liabilities of the couple with respect to child custody, support, visitation, alimony, property, and debts. If the couple decides to divorce at a later date, this decree cannot be converted to divorce decree. A new divorce action is needed.

Social Security trust funds   These include the Old-Age and Survivors Insurance (OASI) Trust Fund, which pays retirement and survivors benefits, and the Disability Insurance (DI) Trust Fund. The funds can be used only to pay benefits and program administrative costs. The trust funds hold money not needed in the current year to pay benefits and administrative costs. By law, they must invest it in interest-bearing securities that are guaranteed by the U.S. government.

SSA-1099   The form that Social Security sends each beneficiary every year. If you are getting benefits on more than one Social Security record, you may get more than one form. The form includes all the benefits you received from the Social Security Administration and adjustments to those benefits. Railroad retirees get an RRB-1099 form instead.

tangible property   Physical property that can be moved.

tax home   Your regular place of business, regardless of where you maintain your family home. It includes the entire city or general area in which your business or work is located.

Index